To Amy + Renee
From mom + Dad
Try Piku food with
Spices from the
Chimp

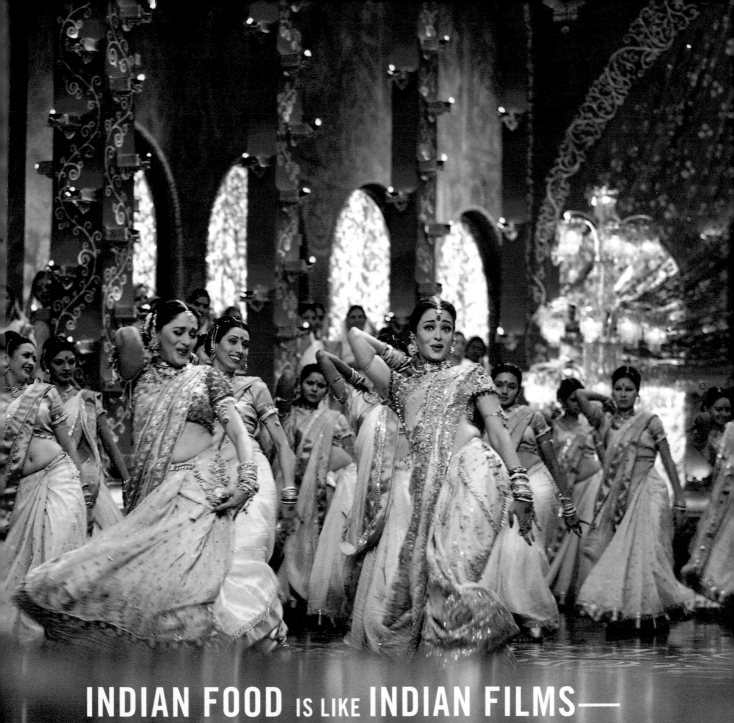

INDIAN FOOD IS LIKE INDIAN FILMS—
BOLD, COLORFUL, AND WAY OVER THE TOP.

BOLLYWOOD KITCHEN

HOME-COOKED INDIAN MEALS PAIRED WITH UNFORGETTABLE BOLLYWOOD FILMS

BY

SRI RAO

PHOTOGRAPHY BY SIDNEY BENSIMON

Houghton Mifflin Harcourt
Boston   New York
2017

*Library of Congress Cataloging-in-
Publication Data*

Names: Rao, Sri, author.
Title: Bollywood kitchen : home-cooked
Indian meals paired with unforgettable
Bollywood films / by Sri Rao.
Description: Boston : Houghton Mifflin
Harcourt, [2017] | Includes index.
Identifiers: LCCN 2017022339 (print) |
LCCN 2017018110 (ebook) | ISBN
9780544971295 (ebook) | ISBN
9780544971257 (paper over board)
Subjects: LCSH: Cooking, Indic. | Motion
pictures—India—Mumbai. |
LCGFT: Cookbooks.
Classification: LCC TX724.5.I4 (print) |
LCC TX724.5.I4 R388 2017 (ebook) |
DDC 641.5954—dc23
LC record available at https://lccn.loc
.gov/2017022339

Book design by Shubhani Sarkar
Food styling by Olivia Mack Anderson
Prop styling by Astrid Chastka

Printed in China
SCP 10 9 8 7 6 5 4 3 2 1

For my mom,

MRS. ANU RAO.

Every meal I eat and every movie I see
will forever remind me of your love.

—BABBU

CONTENTS

ACKNOWLEDGMENTS

In a way, I've been writing this book all my life. It's a tribute to every Indian meal I've eaten since I was a kid, cooked by generous and talented women at whose tables I've had the privilege to sit. Of course, first and foremost is my mom, who brought to America a reverence for food that was instilled in her by my respected grandparents. The irony is, she's never particularly enjoyed cooking, nor does she consider herself very good at it. But as you'll quickly discover once you try these recipes—she deserves more praise than I'll ever be able to give her. I thank her not only for feeding every person who's entered our home for fifty years but also for passing on to me her passion for Bollywood movies. If you think I'm somewhat of an expert on the subject, my mom could fill twenty books like this one with her endless knowledge of the Indian film industry.

Although my dad, Mr. B. Prithvidhar Rao, has never cooked a single thing in my entire life, this book wouldn't exist without him. Sixty years ago, he had the remarkable courage to venture alone to an unknown country across oceans and continents. There were times in those early years when he didn't know where his next meal was going to come from. Yet his perseverance, sacrifice, and hard work became the foundation of a family whose abundance can be witnessed on these beautiful pages. He's always been the quiet, solid anchor at our dinner table. And he's not just *my* dad—for generations to come, we will all look to him as our "founding father."

When I was growing up, we didn't have many relatives in the U.S., so my parents created a family among the tight-knit Indian community in Harrisburg, Pennsylvania. My "aunties" fed me for years—and continue to do so to this day. Memories of their food not only inspired this book, but will forever influence my life as a cook. I can't possibly name them all, but I hold a special fondness for: Hemalatha Venkatadri, Santosh Chadha, Sujatha Gangadhar, Prabhavati Kakarla, Suryakala Venkatadri, Geeta Kumar, and Snober Ketty.

And then there are my real aunties. Although I've only visited my aunts in India a few times, they are always present in my life and in my heart. Each meal they've prepared for me has been packed with intense love because they knew I wouldn't get another chance for years to eat food "cooked by their hand" (as we say in Telugu). Despite our barriers of language and distance, my respect and affection will always be with my pinnis, athas, peddamma, and akkas: Saroja, Aruna, Saraswati, Mallika, Santhi, Padma, Sashi, Lily, Swarna, Rani, and Lata.

This book—and my entire career—wouldn't be possible without my superbly professional team of agents at CAA. I feel the utmost gratitude toward: Ann Blanchard, the Texan tornado whose passion and energy are unbridled, the woman who's been my biggest cheerleader for over a decade; David Larabell, the guy I'm proud to call my book agent, who believed in this first-time author and skillfully landed me a deal in a matter of mere weeks; and David Taghioff, who's made my childhood dreams come true by single-handedly building a career for me in Bollywood, a rarefied feat to say the least.

Thank god for my editor, Justin Schwartz. Over lunch at The City Bakery one afternoon, he somehow agreed to buy this book. He and his team at Houghton Mifflin Harcourt have weathered the journey with me for the last two years. I thank him for believing in my vision and giving me an incredible opportunity that means more to me and my family than he may ever realize.

I hope you'll agree that the book you're holding in your hands is visually captivating. And I have a wonderfully talented design team to thank for that—beginning, as most of my projects do, with my creative director, Shay Zamir. Had it not been for Shay's beautifully designed book proposal, none of this would have happened. Shubhani Sarkar took the helm from there and elegantly designed this book. The cornerstone of it all, though, is the effortlessly stunning photography of Sidney Bensimon, styled by Astrid Chastka and Olivia Anderson (who miraculously cooked every single one of my recipes in just four days).

Speaking of photos, what would this book be without the Technicolor splendor of Bollywood? I am deeply indebted to the producers who graciously lent me the rights to reprint their films' photographs. I send my sincere appreciation to: Apoorva Mehta of Dharma Productions, Siddharth Roy Kapur of Disney UTV, Madhu Mantena of Phantom Films, Rudrarup Datta of Viacom 18, Aabha Sachdev of Sony Pictures, Pranab Kapadia of Eros Entertainment, Shekhar Kapur, Mani Ratnam, Nagesh Kukunoor, and Aashish Singh of Yash Raj Films.

The life of a writer is incredibly challenging, full of rejection and uncertainty. There's no way I could have survived the last twenty years without the support of my closest friends. They've picked me up when I've been knocked down, given me inspiration for new ideas, and—above all else—they've continually believed in me despite what the industry was saying. I owe a round of drinks to: Brian, Emily, Doug, Angie, Shaun, Mary Catherine, Candy, Bill, Maria, Alison, Katherine, Todd and Bess, Nicole, Bleema, Danielle, Jobi, Paul and Sofya, Molly, Abby, Carrie, Steve and Jennifer, Jenn Parsons, Rekha, and Jahnavi.

This book is about my family so I'd like to mention my sister and brother-in-law, Vani and Sachin, along with my beloved niece and nephew, Sheila and Neil. I especially need to thank Sheila, who served as an invaluable sounding board during the writing of this book, having inherited her grandmother's and uncle's passion for Indian food and films. In addition my love goes to my in-laws—Ronnie and Cheryl, Jeff and Michele, Jadyn and Dylan—for embracing me as part of the family and becoming some of the first New Mexicans ever to join the Bollywood fan club.

Finally . . . Jason. We've literally spent hundreds of hours discussing this book. He assuaged my insecurities about being an author, listened to my endless ideas and concerns, provided invaluable feedback, and offered his emotional support through the entire process for close to three years. Most notably, he diligently tasted every single dish I put in front of him—and gained thirty pounds along the way! (He'll never let me live it down if I don't mention he has since lost the "collateral damage," even though I think he's movie-star handsome at any weight.) I talk a lot about my Indian heritage, but it wasn't until I met a white boy named Jason Bratcher that I was able to fully embrace who I am and where I come from. His love has made our family complete. He's my home base, his heart is my safe space. And it's because of him that I am able to tell this story today.

INTRODUCTION

GROWING UP IN MY HOUSE IN SUBURBAN PENNSYLVANIA, THERE WERE TWO CONSTANTS—THE SCENT OF INDIAN FOOD SIMMERING ON THE STOVE IN MY MOTHER'S KITCHEN, AND THE SOUND OF BOLLYWOOD MUSICALS EMANATING FROM THE TV IN THE LIVING ROOM. TO THIS DAY, WHENEVER I SMELL THE WARM AROMA OF DELICIOUS CURRY—AUTHENTIC, HOME-COOKED CURRY, NOT THE GREASY RESTAURANT VARIETY—OR HEAR THE DANCEABLE DRUMBEAT OF POPULAR INDIAN MUSIC, I'M TRANSPORTED BACK TO 413 ALLEGHENY DRIVE.

But it's not just childhood nostalgia. For me, as for most first-generation Indian-Americans, food and films are our primary connection to a motherland we never knew. As a skinny brown kid in an all-white community, I grew up loving Atari and shopping at JCPenney. Were it not for the elaborate dinners my mom served every evening precisely at 6:00, I would know nothing about the complex flavors that fed generations of my ancestors. And were it not for the invention of the VCR, which brought with it a nightly ritual of watching Bollywood movies after dinner, I would be a stranger to the stories, language, and music of my parents' home.

Food and films are a conduit to a culture. They give us a sensory experience of a place, of a people. Indian culture is defined by both its calming spirituality and its joyful zest for life. Nowhere is this more evident than in the earthy spices of an Indian meal or the kitschy, colorful musical numbers of a Bollywood film.

Of course, as a child, it wasn't that deep. All I knew was how I felt. I loved the feeling of the food in my fingers. As my tiny hand mixed rice with luscious meat gravies and outrageously vibrant vegetables, I was transported to another world, beyond my small, working-class town. And when I watched those films, I saw people who looked like me on a TV screen for the very first time. Sure, they spoke a language I didn't initially understand (and randomly broke into song and dance), but I was mesmerized by their journeys because I had a feeling—somehow, innately—that *these were my people.*

(Opposite) Aishwarya Rai holds an eternal flame for her true love in *Devdas* (see page 22).

Cut to today. I've transformed my childhood memories of Indian food and films into my career and passion. I'm one of the only Americans working in Bollywood, having written a major film and produced two others. And as an avid cook, I've translated the traditions of my mother's recipes to my own kitchen in a modern, accessible way.

My parents are pioneers, among the first in the modern wave of Indians to immigrate to the United States. My dad came here to attend college, straight from his hometown in India to the segregated South of 1959 America. At the time, there were only some 10,000 Indian immigrants in the entire country—today, there are over three million.

I can't imagine what life must've been like for them, navigating a truly foreign country in an era when most Americans had never seen an Indian outside the pages of *The Jungle Book*. My dad recalls the first time he encountered signs labeled "white" and "black" next to restrooms in a Greyhound bus station. It was confusing for him, a young man who didn't see himself accurately described by either option (where was the sign for "brown"?). So he hurried into the white restroom and luckily no one bothered to stop him—which unfortunately *wasn't* the case another time at a Virginia lunch counter.

Through the 1960s and '70s, my mom and dad assimilated the best they could, buying a house in the suburbs, having two kids, and learning to navigate the rules

FOR ME, INDIAN FOOD AND FILMS AREN'T

and customs of their new world. But all the while, they clutched firmly to the few remnants of home that they could recreate here—language, religion, and, of course, food and films.

I believe my mom, who didn't work outside the house, saw cooking as her primary contribution to the family and her community, a way to express her love for those around her. Our home is probably like many others in that food is emotional currency. But in an immigrant household, there's an added layer of significance: food is a bloodline. My mom's cooking was a daily reminder to her of her own parents and family—the loved ones she left behind (in a time when there was barely even phone service to India, much less Skype). For me, the food became a way to learn of people whose names I knew but acquaintance I had rarely made.

The movies were a postcard from home for my parents. I remember we would gather in a local college auditorium with just five or six other Indian families to watch a movie one Sunday a month. It was my parents' responsibility to pick up the huge canisters of film reels from the bus station—months-old movies that had made their way around the world, which my mom negotiated to be sent to our town at the end of their run for thirty dollars. I'd watch, enthralled, as one of my aunties carefully threaded the worn-out celluloid through the film projector. Although we kids would spend most of the afternoon running around the lobby and playing with the vending machines, I now understand why my parents and their friends sat contentedly in that theater for hours. Those were the only pictures of home that they would see for years at a time.

(Opposite page)
My mom and dad assimilating into 1960s America.

(Below)
Growing up in Mechanicsburg, PA.

MERELY HOBBIES—THEY'RE MY BLOODLINE.

We've come a long way since then. Indian culture is now in the zeitgeist. From suburban soccer moms practicing yoga to urban hipsters sporting bindis and henna tattoos, Americans have been flirting with all things Indian over the past decade or so. In particular, Indian food has ignited the palate of Americans looking for bold flavors, as well as those seeking a healthful, vegetarian-centric cuisine. Meanwhile, Bollywood films have crept into the ethos with their infectious, hip-shaking rhythms that have been sampled by everyone from Beyoncé to First Lady Michelle Obama.

You don't know Indian. Whether you consider yourself an ardent fan of Indian cuisine or someone who doesn't particularly care for it, I have news for you: Chances are, you've never really tasted Indian food.

To be fair, what you've tasted is food that's primarily from one or two regions of the subcontinent, made by men who immigrated here and opened restaurants trying to replicate dishes from another time and place. Unfortunately, this food bears little resemblance to the food I grew up with—and it's the reason I rarely visit Indian restaurants today.

In this book, I'll introduce you to the food that Indian-Americans like me eat every day. This is home-cooked food, the best of my mom's recipes. You'll notice there isn't a tandoori chicken or tikka masala in sight. That's because we don't cook those restaurant clichés at home. Instead, what you'll find are recipes for dishes you may have never heard of—like keema, a savory, ground beef entrée that turns regular hamburger meat into a sublime experience; or khichdi, a simple, weeknight, lentil-and-rice dish that's perfect for vegetarians, yet robust enough for carnivores.

Because Indians are such a new immigrant group (it was virtually illegal to obtain a visa prior to 1965), we are just now starting to define what Indian food will look like in the United States. My sister and I are among the oldest American-born Indians in this country. So it's up to us and our peers to begin sketching what "Indian" will mean here—how it will be different from the old country—in much the same way that Italian immigrants did a hundred years ago, or Chinese immigrants fifty years ago. Now is the moment when we decide what elements of Indian culture we'll retain, what we'll cast aside, and what we'll adopt from our American home. It's an exciting time for sure.

And one of the first things I'd like to clear up is this: Indian food is *not* difficult to make. The recipes you'll discover in these pages involve ingredients that are readily accessible in your local supermarket and prepared in a straightforward manner suitable for modern American families. The reason for this is simple. When my mom first started cooking in this country, there wasn't an Indian grocery store in sight—even *rice* was a rare commodity (she had to mail-order it from New York City). Out of necessity, the recipes she developed over the years use simple, American ingredients. For the most part, everything in this book can be found in your local grocery store, if not your cupboard. If you've ever cooked Mexican food—or even a regular old pot of chili—chances are you already have most of what you'll need.

But that doesn't mean these recipes lack authenticity. They've simply been streamlined by eliminating fussy steps and obscure components. These dishes have been tried and tested over the last forty years by immigrant families like mine—maintaining the tradition of our roots, but adapting and assimilating like all great American institutions. The result is homemade Indian food you'll enjoy sharing with your family and friends because it's delicious, healthy, *and* easy to prepare.

WELCOME TO BOLLYWOOD, A LAND WHERE EVERYONE TRAVELS WITH BACKUP DANCERS.

The Indian film industry (which derives its nickname from "Bombay + Hollywood") is the most prolific in the world, churning out hundreds of films every year. And, yes, every one of those films is a musical. It's hard to imagine, but whether a romance, thriller, courtroom drama, or sci-fi fantasy, characters in practically every Bollywood movie routinely burst into song. It's a little wacky, but it's incredibly addictive—much like Indian food—which explains why both have millions of fans all over the world.

What's the fascination? Allow me to show you. Interspersed with the recipes in this book, you'll find something equally delicious: the best contemporary Bollywood films, in my opinion. These are the movies I recommend to my own friends. I curated this selection with diligence and care, selecting the films that I feel you'll most enjoy—my lifelong passion laid out for you on the pages that follow.

I'll take you on a tour of the visually captivating, trippy world of Bollywood. We'll cover all the major genres, touch upon milestones in Indian cinema, and get to know the most iconic actors, actresses, and directors.

Bollywood movies are in Hindi, but truly, they have a language all their own. With running times well over two hours and sprawling storylines that can be Shakespearean in scope, they may require more than subtitles for you to navigate your way through the experience. So I've got you covered. I'll put these movies into context for you—explaining the significance of each film, why you might love it, and letting you in on some juicy morsels from behind the scenes.

MAKING THE CUT

It would be safe to say that I spent just as much time selecting the films for this book as I did working on the recipes. I belabored my list for months—starting with close to 200 titles and winnowing it down from there. It was an arduous process during which I watched and re-watched dozens of films, comparing them against one another (and racking up my iTunes bill). Surely, Bollywood enthusiasts will debate my final selection, so allow me to shed some light on the criteria I used.

These are contemporary films. No disrespect to the classics (see page 13), but I chose to focus on the best *modern* Bollywood films. This was mostly a pragmatic decision. In my research, I discovered that many of the best, old-time Bollywood movies are very difficult to view online, and even harder to find with good subtitles. So I begin your tour in the mid-1990s, when Bollywood began a new chapter with glossy, big-budget, internationally successful films like *Dilwale Dulhania Le Jayenge*, *Kuch Kuch Hota Hai*, and *Hum Aapke Hain Koun…!* This was arguably the moment when "contemporary Bollywood" was born.

From that point, I guide you to present-day Bollywood with a representative cross-section of films. The movies in this book provide a comprehensive overview of all the major genres in Bollywood cinema. I've made a point of ensuring that you won't only find romances (the most popular subset), but also a sampling of suspense, comedy, action, and art house flicks. And as much as possible, I've avoided repetition, limiting the number of films with the same actor or director. Instead, after each film's description, I've listed other, similar films you might also enjoy.

I'm excited and confident about the list I've curated for you. It's a culmination of my lifelong passion for Bollywood—everything I know and love about these extraordinary movies is now at your fingertips.

BOLLYWOOD FILMS ARE A KALEIDOSCOPE OF FLAVORS, WHILE INDIAN FOOD IS MELODRAMA ON A PLATE.

A funny thing happens whenever I find myself at an Indian restaurant, usually at the insistence of my non-Indian friends. They scour the menu trying to make sense of it all, and end up ordering items haphazardly—pairing a *vindaloo* with a *korma* and a side of *rogan josh*. What arrives is a mash-up of flavors, the equivalent of assembling a dinner of fried chicken, chicken cordon bleu, and guacamole. Not that my friends seem to mind. They just mix everything together into a mound of sludgy rice and eat it like porridge.

Most Indian restaurants (as well as cookbooks) adopt a Western approach to presenting their dishes—appetizers, soups, entrées, sides. But Indian meals aren't structured that way. Typically, Indians don't eat in courses. Instead, the plate is constructed *as a whole*. In the center is rice or bread, and around it is a selection of proteins, vegetables, and accompaniments with flavors that meld harmoniously.

What you'll find in this book are *complete meals*. I've taken the guesswork out of it for you by creating menus with dishes that complement one another. Each menu is a balance of meat and vegetables, hot and cool, wet and dry. It's the way we eat at my house.

There are dinner menus and brunch menus, menus for parties and menus for kids. Most important, I've made sure that each menu is *doable*. You will *not* be slaving in the kitchen for seven hours trying to prepare an elaborate Indian feast. If, for example, an entrée is a bit time-consuming, I've paired simple sides with it. Every menu in this book had to pass the test of "Would I serve this in my own home?"

And to the vegetarians/vegans out there—I'm here for you. All too often, vegetarians are forced to choose foods that are trying to be *substitutions* for meat and falling short of the "real thing." But in the case of Indian food, vegetables aren't supporting players—they've been the star for over four thousand years. The Hindu religion teaches *ahimsa*, or nonviolence, which frowns upon killing animals, so Indian cuisine has perfected the art of vegetarian cooking. Although almost all of the menus in this book include meat, most also feature a protein-packed lentil or bean dish that could easily serve as your entrée. And there are dozens of heavenly veggie recipes throughout.

IT'S DINNER AND A MOVIE, THE INDIAN WAY.

Along with each meal, I've paired one of my favorite Bollywood films for you to enjoy while you're eating. Much like the food, each film is a symphony of flavors—drama, comedy, music, and action—all rolled into one.

In *Bollywood Kitchen*, I invite you to a party where the food and entertainment are both in Technicolor. These "dinner and a movie" combos are my idea of a great night, and I hope they will be for you, too—whether it's a Saturday evening cocktail party with friends, or a weeknight family supper. It's like culinary school meets film school. But more than anything else—it's a fun ride.

My intention in writing this book is to honor the legacy of my family's immigrant experience. And in so doing, I hope to open a doorway for you to the food, films, music—and joy—that my Indian heritage has to offer our country.

This is an ongoing journey. My relationship with Indian food and films continues to shape my life in subtle, yet profound ways. The first time I brought a boyfriend home to meet my parents, it was understandably a stressful event for my traditional family. But as soon as my mom saw how eagerly Jason devoured her food, she gave a nod of approval and I breathed a sigh of relief. A few years later, we were married on a rooftop in Manhattan, surrounded by both our families, after which we celebrated with an Indian-meets-Americana menu and danced all night to Bollywood music—demonstrating once again that food and films are at the center of every Indian family.

I've only been to India a handful of times and, for all practical purposes, I'm very much an outsider. But I still consider myself deeply connected to my Indian identity. It may be a simplification to say that everything I learned about being Indian I learned through food and films—but there's a lot of truth to that.

I learned the language . . . I learned about family . . . I learned how simple spices can explode with flavor if used with a delicate hand like my mom's . . . I learned to dance, literally and figuratively . . . I learned that when you're Indian, emotions and tastes can be dramatic—something very scary, but potentially liberating, for us Americans. . . .

And more than anything else, I learned about love—both the kind that's accompanied by a sweeping romantic ballad and the kind that's served with a simple plate of rice.

Enjoy the show,

BOLLYWOOD 101

TO THE UNINITIATED, WATCHING A BOLLYWOOD MOVIE FOR THE FIRST TIME CAN BE A BIT DIZZYING. THE MUSIC, THE ACTION, THE MELODRAMA—IT'S ENOUGH TO MAKE YOUR HEAD SPIN—WHICH, I ADMIT, MAY BE PART OF THE FUN. BUT BEFORE YOU JUMP INTO THE WORLD OF DANCING DAMSELS AND HANDSOME HEROES, ALLOW ME TO PROVIDE YOU WITH A BRIEF ROAD MAP TO GUIDE YOU ON THE ADVENTURE.

NO, THEY'RE NOT ACTUALLY SINGING

Many people are surprised to learn that the actors in Bollywood movies are not singers. But they are *excellent* lip-synchers. For those of us accustomed to American musicals, both Broadway and the film variety, we just assume that the melodious voice coming from each actor's mouth is his own.

Not the case in Bollywood. Instead, the voice belongs to what is known as a playback singer. This group of performers has been integral—some might even say imperative—to the success of Bollywood films over the past century. They are the unseen voices behind the screen that belt out thousands of songs every year, while the glory goes to the beautiful actors on-screen who move their lips and shake their hips to match.

That's not to say that playback singers don't have devout followings of their own. It's an elite group for sure, with the same five to ten names popping up in the credits of every film you watch. The most famous playback singer in Bollywood history, Lata Mangeshkar, is nothing short of a national treasure in India. She's been listed in the *Guinness Book of World Records* for having sung thousands of movie songs over the course of her seventy-year career. Even though she no longer records for films, she remains my all-time favorite singer, whose irreplaceable voice is synonymous with Bollywood.

With all respect to Ms. Mangeshkar, it's easy to understand why Bollywood films separate the actors from the singers: Most truly great vocalists aren't necessarily known for their looks. To put it another way, it's very difficult to find actors who are genuine triple threats (performers who can act and sing and dance). When you're producing hundreds of musical films every year, there just aren't enough actors who can juggle all three talents. And while it's possible to teach someone to dance, at least marginally, a great singing voice can't be faked.

So Bollywood separates the two groups of performers and, I would argue, has consequently cultivated some of the best singers in the world. If only we could say the same for the majority of its acting talent.

Speaking of music, one of the reasons that Bollywood movies are so much fun to watch for fans is because we're usually familiar with the music before we see the film. By and large, pop music in India *is* film music. Radio stations and cable TV music channels are continuously playing songs from the latest movie releases. So by the time you go to the theater to see the film, you already know the music and can sing along with the songs on-screen.

PLEASE REFRAIN FROM SILENCE DURING THE SHOW

If there's one piece of advice I have for enjoying the concept behind my book, it is this: Please don't watch these movies the way we watch American movies.

Don't get me wrong. As a writer and director, there is nothing that frustrates me more than people who talk during a film or TV show, disrespecting the hundreds of artists whose time and talent went into that piece of work, regardless of whether or not you happen to be enjoying it. But conversely, there's no better way to express your enjoyment and respect for Bollywood artists than by actively participating with a film as you're watching it. Applause, criticism, running commentary—bring it on.

It's really a matter of self-endurance. These films typically run two and a half hours (older films used to cross the three-hour mark), so there's no way to stay diligently silent for so long without falling into a stupor. And like all things Indian, watching a movie is a communal experience. It's meant to be shared with your family and friends—loudly, if you so choose.

Along the same lines, every movie comes with an intermission. So when the word *interval* flashes on the screen, consider it part of the Bollywood experience to pause your viewing for a social break. Grab another plate of food, serve chai and dessert, or catch up on your text messages before settling back in for the second half of the film (which rarely is as entertaining as the first, so make sure you replenish your cocktail, too).

GODS AMONG THE STARS

We may feel like we live in a celebrity-obsessed culture here in the United States, but we pale in comparison to India. Bollywood stars are akin to gods—literally, in some cases, with makeshift shrines to actors erected in villages and hundreds of millions of fans fiercely devoted to their favorite heroes and heroines.

The current holy trinity of Bollywood are the Khans: Aamir Khan, Shah Rukh Khan, and Salman Khan. Though no relation to one another, these three men have ruled screens and hearts for close to thirty years. Typically, devotees have an affinity for one of the three sacred branches. There's Aamir, the serious actor, Shah Rukh, the romantic leading man, and Salman, the action star of the people.

The granddaddy of them all, though, is Mr. Amitabh Bachchan. Consider him the Zeus of Bollywood, revered by even the biggest demigods themselves. The septuagenarian burst onto the scene in the late '70s/early '80s as "the angry young man," and has continued his reign without interruption ever since. He is perhaps the most famous movie star in the entire world, in sheer number of fans and films. To this day, mobs congregate outside his house every Sunday just to get a glimpse of him for a few moments, waving to his admirers who've been waiting in the sweltering sun for hours.

But it's not just the men. The goddesses of Bollywood have their own pantheon—from the elegant Nargis and Madhubala in the '40s and '50s to divas Rekha and Sridevi in the '80s, dancing queen Madhuri Dixit in the '90s, and current-day global beauties Aishwarya Rai, Deepika Padukone, and Priyanka Chopra (of TV's *Quantico*). Although these leading ladies continue to mesmerize audiences from one era to the next, their individual careers seem to have a shelf life of only around ten years, unlike their male costars. After that point, although they may occasionally find a role of substance, they usually choose instead to seek a suitable (read: wealthy) husband and go into semi-retirement—while their male costars continue to sing and dance on-screen with actresses twenty years their junior. (We could decry sexism more vociferously if we didn't suffer from a similar double standard in Hollywood.)

It's interesting to note that the phenomenon of Bollywood gods isn't confined to India. Stars like Shah Rukh Khan have millions of fans all over the world, in places as diverse as Dubai, Russia, Singapore, and Great Britain. Even in the United States, there have been instances of theater managers having to reprimand audiences for lighting oil lamps and performing religious ceremonies *inside suburban movie theaters* on the opening night of their favorite star's latest film.

So if you find yourself falling in love with one of the larger-than-life personalities in a film from this book—you're not alone. And if you're lucky, you could see them in the flesh. They regularly go on world tours, like the Rolling Stones or Madonna, lip-synching and dancing to your favorite film songs in packed stadiums from New York to Sydney. The best part is, instead of popcorn and hot dogs, the venues serve samosas and mango lassis.

PLEDGING THE FILM FRATERNITY

Although it's a multimillion-dollar business that spans the globe, Bollywood is often referred to within India as a "film fraternity" as opposed to a "film industry." The reason is because it functions as a tight-knit, largely family-run business—an exclusive club that most of its members were born into, and that rarely permits outsiders entry. In this way, Bollywood harkens to a bygone era in Hollywood, when the studio system ruled and producers like Samuel Goldwyn and Louis B. Mayer ran the town.

If you do a Wikipedia search for almost any actor, actress, writer, director, or producer in Bollywood, you'll discover that he is related to one, if not many, other artists in the industry, often going back generations. Some families, like the descendants of Prithviraj Kapoor, form entire dynasties of Bollywood royalty. The Kapoors have been acting since the silent era, with no end in sight. Every decade, the crown is bestowed upon the next prince- or princess-in-waiting, sometimes deservedly so and other times . . . well, not so much.

The fraternity label befits Bollywood in another sense: its social scene. Most of the celebrities in Bollywood grew up together. Their childhood friends, siblings, and cousins are now their costars in both films and gossip websites. Paparazzi regularly snap them partying together or celebrating holidays jointly with their families in a way we don't see with major Hollywood stars. Many also marry within the fraternity, forming supercouples that eventually spawn the next generation of celebrities. It's great fodder for us fans because the romantic storylines behind the scenes can be even more melodramatic than the ones on-screen.

Understandably, it's always been incredibly difficult for new talent without family connections to break into the industry. That's slowly changing, though, as the business itself shifts. Taking a cue from the structure of entertainment companies in America, Bollywood has become more corporatized in the past decade or so. Whereas producers routinely turned to underworld, mob sources to finance their films in the '80s and '90s, these days Hollywood studios like Disney and Fox have partnered with or purchased Indian production companies to get into the Bollywood game. And the money now goes both ways—Indian conglomerate Reliance is the major funder behind DreamWorks Pictures.

WHERE TO FIND THE FILMS

All of the movies in this book are available online, with subtitles, on iTunes, Netflix, Amazon Prime, YouTube, or Google Play. I also recommend checking out a service called Eros Now, which is like the Netflix of Bollywood (you can cancel your subscription at any time). Since streaming availability changes from time to time, in case you can't find one of the films online, you can always purchase a DVD for a reasonable price on Amazon.

By the way, you might notice that your local Indian grocery store has shelves full of DVDs, but I would strongly discourage you from renting them. These are almost certainly pirated copies (despite what the shopkeeper tells you) with very poor picture quality. And what's the point of watching a Bollywood movie if you can't enjoy it in all its Technicolor splendor? Speaking of viewing enjoyment—now you can watch Bollywood on the big screen. These days, all the major films are released worldwide on the same date, opening across America, Europe, the Middle East, and around the world. Chances are, there's one playing at a multiplex near you right now.

And if you fall in love with the songs from a film, you can watch the music videos for free anytime on YouTube. To download a film's soundtrack or individual songs, visit iTunes or check out any number of Bollywood stations and playlists on services like Pandora and Spotify.

A NOD TO THE CLASSICS

Although this book focuses on the best of contemporary Indian cinema, I would be remiss if I didn't pay homage to the beautiful films of Bollywood's yesteryear.

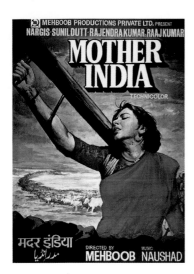

THE GOLDEN AGE

From the late 1940s to the 1960s, Bollywood experienced what many refer to as its Golden Age. The films of this era were delicate classics, replete with melodrama but with dignified sophistication at the same time. Producer, director, and actor Raj Kapoor is undeniably the most famous showman of this period, the Charlie Chaplin of Bollywood. His classics include *Awaara*, *Shree 420*, and *Jaagte Raho*—all of which featured the actress Nargis, with whom he shared a legendary love affair and equally notorious breakup.

Nargis went on to star in *Mother India*, the first Indian film ever to be nominated for an Academy Award. This story of a poor woman who overcomes incredible odds to raise her family could be compared to *Gone With the Wind* for the indelible impact its heroine has had on the hearts of an entire nation. *Mother India* was followed a few years later by an equally groundbreaking epic, *Mughal-e-Azam*, the most expensive, as well as highest grossing, film for decades to come. The story of a Mughal prince (played by the legendary Dilip Kumar) and his forbidden love with a court dancer (the beautiful Madhubala) is still celebrated for its elaborate sets and superb production values.

PARALLEL CINEMA

By the late 1950s, a separate track of filmmaking began to emerge in response to the escapist, musical films of Bollywood. Known as "parallel cinema," the films of this movement focused on social issues and the plight of ordinary Indians. It originally started outside the Hindi film industry by Bengali filmmakers like Satyajit Ray, director of the internationally acclaimed *Apu Trilogies*. Parallel cinema came into prominence within Bollywood in the late '70s and early '80s, through the work of directors such as Shyam Benegal, Basu Chatterjee, and Hrishikesh Mukherjee.

In my view, the greatest accomplishment of parallel cinema is the platform these films gave to female-centric stories. Actresses Shabana Azmi, Smita Patil, and Jaya Bhaduri became the most well-respected and awarded performers of their time (and perhaps since). Their authentic, often gut-wrenching portrayals in films like *Arth*, *Mandi*, *Abhimaan*, and *Kamla* (my personal favorite) are revered by critics and audiences alike. In a country where women have suffered unspeakable inequities, these powerhouse actresses gave voice to discarded sections of society.

THE ANGRY YOUNG MAN

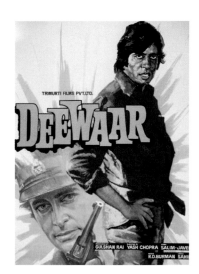

Bollywood's timeline should probably be delineated into two parts—B.B. (before Bachchan) and A.B. (after Bachchan). An unassuming supporting actor in the 1960s, Amitabh Bachchan's life, career, and the future of Bollywood itself changed in 1973 with the release of *Zanjeer*. In the film (the title of which means "chains"), Bachchan plays a new kind of hero—not a hopeless romantic, but an angry young man who violently fights against a corrupt system.

The film, its message—and, above all, its star—struck a chord in India. From there, Bachchan followed with similar characters in blockbuster films like *Deewaar* and *Sholay*, which ranks as the highest grossing Bollywood film of all time (when adjusted for inflation). He ushered in a new type of storytelling, one that focused on violence and injustice. Bollywood exploded with melodrama and action, the ripples of which are still felt today. Along the way, Bachchan himself came to embody all that is Bollywood, a living ambassador of sorts.

THE CAMPY '80S

Depending on whom you ask, the 1980s were either a blight on Indian cinema or the most fun that Bollywood has ever had. The decade got swept away on a wave of polyester mayhem, from disco classics like *Qurbani* and *Disco Dancer* to over-the-top James Bond fantasies like *Shaan* and *Mr. India*.

It was also the era when South Indian filmmakers and actresses took over Bollywood, with a slew of Telugu- and Tamil-language remakes starring Southern beauties like Rekha and Sridevi. These films (such as *Ek Duuje Ke Liye*, *Himmatwala*, and *Tohfa*, to name just a few) were usually family melodramas, with their signature, kitschy musical numbers featuring scantily clad actresses dancing in the rain and leaping from the tops of clay pots.

As a child of the '80s, these were the films that I grew up on, and I *loved* them. One of my very first memories of Bollywood is watching Rekha in a VHS copy of *Mr. Natwarlal*, dancing and romancing her way into my heart. She was absolutely stunning (and continues to be to this day), decked out from head to toe in gorgeous jewelry and costumes that matched her beguiling persona. As an eight-year-old gay boy, I was in heaven. I had found my diva . . . and life has never been the same since.

PARTY SNACKS

Here are some Bollywood morsels to share with your guests while watching the films:

SINGING OUT OF THE GATE. The first Indian film, *Raja Harishchandra* (1913), was silent. But as soon as sound was introduced in 1931 with *Alam Ara*, Bollywood came alive—the film was packed with seven songs.

TO EACH HIS OWN. "Bollywood" only refers to the Hindi-language film industry, based in Bombay (now known as Mumbai). But there are several other regional film industries in India, such as the Telugu- and Tamil-language industries, which produce hundreds of musical films of their own every year.

NO WONDER THEY'RE THREE HOURS LONG. An average film has between five and seven songs, while some successful period dramas and family musicals have been known to contain over a dozen.

IMMACULATE CONCEPTION. Although India is the land that gave us *The Kama Sutra*, the film industry has a strict censor board that regulates the content of all films. Nudity is absolutely not permitted, while even kissing is taboo.

READ MY LIPS. Most Bollywood films are not recorded in sync-sound, the standard filmmaking method of recording actors' voices while filming scenes. Instead, Indian actors face the difficult task of dubbing all their dialogue in a recording studio once the movie is edited.

RED CARPET MANIA. Much like Hollywood, Indians have come to love their awards shows. The annual Filmfare Awards, named for a leading movie magazine, is the most popular, like the Bollywood Oscars. You can watch the shows on YouTube. They're filled with song-and-dance numbers way more fun than anything the Academy has ever put on.

IMITATION IS THE SINCEREST FORM OF FLATTERY. Bollywood has long been criticized for its unauthorized remakes of American and other international films, from *The Silence of the Lambs* and *Memento* to *Mrs. Doubtfire* and *Three Men and a Baby*. Rarely have the original filmmakers succeeded in taking legal action.

NO OFFENSE, DANNY BOYLE. Despite common perception, *Slumdog Millionaire* is *not* a Bollywood movie. It's a British film that just happens to have a musical number in its closing credits, an homage to Bollywood.

MOVE OVER, ZUMBA. If you get the bug to be a Bollywood backup dancer, try taking a Bollywood dance class offered in most major cities and some national gym chains. Also keep an eye out for Bollywood dance nights in clubs all over the United States and Europe.

WHAT'S IN A NAME? The term *Bollywood* is viewed by some in the industry as offensive because it implies that Indian films can't stand on their own without implicit deference to Hollywood. They prefer instead the term *Hindi cinema*.

THAT'S A WHOLE LOTTA RUPEES. The highest grossing Bollywood film as of 2016 is *PK* (2014), grossing $120 million. Although this isn't extraordinary by Hollywood standards, Bollywood as a whole sells *twice as many tickets* as Hollywood worldwide.

CHECK YOUR LOCAL LISTINGS. *Dilwale Dulhania Le Jayenge* is the longest-showing Indian film in history. The romantic musical blockbuster has been playing in one Mumbai theater continuously since it premiered in 1995.

"AND THE OSCAR GOES TO . . . " (WELL, MAYBE SOMEDAY). Three Indian films have been nominated for Academy Awards for Best Foreign Language Film: *Mother India* (1957), *Salaam Bombay!* (1988), and *Lagaan* (2001). None won the prize.

EXOTIC LOCALES. Bollywood has a long tradition of shooting major films in foreign locations, most notably Europe and the United States, but also everywhere from South Africa to Malaysia to Australia. I produced one such film, *New York* (2008), which we shot almost entirely in the United States (with Philadelphia doubling as New York City).

ENGLISH IS INDIA'S OTHER OFFICIAL LANGUAGE. Many Bollywood film scripts are written in English and then later translated into Hindi. Even once they're translated, the scripts still often use English (Roman) characters to phonetically "spell out" the Hindi dialogues. So if you were to get your hands on a script . . . I'm thinking dinner theater?

BANKSY'S GOT NOTHING ON BOLLYWOOD. Hand-painted Bollywood film posters, with their pulp fiction graphics, are a remarkable testament to the artistry of thousands of brilliant but lowly paid poster painters. Though less prevalent on the streets of India today, the art form continues to be a hallmark of the industry itself.

FORGET THE ICE SCULPTURE. You can hire top Bollywood stars to perform your favorite musical number at your upcoming wedding or private party—for a nominal fee of around $1 million. Too pricey? Most will stop by and pose for photos with your guests (sorry, no performance) for a mere $500,000 (plus first-class airfare, of course). Believe it or not, there are plenty of people who do so.

BOLLYWOOD POPCORN

SPICY, MASALA-DUSTED POPCORN

**MAKES 2 BATCHES
(TOTAL SERVINGS 4 TO 6)**

2 teaspoons salt

2 teaspoons ground coriander

2 teaspoons ground cumin

2 teaspoons paprika

1 teaspoon garlic powder

½ teaspoon Indian red chilli powder (or cayenne)

⅔ cup popcorn kernels, divided

1 teaspoon canola oil, divided

4 tablespoons (½ stick) butter, divided

1 teaspoon freshly squeezed lemon juice, divided

The first step to getting your party started is to whip up a few batches of hot and spicy Bollywood popcorn. I like to make this in the microwave because it's much easier than popping on the stove (and requires less oil). Plus, guests can have their own individual bag to season with as much masala spice blend as they choose. This popcorn is salty and savory, and if you prefer a guilt-free alternative, just omit the butter. The spices won't stick quite as well, but it'll still be plenty tasty.

Let the show begin!

Create the Bollywood masala (or spice blend) by mixing together the salt, coriander, cumin, paprika, garlic powder, and red chilli powder in a small bowl.

Measure ⅓ cup of the popcorn kernels into a small bowl and pour over ½ teaspoon of the oil. Stir to coat.

Melt 2 tablespoons of the butter with ½ teaspoon of the lemon juice in the microwave, around 30 seconds.

Pour the kernels into a paper bag and fold over twice. Place the bag on top of a paper towel or plate (to absorb excess oil) and microwave on high for 3 to 4 minutes, until the popping slows to every 3 seconds.

Open the bag carefully and pour the popcorn into a large bowl. Drizzle with the melted butter and toss to coat. Then sprinkle with 1 teaspoon of the masala and toss well. Adjust the salt to taste.

Repeat for a second batch.

DINNER

KEEMA   27
Sublime Ground Beef Curry

NAAN CRISPS   29
Tandoori Pita Chips

RAJMA   30
Hearty Kidney Bean Stew

MOVIE

DEVDAS   22
Lavish, melodramatic love story based on a
literary classic

DEVDAS

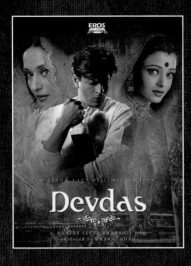

FLAVOR

Breathtaking visuals and lavish musical numbers are the hallmark of this period melodrama. It's a feast for the eyes, and like any good Indian meal—you will *not* leave hungry.

RECIPE

Based on the 1917 novel of the same name, *Devdas* tells the story of a young man (Devdas) and the girl next door (Paro) who's deeply in love with him. But Devdas only sees her as a childhood friend. By the time he realizes his true feelings, it's too late, as Paro's parents have arranged for her to marry another man.

Despondent, Devdas becomes a recluse, drowning his sorrows in booze and living in a brothel. There he meets a ravishing courtesan (Chandramukhi), who becomes devoted to him. But Devdas only has eyes for Paro, the one who got away. The tragic love triangle comes to a climactic end as Devdas descends into an alcoholic spiral.

THE "DISH"

Let's make one thing clear—*Devdas* is not a breezy film. With melodramatic acting and a running time of three hours, *Devdas* is synonymous with everything that's over the top about Bollywood. But that's exactly why I love it. *Devdas* is a visual spectacle. The director, Sanjay Leela Bhansali, is a brand name in Bollywood, known for his operatic style. Nothing tops *Devdas* in terms of gorgeous sets, opulent costumes, and stylized cinematography. Watching the movie feels like seeing a series of lush oil paintings come to life. And the musical numbers are to die for, re-created time and again at every Indian wedding from Mumbai to Mississippi.

Photographs courtesy
Eros International
(pages 20–23, 25)

That's what happens when you pair the two best Bollywood dancers of the last twenty-five years—Madhuri Dixit and Aishwarya Rai. Madhuri (who plays the courtesan) ruled the Indian film industry in the late '80s and '90s, until she passed the baton to former Miss World Aishwarya (who plays the ingénue). Director Bhansali scored a major coup when he announced that *Devdas* would feature these prima donnas going toe-to-toe for the first time. Audiences were so eager to see the stars on-screen together that he added a fierce dance duel between them, even though in the novel the two characters never meet—a significant departure that angered many critics and literary fans.

Devdas was the first Bollywood film to have its premiere at Cannes. Adding to all this fervor was the fact that the film would be Madhuri Dixit's last, before retiring from the industry while her stardom was still at a pinnacle. She moved to Denver, Colorado, with her physician husband, starting a new life as a suburban soccer mom, of all things. Of course, her American neighbors had no clue they were sharing the cul-de-sac with a superstar who had a billion devoted fans. (Not to worry, she eventually grew wistful of the spotlight and returned to Bollywood a decade later.)

Speaking of billions of fans, how can we talk about *Devdas* without discussing its megawatt lead, Shah Rukh Khan? King Khan, as he's known, has reigned over the Bollywood box office for the past three decades and counting. From romantic heartthrob to action star to dark antihero, he's done it all—with his signature, melodramatic acting style. He's been called the biggest movie star in the world by *Forbes* and *Time*, reportedly earning more money than Tom Cruise. Though his portrayal of Devdas is not without its detractors (many find his overwrought performance to be unworthy of such a literary treasure), this film will always hold a spot in the pantheon of Shah Rukh Khan classics.

INGREDIENTS

CAST: Shah Rukh Khan, Aishwarya Rai, Madhuri Dixit
DIRECTOR: Sanjay Leela Bhansali
WRITERS: Prakash Kapadia, Sanjay Leela Bhansali
BASED ON THE NOVEL BY SARAT CHANDRA CHATTOPADHYAY
MUSIC DIRECTOR: Ismail Darbar
RELEASE: 2002

TASTE THIS

If you're a fan of melodramatic romances, sweeping musical numbers, and gorgeous production values, Bollywood's got you covered and then some:

HUM DIL DE CHUKE SANAM (1999) The film that catapulted Sanjay Leela Bhansali to auteur status, this romantic drama has the most lavish musical numbers of the '90s. Though the acting is over the top, Aishwarya Rai's costumes and spectacular dances make this film my absolute favorite guilty pleasure.

UMRAO JAAN (1981) This classic (not to be confused with the 2006 remake) stars the ultimate Bollywood diva, Rekha, in her most stunning role. Based on a nineteenth-century Urdu novel about a real-life courtesan, the film features songs, dances, and dialogues that are poetry in motion.

VEER-ZAARA (2004) Legendary director Yash Chopra's lush love story turns the political conflict between India and Pakistan into a modern-day tale of star-crossed lovers. The boundless romance charts the relationship and separation of an Indian Air Force pilot (Shah Rukh Khan) and a Pakistani politician's daughter (Preity Zinta) over twenty-two tear-soaked years.

KEEMA

SUBLIME GROUND BEEF CURRY

With a movie as luxurious and classic as *Devdas*, you need a meal to match. This is, hands down, my mom's most popular dish, beloved by everyone who has tasted it. It also is a textbook example of American assimilation. Traditionally, the recipe calls for mutton because beef is rarely eaten in India. But when my mom moved to the States, she adapted the dish using hamburger meat to create something that feels familiar and comforting to us as Americans, while at the same time exotic and exciting with its full-bodied flavors.

The mark of good keema is that the ground beef is dry when serving. Occasionally, you may encounter keema in a restaurant that's soaked in tomato gravy, but that's because the chef didn't cook the meat for long enough. If you tend to keema carefully, increasing and decreasing the heat in the final stages, you'll be able to cook off the moisture and be left with crumbles of meat intensely flavored with garlic, ginger, and cloves.

Devdas is perhaps the most iconic film in this book, and I've chosen to serve this meal with it because this recipe is the one that I'm most proud to share with you. It will always remind me of my mom, an expression of her understated gifts as a cook—and a testament to how great Indian-American cuisine can be.

***

Heat a large sauté pan over medium heat. Add the ground beef and sprinkle with the turmeric. Crumble the meat with a wooden spoon and cook to render its fat, 7 to 9 minutes. Remove the meat using a slotted spoon or fine-mesh strainer, allowing the fat to stay in the pan. Set the meat aside.

Discard the grease and wipe the pan dry. Heat the oil over medium-high heat. Add the bay leaves and allow them to begin infusing the oil, about 15 seconds. Add the onions and cook, stirring, until golden brown, about 7 minutes, reducing the heat to medium if necessary to prevent the onions from burning.

Add the garlic and ginger pastes and cook, stirring, for 1 to 2 minutes. Then add the chilli powder, salt, cloves, and cinnamon. Stir the spices into the onions, allowing them to "bloom" (release their oils and flavor) for another minute.

Stir in the tomato to create a thick paste. Cover and simmer until the tomato has completely broken down, 5 to 7 minutes. The sauce should start to "come

SERVES 4 TO 6

2 pounds 85% lean ground beef

½ tablespoon ground turmeric

2 tablespoons canola oil

3 bay leaves

2 medium onions, finely chopped

3 tablespoons garlic paste (or minced garlic)

2 tablespoons ginger paste (or minced ginger)

½ tablespoon Indian red chilli powder (or cayenne)*

2 teaspoons salt

1 teaspoon ground cloves

1 teaspoon ground cinnamon

1 medium tomato, finely chopped

2 teaspoons ground coriander

½ cup chopped cilantro

Lemon, to taste

Cooked rice (any type), for serving

* Use 1 teaspoon for less heat

(Opposite)
Keema
Rajma, p. 30
Naan Crisps, p. 29

together"—you'll notice the oil separating and the sauce pulling away slightly from the sides of the pan.

Return the meat to the pan. Stir well, coating the meat with the spicy tomato sauce. Cook over medium heat for 7 minutes.

Add the coriander. Continue to cook, uncovered, for 15 to 20 minutes, using a fork to crumble the meat until it is dry and granular.

Remove the bay leaves and add the cilantro. Finish with a squeeze of lemon. Adjust the salt and seasonings to taste. (Tip: If you overdid it with the spices, just add a tablespoon of ground, unsweetened coconut to lessen the intensity.) Serve with rice. Keema always tastes better when made a day or two ahead.

NAAN CRISPS

TANDOORI PITA CHIPS

These naan crisps add a delightful crunch to the meal. They're dusted with a simplified tandoori spice blend (the kind you find on tandoori chicken, with its distinctive red, paprika hue). Naan crisps are great for scooping up the rajma stew and ground beef keema. As a fun variation, you could serve this meal nacho style, using the naan crisps as a bed, piling the keema and rajma on top, along with some freshly chopped tomatoes, onions, and a dollop of Greek yogurt or sour cream.

Preheat the oven to 400°F.

In a small bowl, combine all the spices. Mix thoroughly to create a uniform, smooth powder.

Cut the naan into small triangles (I find this easy to do with kitchen scissors). Arrange on a baking sheet and brush both sides lightly with olive oil.

Sprinkle both sides with the spice mixture—a light dusting for mild flavor, a more liberal amount for a robust punch. You will likely have some spice blend left over. Store it in a jar and use when grilling chicken or fish.

Bake the naan crisps for about 10 minutes, until crispy around the edges and lightly charred.

Remove from the oven and sprinkle with sea salt. Serve with the keema and rajma.

SERVES 4 TO 6

1 tablespoon paprika

½ teaspoon salt

½ teaspoon garlic powder

¼ teaspoon ground coriander

¼ teaspoon ground cumin

¼ teaspoon Indian red chilli powder (or cayenne)

¼ teaspoon freshly ground black pepper

One 8- to 10-ounce package naan

Extra-virgin olive oil, as needed

Sea salt, to taste

RAJMA

HEARTY KIDNEY BEAN STEW

SERVES 4

Two 15.5-ounce cans red kidney beans

1 tablespoon canola oil

1 teaspoon black mustard seeds

1 medium onion, finely chopped

1 tablespoon garlic paste (or minced garlic)

½ tablespoon ginger paste (or minced ginger)

2 teaspoons ground cumin

1 teaspoon Indian red chilli powder (or cayenne)

1 teaspoon salt

¼ teaspoon ground turmeric

2 medium tomatoes, diced

¼ teaspoon tamarind paste (optional)

½ tablespoon soy sauce

2 tablespoons chopped cilantro, plus extra for garnish

1 teaspoon ground coriander

Cooked rice (any type), for serving

Greek yogurt (2% or whole) or sour cream, to finish

Pairing this kidney bean stew with ground beef keema has proven to be a delicious combination in my home, something akin to chili con carne. It's hard to believe that simple kidney beans can transform into a dish with so many layers of flavor. Smoky cumin, earthy coriander, warm ginger, and spicy garlic combine to make rajma a true showstopper.

This dish could also stand on its own, without the keema, as a satisfying vegetarian chili served over rice. Rajma is North Indian comfort food—and all you'll need is one bowl of this warm stew to understand why.

Rinse the beans well and drain. Set aside.

In a medium saucepan, heat the oil over medium-high heat. Once the oil is shimmering hot, add the mustard seeds. As soon as the seeds begin to pop, add the onion and cook, stirring, for about 3 minutes, reducing the heat to medium if necessary to prevent the onion from burning. Add the garlic and ginger pastes and cook, stirring, for another minute. Add the cumin, red chilli powder, salt, and turmeric. Stir the spices into the onion, allowing them to bloom, for about a minute.

Stir in the tomatoes. Cover and cook until the tomatoes have broken down, 5 to 7 minutes.

Add the beans and stir. Add 1 cup hot water and bring to a boil. Dissolve the tamarind paste into the hot stew along with the soy sauce. Lower the heat, cover, and simmer for 20 minutes, stirring occasionally.

Add the cilantro and coriander. Use the back of your spoon (or a potato masher) to crush about half of the beans to create a rich gravy. Continue cooking, increasing the heat as necessary, until the sauce is thick and transforms from red to deep brown, another 5 minutes or so.

Adjust the salt and seasonings to taste. Garnish with fresh cilantro and serve in a bowl over the keema and rice. Finish with a dollop of Greek yogurt or sour cream.

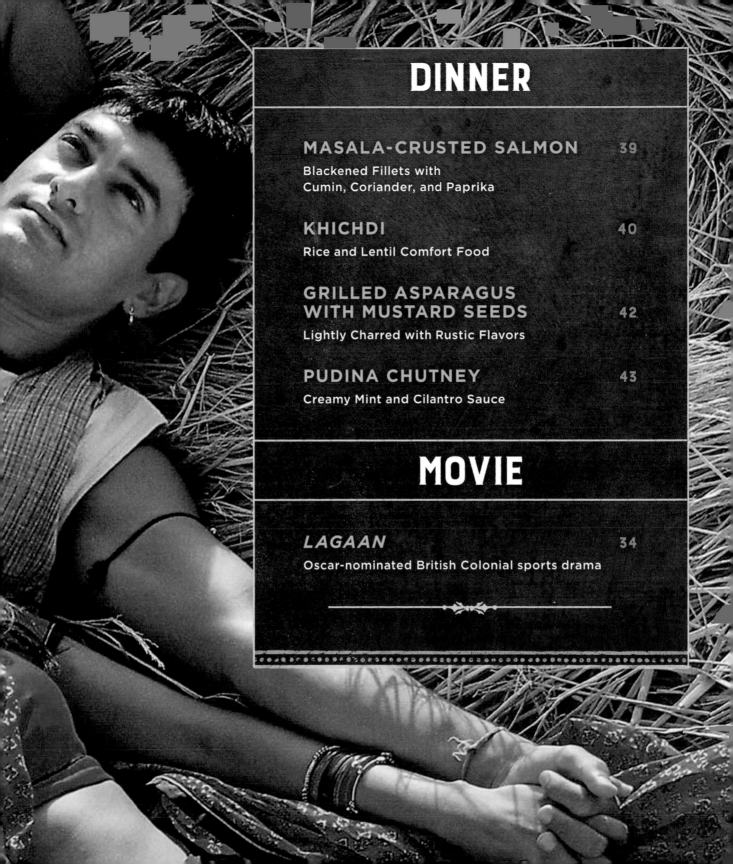

DINNER

MASALA-CRUSTED SALMON
Blackened Fillets with
Cumin, Coriander, and Paprika
39

KHICHDI
Rice and Lentil Comfort Food
40

GRILLED ASPARAGUS
WITH MUSTARD SEEDS
Lightly Charred with Rustic Flavors
42

PUDINA CHUTNEY
Creamy Mint and Cilantro Sauce
43

MOVIE

LAGAAN
Oscar-nominated British Colonial sports drama
34

LAGAAN

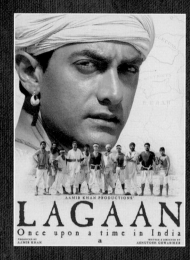

FLAVOR

The only contemporary Bollywood film to be nominated for an Academy Award, this patriotic sports drama is a modern classic.

RECIPE

It's the late 1800s and the British have been occupying India for over 100 years. In a drought-ridden village, a community of poor farmers is unable to pay the exorbitant tax (or *lagaan*) that's imposed upon them by their British colonizers.

When the farmers witness British officers playing a peculiar game called cricket, a courageous young man named Bhuvan accepts a bet from the conniving Commander Russell: If the village can assemble a team and beat the officers in a cricket match, then their tax will be waived for three years. But if they lose, they'll have to pay three times as much. Bhuvan sets out to convince the villagers to join him in beating the Brits at their own game—*after* they first learn how to play.

THE "DISH"

In some ways, the story of *Lagaan* on-screen mirrors the film's journey off-screen. This is a film that's all about Indians competing on the world stage, bucking the odds. It's one of only three Indian films in history to have garnered a nomination for an Academy Award in the Best Foreign Language category. And when the movie's creators walked the red carpet wearing traditional attire, it was a moment of incredible pride for Indians all over the world—including me. It felt like, *finally*, Bollywood had arrived.

At the center of all this attention was Aamir Khan, the star and producer of the film. One of the reigning kings of Bollywood, Aamir shot to fame in the late

1980s with the hit movie *Qayamat Se Qayamat Tak*. He followed that up with a decade of successful romantic dramas that capitalized on his boyish good looks. Beginning with *Lagaan* in 2001, he started taking on complicated, nontraditional roles that showcased his genuine acting talent and made him one of the industry's highest grossing actors ever.

Aamir is something of a maverick. He eschews award shows. He's a notorious perfectionist. He only does one movie a year, transforming his body for each new role. He's a producer and director. And he's an engaged social activist. His landmark TV talk show, *Satyamev Jayate*, bravely started national conversations on taboo topics like rape, domestic violence, and the caste system.

But being an outspoken celebrity comes with a price. In 2015, Aamir made an off-handed comment in reaction to escalating intolerance in India. He said that his wife sometimes worries about their son's future and wonders if they should "move out of India." Those few words sparked a firestorm of controversy. Aamir and his wife were called traitors, politicians used him as a punching bag, and mobs of protestors swarmed his house. Through it all, the actor tried to navigate the hysteria by asserting his allegiance to India while sticking to (and perhaps illustrating) his criticism of intolerance in the country.

There's a reason Bollywood movies are so melodramatic. India is a place where passions run hot and cold.

Lagaan didn't end up winning an Oscar (nor has any other Indian movie to date). The film isn't perfect by any means. The story line is fairly formulaic for a sports movie and the British characters teeter on being caricatures. Nonetheless, it was a milestone for Indians to finally witness one of their beloved Bollywood films take its place in world cinema.

INGREDIENTS

CAST: Aamir Khan, Gracy Singh
WRITER AND DIRECTOR: Ashutosh Gowariker
MUSIC DIRECTOR: A. R. Rahman
RELEASE: 2001

TASTE THIS

Sports and patriotism aren't just for red-blooded Americans. Here are some Bollywood favorites that capitalize on these crowd-pleasing themes:

MOTHER INDIA (1957) Truly the mother of them all, this cinematic gem was the first Indian film to be nominated for an Oscar. Legendary actress Nargis played a poverty-stricken peasant who goes to super-human lengths to raise her sons with integrity, setting the standard for the ideal Indian woman.

RANG DE BASANTI (2006) Aamir Khan takes on the Brits once again in this hugely popular film about a group of college friends making a documentary about radical freedom fighters. The lessons they learn from history give them the courage to take a stand against injustice in their own lives.

DANGAL (2016) Aamir Khan adds another blockbuster sports flick to his repertoire with this biopic. Mahavir Singh Phogat is a one-time wrestler who laments not having any sons to fulfill his championship dreams . . . so he decides to teach his daughters how to compete in a man's world.

MASALA-CRUSTED SALMON

BLACKENED FILLETS WITH CUMIN, CORIANDER, AND PAPRIKA

The British stole a lot of things from India—jewels, natural resources, and, of course, freedom. But one of the few good things to come from colonialism was the spread of Indian cuisine to Great Britain, where it continues to be a thriving art form, home to some of the best Indian restaurants in the world.

Aside from tepid chicken tikka masala (which, rumor has it, was invented in Glasgow by a chef who poured tomato soup over chicken curry), the Brits adapted other Indian dishes in their own, unique way. One such example is kedgeree, an Anglo interpretation of a popular Indian comfort food called khichdi. Kedgeree is made with flaked fish and rice, while khichdi is made with lentils and rice. For this meal, we're deconstructing kedgeree to showcase its flavorful Indian roots.

We begin with this elegant and tasty masala-crusted salmon. Cumin and coriander provide deeply earthy flavors, while paprika and red chilli powder combine to give heat and a beautiful brick color to the fillets. Drizzled with mint chutney, the buttery salmon flakes easily with a fork and melts in your mouth. The best thing about this recipe is that it's remarkably simple to make. Open up a bottle of wine, get a nice sear on the salmon, and dinner will be ready in half an hour.

SERVES 4

- 4 salmon fillets (1½ to 2 pounds total), skinned
- 2 tablespoons paprika
- 2 teaspoons ground cumin
- 2 teaspoons ground coriander
- 2 teaspoons light brown sugar
- 1 teaspoon Indian red chilli powder (or cayenne)
- 1 teaspoon salt
- ½ teaspoon ground turmeric
- Grated zest of 1 lemon
- 1 tablespoon canola oil

Wash and pat dry the salmon fillets.

In a small bowl, mix together the paprika, cumin, coriander, brown sugar, red chilli powder, salt, turmeric, and lemon zest. Rub approximately ½ tablespoon of the spice blend onto each side of the salmon fillets.

Heat the oil in a large nonstick skillet over medium heat. Once the pan is hot, place the fillets in the pan and cook for 4 minutes on the first side. Flip the fillets and cook for an additional 3 to 4 minutes on the second side, or until the desired degree of doneness.

Plate the salmon and drizzle with pudina (mint) chutney.

(Opposite)
Masala-Crusted Salmon
Pudina Chutney, p. 43
Grilled Asparagus with
Mustard Seeds, p. 42
Khichdi, p. 40

KHICHDI

RICE AND LENTIL COMFORT FOOD

SERVES 4

1 cup white rice (any type)

½ cup split moong dal (split mung beans with green husks)

1 teaspoon salt

¼ teaspoon ground turmeric

¼ teaspoon black peppercorns

3 tablespoons butter or ghee (page 298), divided

¼ cup cashews

1 teaspoon cumin seeds

7 to 10 curry leaves*

2 or 3 Indian dried red chillies, broken in half

* Substitute: 3 bay leaves

Khichdi is comfort food. It's what people all over India eat when they're feeling under the weather or want a quick, one-pot supper. It has protein and carbs, a healthy amount of fat, and subtle flavor. When British colonists brought khichdi back home to England, it became a fashionable breakfast food (it was even served by Mrs. Patmore on *Downton Abbey*). They added fish, hard-boiled eggs, and parsley to create a dish called *kedgeree*.

In India, you would never do that. But still, there are plenty of authentic variations—for example, you could add onions, tomatoes, vegetables, or different types of dal (lentils). Also, the consistency can range from quite mushy to dry. This recipe is the way I personally enjoy it, but everyone has his or her own, staunch preferences. However it's presented, khichdi is rich, creamy, and satisfying. That's why it's often fed to babies. And I hope it warms your tummy in much the same way.

In a large saucepan (preferably nonstick), combine the rice and dal. Rinse well several times, until the water starts to become less cloudy (starchy). Then cover with water and soak for 30 minutes.

Drain the rice and dal. Add 5 cups water and bring to a boil over high heat.

Add the salt, turmeric, and peppercorns. Decrease the heat to a gentle boil and cook with the lid slightly ajar, stirring occasionally.

Meanwhile, in a small sauté pan, melt 2 tablespoons of the butter over medium heat. Once the butter is melted, add the cashews and fry until they begin to turn deep brown. Then add the cumin seeds, curry leaves, and red chillies and fry for about 20 seconds. If the butter starts to get too hot, simply stir in a spoonful of the rice-lentils to the pan to temper.

Pour the contents of the sauté pan into the pot of boiling rice and lentils. Stir well. Continue simmering gently until the rice is fully cooked and mushy, with a consistency similar to porridge or grits. (If you need to add more water along the way, feel free to do so.)

Adjust the salt to taste (you'll likely want to add another ½ teaspoon or more). Serve alongside the salmon with a pat of the remaining 1 tablespoon butter on each serving. Inform your guests to discard the curry leaves and red chillies while eating.

GRILLED ASPARAGUS WITH MUSTARD SEEDS

LIGHTLY CHARRED WITH RUSTIC FLAVORS

SERVES 4

1 to 1½ pounds asparagus (20 to 24 stalks), washed and patted dry

1 tablespoon extra-virgin olive oil

1 teaspoon black mustard seeds

½ teaspoon ground cumin

½ teaspoon garlic powder

½ teaspoon salt

½ teaspoon freshly ground black pepper

Grated zest of 1 lemon

Sea salt (optional)

Mustard seeds are one of the most important, yet least recognized, treasures in the Indian spice cabinet. Cumin gets a lot of attention in America, probably because of its popularity in Mexican food. Coriander has become increasingly familiar, perhaps because it goes hand-in-hand with cumin. But black mustard seeds, in my opinion, are yet to have their moment in the spotlight.

That's why I enjoy this grilled asparagus side dish, because mustard seeds are allowed to take center stage. In this simple preparation, you'll begin to get a sense of how the tiny black seeds can really come alive in your mouth, with a slightly sharp, slightly refreshing flavor that tastes like, well . . . mustard. But when paired with other Indian spices, mustard seeds contribute to a unique, rustic flavor profile that is the signature of home-cooked Indian food.

Preheat a grill pan over medium-high heat.

To trim the asparagus, bend the end of each stalk until it snaps. Place the trimmed asparagus in a dish or on a baking sheet. Drizzle with the olive oil. Sprinkle the asparagus with the mustard seeds, cumin, garlic powder, salt, and pepper. Use your hands to toss the stalks in the oil and spices, coating all the pieces evenly.

Place the asparagus on the grill pan, against the grain. Grill for 5 minutes on the first side. Then flip and grill for another 3 to 5 minutes on the other side. (Alternatively, you could broil the asparagus on high for 10 to 15 minutes, until tender, flipping halfway through the cooking time.)

Arrange on a platter. Finish with the lemon zest and sea salt to taste. Serve, alongside a bowl of pudina (mint) chutney, allowing your guests to drizzle some on top if they desire.

PUDINA CHUTNEY

CREAMY MINT AND CILANTRO SAUCE

Mint (*pudina* in Hindi) chutney is a classic condiment in Indian cuisine. It's incredibly versatile, served with everything from kebabs to samosas to street snacks. You'll probably recognize it as the green condiment found on the table in most Indian restaurants. In this menu, the fresh mint with tangy yogurt is the perfect way to cut the buttery richness of our salmon entrée. Cilantro adds another layer of freshness, while ginger and Indian green chilli provide a spicy kick.

With the quantities I've outlined in this recipe, you'll likely have leftover chutney—for which you'll thank me. Store it in the freezer and use it anytime as a healthy dip for veggies, or as a sauce for meat and seafood entrées (it goes great on Kati Rolls, page 125).

SERVES 4 TO 6

1 cup fresh mint leaves

½ cup fresh cilantro (leaves and stems)

½ cup 2% Greek yogurt

1 garlic clove

1-inch piece fresh ginger, peeled and sliced

1 Indian green chilli, cut in half

½ teaspoon salt

½ teaspoon ground cumin

Wash the mint and cilantro. Since the sauce won't be cooked, it's important to wash the herbs well, to rinse off any grit that may be stuck to the leaves or stems.

Place the mint, cilantro, yogurt, garlic, ginger, chilli, salt, and cumin in a blender and puree until smooth, adding up to 1 tablespoon water if needed. You will probably need to stop the blender a few times and stir the contents to get things going.

Adjust the seasonings to taste. Store leftovers in the fridge for up to a week, or in the freezer for months.

DINNER

PALAK CHICKEN   51
Velvety Spinach and Chicken Curry

CHANA MASALA   53
Classic North Indian Chickpeas

GOBI MATAR   54
Cauliflower Sautéed with Peas and Tomatoes

KHEER   55
Creamy Rice Pudding

MOVIE

NH10   46
Terrifyingly good suspense thriller

NH10

FLAVOR

You may regret having eaten a big dinner once you start watching this gut-wrenching, terrifying suspense thriller.

RECIPE

National Highway 10 (or NH10) is a 250-mile stretch of road leading out of the capital, New Delhi, to the northern border of India. A young, successful couple, Arjun and Meera, decide to take a weekend road trip. They pack up their car and take off into the scenic countryside.

Arjun and Meera aren't very far along NH10 when they enter a different world—that of rural India. At a roadside truck stop, they become unwittingly embroiled in a local skirmish. Their trip takes a severe detour as they're dragged off the main road (literally and figuratively) into violent backwaters ruled by tribal justice. And these city slickers might not get out alive.

THE "DISH"

Anyone who has ever been to India can tell you that it's a land of extremes. Many people comment that it feels like there are "two Indias." There's the India you experience inside your hotel, full of gilded corridors and exquisite luxuries. And then there's the India you discover when you step outside, smacked in the face with heat and pollution. Men, women, and even children work in menial labor—breaking stones with pickaxes and carrying bricks on their heads. They are the inhabitants of the *other* India—the roughly 300 million people who live on $1 per day.

NH10 captures this dichotomy in a visceral way. As the movie opens, we identify with Arjun and Meera. They're beautiful, sophisticated, and upwardly

Photographs courtesy
Phantom Films (pages
44–47, 49)

mobile. They could just as easily be a young couple living in New York instead of New Delhi. We start to fall into the lull of globalization—the media-hyped message that you can go anywhere in the world today and still feel at home, with easy access to Twitter, FaceTime, and Starbucks. Just log on to Airbnb and pack your bags! But it's only a few miles out of the city—and a few minutes into the movie—when we're hit with reality.

The film is a thrill ride. There will definitely be moments when you'll want to curl up under a blanket or cover your eyes—and that's all part of the fun. But *NH10* also provides a sharp commentary about the clash of class and modernity that's happening in India and other places around the world today. As much as we'd like to shove this unfortunate truth under the rug, we see every day the mounting, often violent friction of old vs. new, East vs. West, and evangelical vs. secular.

The star of the film is Anushka Sharma, and she deserves major props. Not only does she turn in a brutal performance, but she's also the producer of the film. Unlike most other actors, Anushka is not from a film family (she started out as a model). She has built her successful career on the merits of her talent alone, a claim that few other Bollywood stars can make.

I had the opportunity to work with Anushka in *Badmaash Company*. Although our film was unfortunately one of her only failures, she was an energetic and consummate professional through and through. It came as no surprise to me that she added producer to her resume at such a young age (twenty-six), and that too with a shrewd film like *NH10*, which was low-budget and high-profit.

INGREDIENTS

CAST: Anushka Sharma, Neil Bhoopalam
DIRECTOR: Navdeep Singh
WRITER: Sudip Sharma
RELEASE: 2015

TASTE THIS

To be honest, I can't think of any Bollywood movie that's as scary as *NH10*, but these (sometimes campy) thrillers will keep you on the edge of your seat:

NEERJA (2016) Fashion icon Sonam Kapoor stars as Neerja Bhanot, a twenty-two-year-old flight attendant who stared down Palestinian terrorists and saved hundreds of lives aboard Pan Am Flight 73 in 1986. As someone who hates to fly, I just can't bring myself to watch this chilling true story.

KAUN (1999) This psychological suspense film from Bollywood's horror maven Ram Gopal Varma has only three characters. It's a rainy night with a serial killer on the loose and a young woman is home alone when the doorbell keeps ringing (the title means "Who's there?"). Urmila Matondkar's performance as the frightened woman is truly eerie.

GUMNAAM (1965) Based on Agatha Christie's *And Then There Were None*, this murder mystery is pure camp classic, a favorite of old-school Bollywood. The psychedelic musical numbers alone are worth the price of admission.

PALAK CHICKEN

VELVETY SPINACH AND CHICKEN CURRY

This menu is quintessentially North Indian, the kind of hearty meal you might find at a truck-stop café (called a *dhaba*) along NH10. The centerpiece is this delightful palak chicken, sometimes called saag chicken (*palak* means "spinach" while *saag* refers to any leafy greens, including spinach, but also mustard leaves and collard greens).

I love recipes that blend meat and vegetables together. Whether it's this spinach-chicken curry or other variations, like pumpkin-beef curry or eggplant-chicken curry, I find that the deep spiciness of meat offset with the subtle sweetness of vegetables makes for a wonderful juxtaposition of flavors.

In this preparation, you're welcome to brown the chicken pieces before adding them to the pan, but I don't find it to be necessary. The difference in flavor is marginal when the chicken is cooked in a curry with so many spices. It's only a matter of texture, and since we're looking for a smooth, silky feel, I find that browning the chicken works against that objective.

Along the same lines, I prefer to use frozen spinach to fresh because it provides a moist environment for the chicken, and, when combined with yogurt, creates a creamy sauce without relying on heavy cream. Speaking of which, don't be fooled by the spinach dishes you encounter in Indian restaurants—there's nothing healthy about them, as they are usually swimming in milk fat. My palak chicken recipe is just as rich, but with none of the guilt.

Thaw the spinach on the countertop or in the microwave.

Meanwhile, heat the oil in a Dutch oven or large saucepan over medium heat. Add the bay leaf and allow it to begin infusing the oil, about 15 seconds. Add the onion and cook, stirring, until golden, 7 to 9 minutes, reducing the heat as necessary. You want the onion to *slowly* turn golden and develop a mellow flavor (as opposed to deeply browning as we would for a classic chicken curry).

Add the garlic and ginger pastes and cook, stirring, for another 2 minutes. Then add 1½ teaspoons of the salt, the red chilli powder, cumin, ½ teaspoon of the turmeric, the cinnamon, and cloves. Allow the spices to bloom in the oil for about a minute.

SERVES 4 TO 6

Two 10-ounce packages frozen chopped spinach

2 tablespoons canola oil

1 bay leaf

1 large onion, finely chopped

2 tablespoons garlic paste (or minced garlic)

1 heaping tablespoon ginger paste (or minced ginger)

2 teaspoons salt, divided

1 teaspoon Indian red chilli powder (or cayenne)

1 teaspoon ground cumin

1 teaspoon ground turmeric, divided

½ teaspoon ground cinnamon

½ teaspoon ground cloves

1 medium tomato, diced

2 pounds boneless, skinless chicken thighs (or breasts), cut into 1- to 1½-inch chunks

2 tablespoons Greek yogurt (2% or whole)

½ tablespoon ground coriander

Naan, roti, or paratha for serving

(Opposite, clockwise from top-left) Chana Masala, p. 53 paratha, p. 292 Palak Chicken Gobi Matar, p. 54

Stir in the tomato. Cook, stirring, for about 3 minutes, until the tomato has started to break down.

Add the spinach to the pan. Increase the heat to medium-high and break up the spinach while stirring it into the tomato-onion paste (sometimes it can be helpful to use a fork to break it up). Season with the remaining ½ teaspoon salt. Stir well. Cover and simmer for 5 minutes.

Season the chicken with the remaining ½ teaspoon turmeric and add to the pan. Stir well to incorporate. Decrease the heat, cover, and simmer, stirring occasionally, for 10 minutes.

Remove the bay leaf. Stir in the yogurt and coriander. If you're making the dish a day ahead, turn off the heat at this point. Cool before refrigerating and then finish cooking before you serve.

Increase the heat and continue cooking, uncovered, stirring occasionally, for 15 minutes.

Check and adjust the seasonings (you might want to add another pinch or two of salt). The spices will mellow after a few minutes, but if you find that it's still too hot for your liking, just add more yogurt. Allow the meat to rest for 5 minutes before serving with naan, roti, or paratha.

CHANA MASALA

CLASSIC NORTH INDIAN CHICKPEAS

This is perhaps the most popular vegetarian dish in all of North India. Hearty chickpeas (*chana*) are simmered in tomatoes, onions, and an Indian spice blend (*masala* in Hindi). It's imperative that you serve this with soft roti or naan because there's nothing more satisfying and comforting than savory chickpeas and bread (as anyone who enjoys hummus and pita can attest). In fact, chana masala makes for a great entrée or nutritious lunch all by itself. My hope is that you'll add this recipe to your repertoire of healthy, tasty, and easy-to-prepare dishes that you can go back to again and again.

In a medium saucepan, heat the oil over medium-high heat. Once the oil is shimmering hot, add the mustard seeds. As soon as the seeds start to pop, add the onion and cook, stirring, for about 3 minutes, reducing the heat to medium if necessary to prevent burning.

Add the garlic and ginger pastes and cook, stirring, for another minute. Then add the cumin, red chilli powder, salt, and turmeric. Stir the spices into the onion, and allow them to bloom for about a minute.

Add the tomato and stir well to create a thick paste. Cover and simmer until the tomato has broken down, 3 to 5 minutes.

Add the chickpeas to the pan, increase the heat, and stir well. Dissolve the tamarind paste in 1 tablespoon of warm water and add to the pan. Cover tightly and simmer, stirring occasionally, for 20 minutes.

Add the cilantro and coriander. Use the back of your spoon to crush one-fourth to one-half of the chickpeas. You want a portion of the chickpeas to break down and mix with the onion and tomato to create a thick and flavorful gravy. Cover, decrease the heat, and simmer for another 5-10 minutes, stirring occasionally, until deeply brown in color.

Adjust the seasonings to taste (if you'd like to add more salt, try soy sauce instead—it adds saltiness while deepening the color of the dish). Serve with naan, roti, or paratha.

SERVES 4 TO 6

1 tablespoon canola oil

½ tablespoon black mustard seeds

1 medium onion, finely chopped

1 tablespoon garlic paste (or minced garlic)

½ tablespoon ginger paste (or minced ginger)

2 teaspoons ground cumin

1 teaspoon Indian red chilli powder (or cayenne)

1 teaspoon salt

½ teaspoon ground turmeric

1 medium tomato, diced

Two 15.5-ounce cans chickpeas, rinsed and drained

¼ teaspoon tamarind paste (optional)

2 tablespoons chopped cilantro

½ tablespoon ground coriander

Naan, roti, or paratha, for serving

GOBI MATAR

CAULIFLOWER SAUTÉED WITH PEAS AND TOMATOES

SERVES 4 TO 6

1 head cauliflower

1 tablespoon canola oil

½ tablespoon black mustard seeds

½ tablespoon cumin seeds

1 bay leaf

1 medium onion, finely chopped

1 tablespoon garlic paste (or minced garlic)

1 tablespoon ginger paste (or minced ginger)

½ teaspoon Indian red chilli powder (or cayenne)

1 teaspoon salt

½ teaspoon ground turmeric

1 medium tomato, diced

1 cup frozen peas

2 tablespoons chopped cilantro

1 teaspoon ground coriander

Fresh mint, for garnish

Naan, roti, or paratha, for serving

Continuing with our roadside meal, this tasty side dish is one of the few restaurant staples that I consider healthy enough to serve at home. Crunchy cauliflower florets (*gobi*) are simmered in spicy tomato sauce and dotted with sweet peas (*matar*). The amount of time you cook this is up to you. Some people like to do a relatively quick stir-fry, to keep the cauliflower crisp, while others (like me) enjoy the cauliflower when it's quite tender, melting into the tomatoes and spices. In either case, the peas only need a few minutes at the end, just enough time to add a vibrant green finish to the dish.

Wash the cauliflower and cut into small-medium florets with very short stalks. Dry well on paper towels.

In a medium saucepan, heat the oil over medium-high heat. Once the oil is shimmering hot, add the mustard seeds, cumin seeds, and bay leaf. As soon as the mustard seeds begin to pop, add the onion and cook, stirring, reducing the heat to medium if necessary to prevent burning, for 3 minutes.

Add the garlic and ginger pastes and cook, stirring, for another minute. Then add the red chilli powder, salt, and turmeric. Stir the spices into the onion, allowing them to bloom for about a minute.

Add the tomato and stir well to create a thick paste. Cover and simmer gently until the tomato has broken down, 3 to 5 minutes.

Add the cauliflower to the pan, increase the heat, and stir well to coat all the pieces with the spicy paste. Then cover, lower the heat, and simmer, stirring occasionally, until the cauliflower is cooked to the desired tenderness (personally, I like the cauliflower to be quite soft, which takes about 20 minutes).

Add the frozen peas (no need to thaw), cilantro, and coriander. Turn up the heat and stir to combine. Cook, uncovered, until the peas have cooked through, a few more minutes.

Adjust the seasonings to taste. Remove the bay leaf and serve, garnished with a few sprigs of mint, accompanied by naan, roti, or paratha.

KHEER

CREAMY RICE PUDDING

It seems as though every culture has its version of rice pudding. So it should come as no surprise that Indians do too, considering how important rice is in our cuisine. Kheer is incredibly popular in India, particularly in North India, in the region of NH10. It has transferred successfully into Indian-American homes, perhaps because it's much simpler to make than most other Indian desserts. It's decadent and comforting, suitable for family as well as guests.

There's a popular variation of this dessert in South India, called payasam, which is made with toasted, broken vermicelli in place of rice. Speaking of variations, if you happen to have saffron in your spice cabinet, you should soak a pinch in milk and add it to the kheer for a wonderful, luxurious color.

Some people prefer to eat kheer warm, while others like it cold. If you would like to try it hot, ladle it immediately into pudding bowls and garnish with chopped pistachios. Personally, I enjoy it cold, so I transfer the finished kheer from the stove to a serving dish, cool it completely, and then refrigerate. When it comes out of the fridge a few hours later, it will have thickened, so just stir it, perhaps with a spoonful or two of milk, to reach the desired consistency.

SERVES 4 TO 6

¼ cup **white rice (any type)**

4 cups **whole milk**

2 tablespoons **unsalted butter or ghee (page 298)**

2 tablespoons **sliced almonds**

2 tablespoons **golden raisins**

¾ cup **sweetened condensed milk**

¼ teaspoon **ground cardamom**

Chopped unsalted pistachios, for garnish

Add the rice to a medium saucepan with a heavy bottom (I prefer to use nonstick). Rinse well several times, until the water starts to run clear. Drain.

Cover the rice with the milk and bring to a boil over medium heat; be careful to keep the heat gentle or else the milk will burn. Stir occasionally as the milk is heating to make sure neither the rice nor the milk sticks to the bottom of the pan. After the milk has come to a boil, decrease the heat to a rapid simmer. Cook the rice, stirring very often, until tender, about 20 minutes. Keep a close eye on it, reducing the heat if necessary.

Meanwhile, melt the butter in a small skillet over medium-low heat. Once the butter is melted, add the almonds and raisins and cook, stirring occasionally, over a gentle heat (between medium and medium-low) until the raisins are plump and the almonds golden, about 3 minutes. Remove from the heat.

Stir the condensed milk into the pan with the rice. Add the almonds and raisins (along with the melted butter). Add the cardamom. Stir all the ingredients together and bring back to a gentle boil.

Decrease the heat and simmer, stirring often, for 10 minutes as the kheer thickens. Taste. If you find it to be too sweet for your liking (as Indian desserts can be), simply add more whole milk.

Serve, warm or chilled, in pudding bowls, garnished with chopped pistachios.

DINNER

SHRIMP CURRY 65
Shrimp in Rich Gravy of Poppy Seeds and Tamarind

BHINDI MASALA 67
Okra Sautéed with Dry Spices

BLACK-EYED PEAS 69
Warm Relish Simmered with Mustard Seeds, Cumin, and Coriander

MOVIE

YEH JAWAANI HAI DEEWANI 60
Modern, coming-of-age romance with a killer soundtrack

YEH JAWAANI HAI DEEWANI

FLAVOR

With irresistible dance music and a youthful spirit (not to mention a sexy lead couple), this coming-of-age drama about a group of friends is like happy hour at your favorite college pub.

RECIPE

The title of this film translates as *This Youth Is Crazy*. It follows a group of four college friends on a trekking expedition in the Himalayas. The shy, nerdy girl (Naina) develops a crush on the charismatic, popular boy (Bunny), who coaxes her out of her shell. Opposites certainly attract, but mere attraction might not be enough for two people with different life ambitions to end up together.

The gang reunites eight years later at the wedding of one of the friends (Aditi). As times have changed, so have their lives. Over the course of the wedding weekend, they're faced with the choices that come with adulthood—trading dreams for reality, but perhaps finding deeper happiness in the end.

THE "DISH"

This is not your father's Bollywood. *Yeh Jawaani Hai Deewani* is part of a new wave of Bollywood stories, one that reflects a country on the move (which was first depicted in the seminal 2001 coming-of-age drama, *Dil Chahta Hai*). The characters in this film represent the youth of modern India, where guys and girls interact freely, hold down careers, and enjoy traveling with friends—basically, a generation that's becoming more Westernized in lifestyle and attitudes.

The film deftly captured this youthful spirit to become one of the top ten box office moneymakers in Bollywood history. Its success was fueled, at least in part, by the off-screen relationship between its red-hot leads, Ranbir Kapoor and Deepika Padukone. These media darlings are aspirational ambassadors for their generation, their every move watched and copied by hundreds of millions of admiring young fans.

But the thing that makes this film so juicy is the fact that it reunited the couple after a very public breakup. What's more, the stars were quite open about discussing their relationship in the press. This type of frankness about romance had perhaps never before been seen in Bollywood.

Of course, affairs between Bollywood stars are nothing new. But in the past, these relationships were rarely admitted in public, unseemly in a country where the vast majority of marriages are arranged. The fact that Ranbir and Deepika not only acknowledged that they were once involved, but also discussed the realities of trying to maintain a friendship post-breakup, signaled to the country's youth that perhaps love need not lurk in the shadows.

Everything about this film is youthful and modern, from the music to the fashion—and even the angsty coming-of-age problems the characters face. Gone are the days when Bollywood characters struggled to put food on the table. In this film, they're traipsing through the streets of Paris, or on vacation with their buddies, bemoaning the pressures of "growing up." First world problems, for sure.

You may notice another "Westernized" aspect of the film: its costar, Kalki Koechlin. Born in India to French parents, Kalki is a white girl who speaks Hindi. She may seem out of place at first glance, but in some ways she personifies the globalization that India is undergoing.

Directed by twenty-nine-year-old wunderkind Ayan Mukerji, *Yeh Jawaani Hai Deewani* is a fresh, fun romp that isn't worried about being "serious cinema." But with its carefree spirit, it may actually be making a serious statement.

INGREDIENTS

CAST: Ranbir Kapoor, Deepika Padukone, Aditya Roy Kapoor, Kalki Koechlin
WRITER AND DIRECTOR: Ayan Mukerji
MUSIC DIRECTOR: Pritam
RELEASE: 2013

TASTE THIS

If modern, youthful friendships and star-crossed lovers are your thing, then take a spin with these other contemporary coming-of-age stories:

JAB WE MET (2007) Undoubtedly the best romantic comedy in contemporary Bollywood, this film took India by storm. The songs, the beautiful young stars (who were a couple in real life), even the combining of English with Hindi in the film's title (translation: *When We Met*)—everything about this film set a new standard for falling in love in the twenty-first century.

ZINDAGI NA MILEGI DOBARA (2011) Time to pack your bags for a gorgeous road trip through the Spanish countryside. Three best buddies who've drifted apart over the years decide to take one final hurrah that reconnects them with one another and their lost zest for life.

KAI PO CHE! (2013) Based on a best-selling novel, this touching drama follows three small-town buddies who open a sports shop as a way to break free from their middle-class lives. However, religious differences and political violence threaten to destroy their dreams and their friendship.

SHRIMP CURRY

SHRIMP IN RICH GRAVY OF POPPY SEEDS AND TAMARIND

In the film, Ranbir Kapoor's character "finds himself" on the streets and waterways of Paris. Many people aren't aware of the connection between France and India. Pondicherry, the port city where Kalki Koechlin was born to French parents, was occupied by France for close to 300 years. As a result, Pondicherry is home to a unique blend of food influences, including a little-known cuisine called "Indian Creole."

Having never been to Pondicherry myself, I can't claim that this recipe is 100 percent authentic, but instead this menu is my playful interpretation of Indian Creole. It begins with this shrimp curry, a dish you might encounter in the region once known as French India and loaded with the exotic flavors of mustard seeds, curry leaves, and coconut.

But it's the poppy seeds and tamarind that make this recipe most distinctive. Tamarind gives the curry a wonderfully sour taste, while poppy seeds create a velvety texture that's slightly sweet and nutty. Although white poppy seeds are preferable for their color and milder flavor, you can always use black poppy seeds if that's more readily available to you.

In a mixing bowl, combine 1 tablespoon of the garlic paste, 1 tablespoon of the ginger paste, ½ teaspoon of the salt, the red chilli powder, and the turmeric. Mix the spices together to create a thick paste. Add the shrimp to the bowl and stir to coat well. Set aside.

In a large sauté pan, gently toast the coconut powder and poppy seeds over medium heat, stirring occasionally, until light brown and fragrant, about 2 minutes. Pour into a spice mill and grind to a fine powder. (If you don't have a spice mill handy, don't worry about grinding the poppy seeds and coconut. The sauce will be slightly coarse, but taste about the same.)

Wipe the sauté pan clean and heat 1 tablespoon of the oil over medium heat. Add the shrimp and cook, tossing occasionally, just until they start to turn pale pink, about 4 minutes. Be careful not to overcook at this point because the shrimp will continue to cook later in the sauce. Return the shrimp to the mixing bowl.

SERVES 4

1½ tablespoons garlic paste (or minced garlic), divided

1½ tablespoons ginger paste (or minced ginger), divided

1 teaspoon salt, divided

½ teaspoon Indian red chilli powder (or cayenne)

½ teaspoon ground turmeric

1¼ pounds medium shrimp, peeled and deveined, tails removed

¼ cup coconut powder

1 tablespoon white poppy seeds

2 tablespoons canola oil, divided

1 teaspoon black mustard seeds

7 to 10 curry leaves

2 Indian green chillies, cut in half (if you don't want as much heat, leave one or both chillies whole, or omit them altogether)

1 medium red onion, finely chopped

½ teaspoon ground cumin

1 teaspoon ground coriander

½ teaspoon tamarind paste

¼ cup chopped cilantro

Cooked rice (any type), for serving

(Opposite, clockwise from top-right)
Shrimp Curry; Bhindi Masala, p. 67; Black-Eyed Peas, p. 69

In a medium saucepan, heat the remaining 1 tablespoon oil over medium-high heat. Once the oil is shimmering hot, add the mustard seeds, curry leaves, and green chillies. As soon as the mustard seeds begin to pop, add the onion and cook, stirring, until dark brown on the edges, about 5 minutes.

Decrease the heat and add the remaining ½ tablespoon garlic paste, ½ tablespoon ginger paste, ½ teaspoon salt, the ground cumin, and the poppy seed–coconut powder mixture. Cook, stirring, for 1 to 2 minutes.

Pour in 1 cup hot water and stir well to create a sauce. Add the coriander and dissolve the tamarind paste into the sauce. Bring the sauce to a bubble, then cover, decrease the heat, and simmer, stirring occasionally, for 7 to 10 minutes. As the sauce thickens, add another ½ to 1 cup hot water.

Taste the sauce and adjust the seasonings. If it's too spicy, add water to dilute. Add the shrimp and stir gently. Sprinkle the cilantro over the top. If you're making the dish ahead of time, stop at this point and finish cooking before serving.

Cover and simmer for a final few minutes, just long enough for the shrimp to finish cooking, about 5 minutes. Allow the dish to sit, covered, until you're ready to serve so the shrimp can fully absorb the delicious sauce.

Remove the green chillies and ladle the shrimp and sauce over rice. Inform your guests to discard the curry leaves while eating.

BHINDI MASALA

OKRA SAUTÉED WITH DRY SPICES

The next component of our Indian Creole menu is—what else?—okra. My partner, Jason, loves okra (*bhindi*), so we make it quite often, but I realize that many people are ambivalent toward it because of its "slimy" consistency. I'm happy to report, though, that I've found three techniques to address this issue.

First, it's important to dry the okra very well after washing. I spread them out on kitchen towels and leave them to air-dry for 20 minutes or so. Second, I start the recipe by pan frying the cut okra pieces in a little bit of oil over very high heat. I find this method of pre-cooking the okra greatly decreases its stickiness. Granted, this also adds oil to the dish, so if that's something you're concerned about, by all means skip this step (you'll just need to increase your cooking time later in the process so the okra gets tender). Finally, I choose *not* to add tomatoes to my recipe, even though they're quite common in Indian okra preparations, because the juice and pulp from the tomato only exacerbate the slime quotient.

All in all, these techniques have greatly improved my okra game—so much so that I'm confident you'll like this dish even if you've never considered yourself a fan of slimy green veggies.

Wash the okra and dry on kitchen towels. Leave them to air-dry further for about 20 minutes. You want the okra to be as dry as possible before slicing.

Trim the stems and tails on the okra and cut into thick slices (roughly ½ inch).

Heat 2 tablespoons of the oil in a large sauté pan over high heat. Once the oil is very hot, add the okra and cook, stirring, until bright green and slightly charred, 6 to 8 minutes; season with ¼ teaspoon of the salt along the way. Remove to a plate.

Heat the remaining 1 tablespoon oil in the same pan over medium heat. Once the oil is shimmering hot, add the mustard seeds. As soon as the seeds start to pop, add the onion and cook, stirring, until golden, 3 to 5 minutes, reducing the heat if necessary.

SERVES 4

1 pound okra

3 tablespoons canola oil, divided

¾ teaspoon salt, divided

1 teaspoon black mustard seeds

1 medium onion, finely chopped

1 teaspoon garlic powder

1 teaspoon ground cumin

½ teaspoon ground ginger

½ teaspoon Indian red chilli powder (or cayenne)

¼ teaspoon ground turmeric

1 lemon, cut in half, divided

2 tablespoons coconut powder

1 teaspoon ground coriander

Roti or naan, for serving

Add the garlic powder, cumin, ginger, red chilli powder, turmeric, and the remaining ½ teaspoon salt. Allow the spices to bloom for about a minute. Then return the okra to the pan and toss with the onion to coat well. Add a squeeze of lemon. Cook, stirring, for 3 to 5 minutes. Then add the coconut powder and coriander and stir to combine. Cook until the desired tenderness is achieved, another few minutes.

Adjust the seasonings to taste. It's best to let the dish sit for a half hour or longer, if possible, to allow the flavors to develop more fully. Just reheat quickly before serving with roti or naan. Cut the remaining lemon into wedges, and use to garnish the dish.

BLACK-EYED PEAS

WARM RELISH SIMMERED WITH MUSTARD SEEDS, CUMIN, AND CORIANDER

For the final leg of our trip to Creole country via Air India, get a taste of this bold interpretation of the classic Creole ingredient, black-eyed peas. Calling this a "relish" may be a bit of an understatement, though, because it could easily double as a protein-rich entrée when served over rice or with warm naan/roti. It's incredible to believe that humble beans can be transformed into a dish with this much depth of flavor using just a few simple spices. And for a saucy variation, simply add one medium tomato, diced, simmered with the spices before adding the black-eyed peas (but if you choose this version, omit the tamarind/lemon since the tomato provides plenty of tang).

Indians are never ones to turn their backs on superstition, so as soon as my mom heard about the Southern tradition, she started making this dish every New Year's Day for good luck. I don't know about luck, but this recipe will certainly bring you hearty nourishment, on the first day or any day of the year.

SERVES 4 TO 6

Two 15.5-ounce cans black-eyed peas

2 tablespoons canola oil

1 teaspoon black mustard seeds

1 medium onion, finely chopped

1 tablespoon garlic paste (or minced garlic)

½ tablespoon ginger paste (or minced ginger)

1 teaspoon ground cumin

½ teaspoon Indian red chilli powder (or cayenne)

¼ teaspoon ground turmeric

½ teaspoon tamarind paste*

1 teaspoon ground coriander

½ teaspoon salt

Chopped cilantro, for garnish

* Substitute: juice of 1 lemon + ½ tablespoon soy sauce

Rinse and drain the black-eyed peas. Set aside.

In a medium saucepan, heat the oil over medium-high heat. Once the oil is shimmering hot, add the mustard seeds. As soon as the seeds start to pop, add the onion and cook, stirring, until golden, 3 to 5 minutes.

Add the garlic and ginger pastes, decrease the heat to medium, and cook, stirring, for 1 minute. Then add the cumin, red chilli powder, and turmeric. Stir the spices into the onion, allowing them to bloom for another minute.

Add the black-eyed peas to the pan, increase the heat, and cook, stirring, for about 3 minutes.

Dissolve the tamarind paste in ¼ cup warm water and add it to the pan. Lower the heat, cover, and simmer, stirring occasionally, for 10 minutes.

Stir in the coriander and salt. Cover and continue simmering until the beans are slightly mushy, around 10 minutes.

Adjust the salt and seasonings to taste. Garnish with fresh cilantro and serve alongside the shrimp curry.

(Opposite)
Black-Eyed Peas

DINNER

GEETA'S ROAST CHICKEN 77
Whole Chicken Marinated in Spicy Yogurt and Nuts

SWEET AND SAVORY PUMPKIN 79
Simmered with Indian Green Chillies, Sesame, Coconut, and Brown Sugar

BAGARA ANNAM 81
Tasty Cashew Fried Rice

MOVIE

KAPOOR & SONS 72
Funny and heartbreakingly real family drama

KAPOOR & SONS

FLAVOR

Anyone who has sat through a dysfunctional family dinner will be able to relate to the pathos, humor, and love in this realistic drama.

RECIPE

Two brothers, one living in London (Rahul), the other living in New Jersey (Arjun), receive news from back home that their grandfather has suffered a heart attack. The guys return to India and straight back into old family dynamics. Rahul is the successful elder brother who can do no wrong, while Arjun is the screw-up who can't seem to get his life together.

When Arjun falls for a girl in town (Tia), another wrench gets thrown into the brothers' already strained relationship. Add to that mom and dad's rocky marriage and you've got all the elements for a disastrous family reunion—one that will bring to light painful truths that have been kept secret for too long.

THE "DISH"

I had already finished my selection of films for this book when my mom and I went to see *Kapoor & Sons*. By the time we walked out of the theater, we both knew that I had to make space for this movie in my book.

Family dramas are as old as Bollywood itself. But typically, families in Bollywood are large, happy, and constantly singing and dancing together. In the case of *Kapoor & Sons*, though, writer-director Shakun Batra has created a family that is realistic and relatable. Their subtle interactions—layered with habitual patterns, years of resentment, and unresolved feelings—are palpable to anyone who's gone home for Thanksgiving or Christmas.

With all its nuance, *Kapoor & Sons* tackles some weighty issues, including betrayal and infidelity, but its most significant contribution to Indian cinema is that it's the first mainstream Bollywood movie to portray a gay character with truth and integrity. That's no small feat in a country where homosexuality is still illegal.

Being gay is the ultimate taboo in India. It's a topic that's rarely even discussed—and Bollywood is no exception. For an industry that has churned out *tens of thousands* of movies, I can count on one hand the films that have featured LGBT characters. And despite claims that there are gay and lesbian members of the film industry, I can't mention any names in this book because none is out to the public.

The irony is, India has an ancient culture that was actually accepting of homosexuality. Remember, this is the land that brought us the *Kama Sutra*. Sacred Hindu texts dating back thousands of years tell stories of characters who have a range of sexual orientations and gender identities—and they were fully accepted, even revered, for it. Unfortunately, when the British arrived in India, they brought with them their Victorian morals, which condemned homosexuality—writing the laws that are still upheld in India today. After a century of colonialism, these repressive and bigoted beliefs have been embraced in Indian culture and mistakenly ascribed to Hinduism.

That's why a film like *Kapoor & Sons* is so groundbreaking. The gay character in this film is a fully rounded person, with problems and faults that have nothing to do with his sexuality. And the family's response to his secret is incredibly realistic. Western viewers may find that the film "tiptoes" around the subject, but from an Indian perspective, this film is a radical step to furthering dialogue within the country.

The response to the movie is testament to that. *Kapoor & Sons* was met with very little controversy. In fact, it became one of the biggest hits of the year by painting a picture of a family that audiences could identify with. This is the kind of insightful, true-to-life film that's an example of how powerful cinema can be.

INGREDIENTS

CAST: Sidharth Malhotra, Fawad Khan, Alia Bhatt, Ratna Pathak, Rajat Kapoor, Rishi Kapoor

DIRECTOR: Shakun Batra

WRITERS: Ayesha Devitre Dhillon, Shakun Batra

RELEASE: 2016

TASTE THIS

Bollywood has little experience telling stories with LGBT characters. In addition to the groundbreaking work of indie filmmaker Onir, here are some of the very few films that have dipped their toe into these waters:

FIRE (1996) Technically not a Bollywood movie, this highly acclaimed film from Indo-Canadian director Deepa Mehta depicts two sisters-in-law who fall in love in a middle-class Indian family. When the movie released in India, protesters ransacked theaters and hurled death threats at the filmmakers.

ALIGARH (2016) Based on a 2010 true story, this must-see drama is about a college professor who's caught having sex with another man in his apartment. Dr. Ramchandra Siras was suspended from his job, fought for his rights in court, and watched his life tragically unravel.

BOMBAY TALKIES (2013) In this anthology film, four contemporary directors come together to tell short stories in commemoration of Bollywood's centenary. One segment (directed by superstar filmmaker Karan Johar) explores the lives of gay men in cosmopolitan Mumbai, while another segment tells the poignant story of a trans child in love with Bollywood dancing.

GEETA'S ROAST CHICKEN

WHOLE CHICKEN MARINATED IN SPICY YOGURT AND NUTS

Big family dinners were always extra special when my aunt, Geeta, brought her sig-nature roast chicken. On Thanksgivings, I would make turkey with all the traditional, American trimmings, while Geeta would bring a beautiful chicken to add some requi-site Indian flavors to the table. Of course, I still remember hers being more succulent and tasty than all my attempts in the years since, but I suppose that's always the case when you're trying to replicate a family favorite.

Nonetheless, this dish is a knockout. And there's nothing subtle about it. Like a good Bollywood movie, it packs a delicious punch. The crust should be thick and dark, the result of a decadent marinade of yogurt, nuts, garlic, ginger, and spices. I strongly recommend marinating the chicken overnight to ensure a tender, juicy bird. And be sure to serve it with Pudina (mint) Chutney (page 43) to balance the chicken's spicy flavors with a refreshing, cool sauce.

Geeta's roast chicken has been a centerpiece of many large family dinners at our house. Its bold flavors were exactly what was needed to stand up to the melodrama that inevitably unfolded around the table. Kapoor & Sons got nothing on us.

Clean the chicken by removing the giblets, cutting away any excess fat, rinsing the inside and out, and patting dry.

Grind the nuts to a fine powder, along with the coconut powder and poppy seeds, in a food processor or spice mill.

In a large mixing bowl, whisk together the powdered nuts with the yogurt, garlic and ginger pastes, oil, salt, red chilli powder, coriander, cumin, turmeric, cinnamon, and cloves to create a thick marinade.

Coat the chicken with the marinade. Also get underneath the skin and mas-sage the marinade into the breast area. This step will get a little messy, but the best way to a tasty and juicy chicken is to slather on the marinade, covering the entire bird with a thick coating. Wear latex gloves if you feel that will help.

Place the chicken in a large bowl or on a platter, cover loosely with plastic wrap, and refrigerate for at least 6 hours or, ideally, overnight.

SERVES 6 TO 8

1 roasting chicken (6 to 8 pounds)

¼ cup cashews

¼ cup almonds

¼ cup coconut powder

2 tablespoons white poppy seeds

1½ cups 2% Greek yogurt

3 tablespoons garlic paste (or minced garlic)

2 tablespoons ginger paste (or minced ginger)

2 tablespoons canola oil

1 tablespoon salt

1 tablespoon Indian red chilli powder (or cayenne)

1 teaspoon ground coriander

1 teaspoon ground cumin

1 teaspoon ground turmeric

½ teaspoon ground cinnamon

½ teaspoon ground cloves

2 lemons, plus extra for serving

1 medium onion, cut into slices or rings (not too thin)

¼ cup chopped cilantro

Pudina Chutney (page 43), for serving

(Opposite, clockwise from top-left)
Bagara Annam, p. 81; Sweet and Savory Pumpkin, p. 79; Geeta's Roast Chicken

Preheat the oven to 375°F. Remove the chicken from the refrigerator about an hour prior to cooking.

Scrape some of the marinade off the chicken (the yogurt tends to burn), but reserve all the excess in the bowl in the refrigerator. Cut the lemons in half and stuff inside the chicken cavity. Place the chicken on a rack in a roasting pan. (If you don't have a rack, use root vegetables like carrots, potatoes, or onions to create a bed upon which to set the chicken, preventing it from soaking in its own fat and allowing heat to circulate all around.)

Place the chicken in the oven and bake for about 20 minutes per pound, or until the internal temperature at its thickest part reaches 180°F. (If you don't have a meat thermometer, slice into the chicken between a leg and thigh—it's done when the juices run clear.)

In the final 20 minutes, brush the chicken with the remaining marinade and cover it with the sliced onion. Bake (or broil) until the exterior turns dark brown and crusty.

Remove the chicken from the oven, cover with aluminum foil, and allow it to rest for 20 to 30 minutes. Sprinkle with the cilantro and garnish with wedges of lemon. Serve with the mint chutney.

SWEET AND SAVORY PUMPKIN

SIMMERED WITH INDIAN GREEN CHILLIES, SESAME, COCONUT, AND BROWN SUGAR

One of the things I love most about Indian cooking is how we can take an ingredient that's ordinary or familiar and transform it into something new and unexpected. For example, you may have eaten pumpkin all your life, but I can guarantee you've never tasted it quite like this.

Chunks of pumpkin are flavored with a mellow, nutty blend of sesame seeds, coconut, and brown sugar. Meanwhile, fiery green chillies and mustard seeds provide a sharp counterbalance. The overall effect is a sweet and savory dish that elevates pumpkin beyond the usual desserts to which we've become accustomed.

And of course, pumpkin pairs beautifully with roast chicken, another nod to Thanksgiving dinners in my Indian-American family. But if it happens not to be pumpkin season, this recipe is equally delicious with butternut squash, which you can usually purchase year-round.

SERVES 6 TO 8

One 4-pound pumpkin

2 tablespoons canola oil

2 teaspoons black mustard seeds

10 to 12 curry leaves

3 or 4 Indian green chillies, cut in half

1 large onion, chopped

1 tablespoon ginger paste (or minced ginger)

2 teaspoons ground cumin

1 teaspoon salt

½ teaspoon ground turmeric

¼ teaspoon ground cinnamon

¼ cup sesame seeds

2 tablespoons coconut powder

2 tablespoons light brown sugar

Indian red chilli powder (or cayenne), to taste

Using a very sharp knife, cut the stem off the pumpkin, creating a flat base so the pumpkin sits squarely on your cutting board. Then go around the perimeter and cut off the rind, in strips from top to bottom, similar to the way you would supreme an orange. Cut the pumpkin into quarters lengthwise and remove the seeds and fiber. Finally, cut each quarter into 1-inch chunks.

Heat the oil in a very large saucepan over medium-high heat. Once the oil is shimmering hot, add the mustard seeds, curry leaves, and green chillies. As soon as the mustard seeds start to pop, add the onion and cook, stirring, until softened, about 3 minutes.

Decrease the heat and add the ginger paste, cumin, salt, turmeric, and cinnamon and cook, stirring, for 1 to 2 minutes.

Add the pumpkin to the pan and stir well for several minutes, until the pumpkin pieces are well coated with the spicy onion. Cover, decrease the heat, and simmer for 10 minutes.

Meanwhile, gently toast the sesame seeds and coconut powder in a dry skillet over medium heat until lightly golden and fragrant, about 3 minutes. Grind in a spice mill to create a smooth powder.

Add the sesame-coconut powder to the pumpkin along with the brown sugar and stir well. Cover and continue to simmer, stirring occasionally, until the pumpkin is very tender, 10 to 15 minutes. Some of the smaller chunks should turn to mush, while the majority retain their shape but are soft all the way to the center. Feel free to add ¼ to ½ cup water to help the dish come together.

Adjust the seasonings to taste. The beauty of this dish is the balance of sweet, spicy, and salty, so play around by adding brown sugar, salt, or red chilli powder to your liking. Transfer to a large serving bowl and present alongside the roast chicken on a platter. Inform your guests to remove the green chillies and curry leaves while eating.

BAGARA ANNAM

TASTY CASHEW FRIED RICE

Our roast chicken dinner is complete with this savory fried rice, our go-to recipe at all family get-togethers. Dotted with cashews and fragrant with spices, it serves as an earthy palette for your meal, without overshadowing the other dishes.

The key to achieving deep flavor and color is to brown the onion very well. Sautéing the onion over fairly high heat for several minutes—to the point of getting charred on the edges—provides a rich base in which to toast the rice. Combined with ground cloves, the rice takes on a luxurious brown color that makes bagara annam befitting of a feast.

SERVES 6 TO 8

3 cups basmati rice

3 tablespoons canola oil

3 bay leaves

3-inch cinnamon stick

3 Indian green chillies, cut in half

1 medium onion, roughly chopped, plus extra for garnish

½ cup cashews

2 tablespoons garlic paste (or minced garlic)

1 tablespoon ginger paste (or minced ginger)

1 teaspoon ground coriander

½ teaspoon ground cloves

2 teaspoons salt

¼ cup chopped cilantro

Lemon wedges, for serving

Rinse the rice well several times until the water starts to become less cloudy (starchy). Cover with water in a bowl and set aside to soak.

In a large, wide saucepan (preferably nonstick), heat the oil over medium-high heat. Add the bay leaves, cinnamon stick, and chillies. Allow them to infuse the oil for about a minute. Add the onion and cook, stirring, until deeply brown and charred around the edges, 5 to 7 minutes.

Add the cashews and cook, stirring, until golden, about 2 minutes. Decrease the heat to medium, add the garlic and ginger pastes, and cook, stirring, for another minute. Then add the coriander and cloves and stir.

Drain the rice well and add it into the pan. Season with the salt. Increase the heat to medium-high and cook, stirring the rice with the onion and spices, until it becomes toasted and deeply brown, about 3 minutes.

Pour 6 cups hot water into the pan. Stir well, scraping up the brown bits from the bottom of the pan. Add the cilantro and bring to a boil. Decrease the heat to the lowest setting, cover tightly, and cook undisturbed for 30 minutes.

Fluff the rice with a fork. Bite on a few grains to see if they are fully cooked. If it's still al dente, cover and continue to cook for a few more minutes. If the rice is cooked, but soggy, continue to heat uncovered until the excess water has evaporated.

Adjust the salt to taste. If you'd like to add more salt, try soy sauce instead—it will provide saltiness while deepening the color of the rice. Tumble the rice onto a serving platter. Remove the bay leaves and chillies. Garnish with your choice of lemon wedges, onion slices, and/or hard-boiled eggs, cut in half lengthwise.

DINNER

HOMESTYLE CHICKEN CURRY — 89
Bone-In Chicken Braised in Rich Tomato Gravy

PAN-ROASTED BRUSSELS SPROUTS — 91
Tossed with Crunchy Peanuts

MANGO CHEESECAKE — 92
Tangy Cheesecake with a "Tea Biscuit" Crust

MOVIE

DOR — 84
Delicate indie film about the compassion of strangers

FLAVOR

This art house flick set in the gorgeous deserts of Rajasthan is like an amuse-bouche—a delicious morsel that's tiny in size, but deep in flavor.

RECIPE

Dor is the story of two women whose lives become intertwined by dire circumstance (the title means "string," as in the thing that connects people or situations). Meera is a young woman living in the rural desert of Rajasthan state, strictly confined by the customs of her traditional Hindu family. Zeenat, a Muslim, is a more progressive woman from a mountain state to the north.

The two women seemingly have nothing in common, except that Zeenat desperately needs Meera's help to save her husband's life. It is this unlikely connection—and the redemption it offers them both—that is the heart of *Dor*.

THE "DISH"

India's independent film scene, called "parallel cinema," enjoyed its heyday in the late '70s/early '80s. During that era, a slew of hard-hitting films with social commentary were made by filmmakers like Shyam Benegal, featuring acclaimed actors including Smita Patil, Naseeruddin Shah, and Shabana Azmi, who turned in gritty, realistic performances. The films, which often did not contain any songs, were a response to Bollywood's escapist entertainment.

Dor is an example of parallel cinema in more recent times. Its director, Nagesh Kukunoor (who makes a cameo in the film as the factory owner), produces low-budget films that are noted for their subtle realism and for shining a spotlight on characters outside the mainstream of Indian society. For example, his most famous film, *Iqbal*, is the story of a deaf boy who dreams of playing cricket for the Indian national team. (Interestingly, Kukunoor went to grad school in the United States and worked here as an engineer, saving his money to go home and finance his first film, *Hyderabad Blues*, a romantic comedy about a guy who struggles to readjust to India after returning from America.)

In *Dor*, Kukunoor presents the struggle of two women from very different backgrounds, but with a common thread between them. For viewers who are unfamiliar with traditional Indian culture, it may be surprising to see the plight of the widow in this story. In many parts of India—not just remote villages, but towns and cities as well—widows are seen as burdens to their families. The death of a woman's husband, often the primary breadwinner, makes her persona non grata. For a poignant, unforgettable movie about widows in India, I highly recommend Deepa Mehta's Oscar-nominated film *Water*.

As Bollywood evolves, more films these days are experimenting with form and content, and doing so with commercial success. Young Indian audiences have been weaned on Hollywood films and TV shows, which are widely accessible today at theaters and online (at least for those living in cities). In turn, these audiences—and the filmmakers in their peer group—are increasingly receptive to Hindi films that break the norms of Bollywood. Films with female protagonists, taboo subject matter, or pointed social commentary have proven quite popular in recent years. In fact, many of the films in this book are part of that trend.

In other words, parallel cinema is converging with the mainstream in Bollywood.

INGREDIENTS

CAST: Ayesha Takia, Gul Panag, Shreyas Talpade
WRITER AND DIRECTOR: Nagesh Kukunoor
INSPIRED BY THE MALAYALAM FILM *PERUMAZHAKKALAM*
MUSIC DIRECTOR: Salim-Sulaiman
RELEASE: 2006

TASTE THIS

I love stories about unexpected encounters. These superbly crafted "parallel cinema" films explore the surprising and monumental effect one chance meeting can have on your life:

MR. & MRS. IYER (2002) This English-language indie from respected director Aparna Sen tells the story of a Hindu woman and Muslim man who are thrown together on a traumatic bus journey. Touching on issues of religious violence, feminism, and prejudice, the film offers a sensitive treatment of some very weighty issues, from one of India's few female directors.

RAINCOAT (2004) This incredibly delicate drama is based on the O. Henry short story "The Gift of the Magi." Aishwarya Rai, in perhaps her best (and totally unglamorous) performance to date, stars as a simple housewife who shares a platonic but deeply moving encounter with a former lover on one rainy day.

IJAAZAT (1987) This oft-forgotten art film is a delicate gem, starring my favorite actress, Rekha. An ex-husband and -wife meet unexpectedly in a train station and, over the course of one night, revisit their past. The title of the film means "permission," and refers to the final, touching scene that has lingered with me for years.

HOMESTYLE CHICKEN CURRY

BONE-IN CHICKEN BRAISED IN RICH TOMATO GRAVY

In keeping with the bucolic setting of *Dor*, I present this rustic, comforting dish. This classic entrée is what Indians mean when they say "chicken curry." There are countless variations from region to region and household to household, but the fundamentals of every homestyle chicken curry are the same—bone-in chicken swimming in a luscious tomato gravy. This particular version is distinctive because of its ground nuts, which provide a rich sweetness to counterbalance the tangy tomatoes.

This is the kind of meal where you take the pot straight to the table and everyone digs in, family style. With homestyle chicken, it's all about the gravy. There's nothing more satisfying than basmati rice soaked in it, or soft roti sopping it up. After dinner, you'll feel like sitting around a desert campfire and telling stories in the chilly nighttime air.

Heat 1 tablespoon of the oil in a very large braising pan or Dutch oven (ideally, the pan should be wide enough to fit all the chicken thighs in a single layer) over medium-high heat. Meanwhile, season the thighs with the turmeric and ½ teaspoon of the salt. Place the thighs in the pan, meaty side down, and sear for 7 to 10 minutes, then flip and sear for 3 minutes on the other side. Remove the chicken to a plate.

In the same pan, heat the remaining 1 tablespoon oil. Add the bay leaves, green chillies, and cinnamon stick. Allow them to begin infusing the oil, about 30 seconds.

Add the onion and cook, stirring, until deeply browned, 3 to 5 minutes.

Add the garlic and ginger pastes and cook, stirring, for 1 minute, reducing the heat if necessary to prevent burning. Then add the remaining 1 teaspoon salt, the red chilli powder, and the cloves and allow the spices to bloom for another minute.

Stir in the crushed tomatoes. Cover and simmer until droplets of oil separate from the sauce, indicating that the tomatoes are well cooked, 7 to 10 minutes.

Meanwhile, pulse the peanuts in a spice mill to create a fine powder.

Add the peanut powder to the sauce and stir well. Add the yogurt and stir to create a creamy paste. Then add 1 cup hot water and stir to create a sauce. Bring the sauce to a bubble.

SERVES 4

2 tablespoons canola oil, divided

8 bone-in chicken thighs (about 3 pounds), skin removed (of course, you're welcome to leave the skin on if you prefer)

½ teaspoon ground turmeric

1½ teaspoons salt, divided

2 bay leaves

2 Indian green chillies, cut in half (or an additional ½ teaspoon Indian red chilli powder or cayenne)

3-inch cinnamon stick, or ½ teaspoon ground cinnamon, added with other spices

1 large onion, finely chopped

2 tablespoons garlic paste (or minced garlic)

1 heaping tablespoon ginger paste (or minced ginger)

½ teaspoon Indian red chilli powder (or cayenne)

½ teaspoon ground cloves

¾ cup crushed tomatoes

¼ cup peanuts

2 tablespoons Greek yogurt (2% or whole)

½ cup chopped cilantro

1 teaspoon ground coriander

Cooked basmati rice or Bagara Annam (page 81), for serving

Place the chicken pieces back in the pan, nestling them into the sauce. Cover and simmer for 20 minutes, occasionally rearranging the thighs, flipping them, and spooning over the sauce.

Add the cilantro and coriander. If you're making the dish a day ahead (which I highly recommend), stop at this point. Cool completely and refrigerate.

Cover the pan and simmer until the sauce has turned from red to deep orange-brown, 10 to 15 minutes. Adjust the seasonings to taste. If it's too spicy, simply add another spoonful of yogurt. Remove the green chillies, bay leaves, and cinnamon stick. Take the pan directly to the table and serve family style over basmati rice or Bagara Annam (page 81).

PAN-ROASTED BRUSSELS SPROUTS

TOSSED WITH CRUNCHY PEANUTS

To balance the depth and richness of the chicken curry, I like to serve these crisp and healthy Brussels sprouts. Not to be overshadowed, the Brussels sprouts are packed with flavor and can hold their own aside the chicken. They make for a beautiful presentation, these forest green pearls offsetting the burnt amber gravy of the curry.

SERVES 4

1½ pounds Brussels sprouts

2 tablespoons canola oil, divided

1 teaspoon black mustard seeds

1 medium red onion, finely chopped

½ tablespoon garlic paste (or minced garlic)

½ tablespoon ginger paste (or minced ginger)

1 teaspoon ground cumin

1 teaspoon salt

½ teaspoon Indian red chilli powder (or cayenne)

¼ teaspoon ground turmeric

¼ cup chopped peanuts

Lemon, to taste

Wash the Brussels sprouts and remove any outer layers that are wilted. Trim the stems and cut in half lengthwise.

Heat 1 tablespoon of the oil in a very wide sauté pan or cast-iron skillet over medium-high heat. Place the Brussels sprouts, cut side down, in the pan in a single layer (you may need to do this in two batches). Cook, without moving, until the cut sides get a nice, dark brown char on them, about 5 minutes. Remove to a dish.

Heat the remaining 1 tablespoon oil in the same pan. Once the oil is shimmering hot, add the mustard seeds. As soon as the seeds begin to pop, add the onion and cook, stirring, for about 2 minutes. Add the garlic and ginger pastes, decrease the heat to medium, and cook, stirring, for another minute. Then add the cumin, salt, red chilli powder, and turmeric and allow the spices to bloom for about 30 seconds.

Return the Brussels sprouts to the pan and sprinkle with the peanuts. Toss gently to coat the sprouts well with the onion and spices. Cover and simmer for 3 minutes, just until the sprouts have reached the desired tenderness.

Adjust the seasonings. Finish with a squeeze of lemon, if desired. Take the pan directly to the table and serve alongside the chicken curry.

(Opposite)
Pan-Roasted
Brussels Spouts

MANGO CHEESECAKE

TANGY CHEESECAKE WITH A "TEA BISCUIT" CRUST

SERVES 6 TO 8

FOR THE FILLING

1½ pounds frozen mango chunks (or 3 or 4 very ripe mangoes)

20 ounces cream cheese

4 large eggs

1¼ cups sugar

4 ounces sour cream

¼ teaspoon ground cardamom

1 tablespoon cornstarch (optional)

FOR THE CRUST

1½ cups crushed tea biscuits (crush in a food processor or place in a plastic bag and beat with a rolling pin)

½ cup crushed, unsalted cashews (crush in a food processor or place in a plastic bag and beat with a rolling pin)

¼ cup sugar

8 tablespoons (1 stick) unsalted butter, melted

Sweetened coconut flakes, for garnish (toasted, if desired)

What better way to end a family-style meal than with a big dessert?

Every Indian-American kid knows something about "biscuits." No, not the Southern kind smothered in gravy. For Indians, "biscuits" refer to sugar cookies that are the classic companion for afternoon chai. I think we all grew up hearing about our parents' favorite, Parle Glucose biscuits, which I imagine were to our parents what Oreos were to us. When I actually tasted my first, authentic Glucose biscuit on a trip to India, I cannot say that I was smitten.

In any case, the crust of this mango cheesecake is an homage to the ever-adored Indian "biscuit," which is what I use in place of graham crackers (along with a hint of that other staple of Indian desserts—cashews). You can certainly buy Parle Glucose biscuits at an Indian grocery store, but I choose instead to use regular, supermarket tea biscuits (e.g., Nabisco Social Tea), which is what my parents serve with chai to this day.

I have to give a nod to my sister, Vani, for inspiring this dessert. She would be the first to acknowledge that she's *not* a cook, but mango cheesecake is the one dish you can count on her to bring to a family potluck—and everyone loves it. The idea of cheesecake is familiar for kids, while the flavors of mango, nuts, and cardamom are sophisticated for adults. It's a delicious way to cap off this homestyle meal.

FOR THE FILLING: If using frozen mangoes, thaw them in the microwave. Also set out the cream cheese to soften.

Preheat the oven to 350°F. Grease a 9-inch springform pan with butter or cooking spray. Wrap the bottom and sides of the pan with aluminum foil (to prevent the contents from seeping out in the oven).

FOR THE CRUST: In a food processor or mixing bowl, combine the crushed tea biscuits, cashews, and sugar with the melted butter to form crumbs the consistency of wet sand. Press the crumbs evenly onto the bottom of the springform pan. Bake for 8 to 10 minutes, just until slightly golden. Set aside to cool.

Meanwhile, create a mango puree by blending the mango pieces (make sure they are fully thawed) in a blender until completely smooth. Measure 2 cups puree and set aside.

Using a stand mixer or hand mixer, gently beat the eggs with the sugar. Add the cream cheese and sour cream and beat until smooth. Then add the 2 cups mango puree, cardamom, and cornstarch and beat until well combined and creamy. It's okay if there are some specks of cream cheese visible in the filling.

Once the crust is cool to the touch, pour the filling into the pan. Bake for 1 hour and 30 minutes to 1 hour and 45 minutes, until the edges are set and lightly brown.

Turn off the oven and crack the door so the cheesecake can begin cooling slowly.

After an hour or so, remove the cake from the oven and cool completely. Then refrigerate overnight until it is set.

Top the cheesecake with coconut flakes (this is also a good way to cover any cracks that may have formed). Slide a knife around the perimeter of the cheesecake and remove it from the springform pan. Scrvc while still chilled.

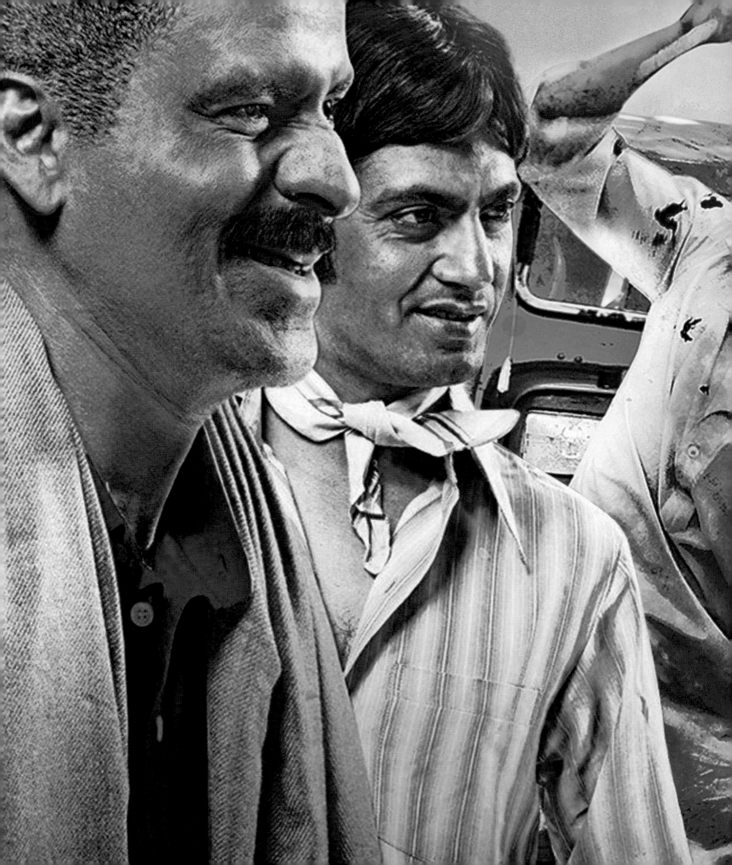

DINNER

BOLLYBURGERS   101
Succulent, Spicy Hamburgers with Mango Salsa

SWEET POTATO FRIES   102
Oven-Baked Wedges with
Garlic-Cilantro Dipping Sauce

MANGO LASSI   104
Tangy Mango Milkshake

MOVIE

GANGS OF WASSEYPUR   96
Sprawling, pulp-fiction crime saga

GANGS OF WASSEYPUR

FLAVOR

This five-and-a-half-hour crime saga is like an all-you-can-eat buffet of gangsters, shootouts, and gruesome revenge.

RECIPE

Wasseypur is a coal-mining town in rural northeast India. The film begins in the present day, but jumps back to colonial times, where we meet Shahid Khan, a local thug who impersonates an infamous bandit to loot trains carrying goods for the British East India Company. His deceit does not go over lightly with the real bandit, who murders all of Shahid Khan's cohorts.

Thus begins an unending cycle of savage reprisals that continue for eight decades. Similar to *The Godfather*, *Gangs of Wasseypur* is a sprawling tale of interwoven subplots that span three generations of ruthless characters. It's a story of crime and politics, violent through and through, but deeply human at the same time.

THE "DISH"

First things first—don't be intimidated by this film's massive running time. Special for American audiences, the producers portioned the epic into eight, 40-minute "episodes," which are available on Netflix, so you can binge-watch it like your favorite TV show.

But let me also make clear—this movie isn't for everyone. For those (like me) who aren't keen on violence, it's probably not your cup of tea. But if you're a fan of Quentin Tarantino or Francis Ford Coppola, then chances are you're going to love it. American critics have described *Gangs of Wasseypur* with such superlatives as

"quite possibly one of the best gangster movies ever made." When the film screened at Cannes and Sundance, it signaled to the world that there was something really cool brewing in Bollywood.

Director Anurag Kashyap is the poster boy for a new wave of Indian cinema. Kashyap began his career as a writer and got his big break developing the script for *Satya*, a film that is regarded as Bollywood's best crime drama. A decade later, he began his feature directorial career in earnest with a string of unapologetic, hard-hitting dramas like *Black Friday*, *Dev D*, and *That Girl in Yellow Boots*. Kashyap's signature style employs guerrilla filmmaking, shooting in real locations on shoestring budgets and allowing for ample improvisation among his actors. The overall effect is a gritty, realistic, un-Bollywood portrayal of modern India, featuring characters whose lives are peppered with addiction, violence, and sexuality.

Kashyap's impact on Indian cinema has gone beyond his work as a director, though. As a producer and partner in Phantom Films, he has arguably been even more influential, mentoring a cohort of edgy, new filmmakers. Movies like *NH10*, *The Lunchbox*, and *Queen* (see pages 46, 254, and 266) break the constraints of typical Bollywood fare, garnering critical acclaim both within and outside India. And Anurag Kashyap has had his hands in all of these films, along with many others, giving voice to a new generation of Indian auteurs.

One of my goals in writing this book was to introduce Western audiences to contemporary Indian cinema and demonstrate that "Bollywood" is no longer relegated to the cliché, kitschy musical (not that there's anything wrong with that). Anurag Kashyap is blazing ahead with movies that are Indian in content but undeniably international in quality and tone. And I'm confident his brand of filmmaking will only become more prominent in the future.

INGREDIENTS

CAST: Manoj Bajpayee, Piyush Mishra, Jameel Khan, Jaideep Ahlawat, Richa Chadda, Reema Sen, Nawazuddin Siddiqui
DIRECTOR: Anurag Kashyap
WRITERS: Zeishan Quadri, Akhilesh Jaiswal, Sachin Ladia, Anurag Kashyap
MUSIC DIRECTOR: Sneha Khanwalkar
RELEASE: 2012

TASTE THIS

Bollywood has its own sordid history with the underworld (long the source of film financing), so movies about the mob are perhaps a perfect fit:

SATYA (1998) The first installment in director Ram Gopal Varma's "gangster series" has been called a modern masterpiece, exploring the violence and humanity of criminals in a way never before seen in Indian films. Its slick and unapologetic portrayal of the Bombay mafia is said to have been an inspiration for Danny Boyle's *Slumdog Millionaire*.

COMPANY (2002) Ram Gopal Varma continues his homage to the Bombay mafia by examining the economic workings of the underworld. A young man joins a crime organization with the hopes of making it big, and rises through the treacherous ranks of the "company."

UDTA PUNJAB (2016) This hard-hitting crime drama with interconnecting story lines explores the drug crisis in the state of Punjab. The filmmakers (including producer Anurag Kashyap) became embroiled in a highly publicized, but ultimately successful, battle with India's censor board, which demanded extensive cuts to the film because of its unapologetic content.

BOLLYBURGERS

SUCCULENT, SPICY HAMBURGERS WITH MANGO SALSA

This hamburger recipe is perfect for Guys' Movie Night, exactly the kind of meal you want to pair with gangsters, gunfights, and gore. It's packed with robust spices—garlic, ginger, coriander, cinnamon, cloves, and red chilli—which come together seamlessly to create an incredibly savory burger experience. The secret to keeping it juicy is to grate an onion directly into the meat. Topping it all off is a spicy/sweet mango salsa that counterbalances the burger with fresh, tropical flavors.

Living in Manhattan, I don't have an outdoor grill, so I use a cast-iron skillet or grill pan. But if you're fortunate enough to be able to cook outside, these burgers would be even more delicious with a hit of smoky charcoal. And if your butcher happens to carry ground lamb, that's another man-pleasing variation to try.

Preheat a cast-iron grill pan or skillet over high heat.

In a large mixing bowl, combine the ground meat with the onion, cilantro, garlic and ginger pastes, salt, coriander, red chilli powder, cinnamon, and cloves. Use your hands to work the spices into the meat.

Divide the meat into 4 equal parts. Form each quarter into a patty. Press down the center of each patty with your thumb to create a dimple (which will flatten when cooked).

Brush each patty with oil and place on the hot skillet. Cook for 4 minutes on the first side, then flip and cook the other side over medium-high heat for an additional 4 minutes (for medium-rare) or 6 to 8 minutes (for medium-well).

Meanwhile, for the salsa, combine all the ingredients for the mango salsa in a mixing bowl. Adjust the seasonings to taste.

Serve the burgers on toasted buns with all the traditional fixings, plus a generous helping of mango salsa—or, serve the salsa on the side as a refreshing salad.

SERVES 4

1½ pounds ground chuck beef

½ medium onion, grated

3 tablespoons chopped cilantro

½ tablespoon garlic paste (or minced garlic)

½ tablespoon ginger paste (or minced ginger)

1 teaspoon salt

½ teaspoon ground coriander

½ teaspoon Indian red chilli powder or cayenne (use a little more if you want it spicy)

¼ teaspoon ground cinnamon

¼ teaspoon ground cloves

Canola oil

Toasted hamburger buns, for serving

FOR THE MANGO SALSA

1 cup finely chopped, ripe mangoes (or frozen, thawed)

½ pint grape tomatoes, quartered

½ small red onion, finely chopped

2 tablespoons finely chopped fresh mint

½ teaspoon salt

1 Indian green chilli, minced

Juice of ½ to 1 lime, to taste

(Opposite)
Bollyburger; Sweet Potato Fries, p. 102

SWEET POTATO FRIES

OVEN-BAKED WEDGES WITH GARLIC-CILANTRO DIPPING SAUCE

SERVES 4

2 pounds sweet potatoes

1 teaspoon paprika

½ teaspoon salt

½ teaspoon ground cumin

½ teaspoon ground coriander

¼ teaspoon Indian red chilli powder (or cayenne)

2 tablespoons extra-virgin olive oil

Sea salt, to taste

FOR THE DIPPING SAUCE

1 cup 2% Greek yogurt

¼ cup finely chopped cilantro

¼ teaspoon garlic powder

¼ teaspoon salt

You gotta have fries with that burger. I like to switch things up a little by serving these sweet potato fries instead of regular French fries. For one thing, they're baked, so no need to break out the deep fryer. But more important, the touch of sweetness is a nice complement to the savory burger. These fries are dusted with earthy spices and served with a simple, garlic-cilantro dipping sauce. You might want to consider making an extra batch for snacking while watching the show.

Preheat the oven to 450°F. Line a baking sheet with aluminum foil.

Wash and peel the sweet potatoes (or leave the skin on if you prefer). Cut them in half lengthwise, then cut each half into 3 to 5 wedges or spears. Place the potatoes on the baking sheet.

In a small mixing bowl, combine the paprika, salt, cumin, coriander, and red chilli powder. Mix well with a fork.

Drizzle the olive oil over the potatoes and toss to coat. Then sprinkle the spice blend on top and use your hands to coat all the potatoes evenly. Spread the potatoes in an even layer.

Bake for 15 minutes, then flip and bake for an additional 10 minutes, until the potatoes are dark brown and the edges crispy.

Meanwhile, for the dipping sauce, mix the yogurt, cilantro, garlic, and salt in a small bowl. Thin the sauce with a teaspoon or two of water as needed.

Remove the fries from the oven and sprinkle with sea salt. Transfer to a platter and serve with the dipping sauce. Leftover sauce can be refrigerated and makes for a great, healthy dip with fresh veggies.

MANGO LASSI

TANGY MANGO MILKSHAKE

SERVES 4

4 cups frozen mango chunks

4 cups Greek yogurt

2 cups milk

2 tablespoons honey

¼ teaspoon salt

Ground cardamom,
for garnish

Chopped pistachios,
for garnish

What goes better with burgers than milkshakes, right? Well, try this Indian variation. They're more tart than sweet (since they're made with yogurt), with just a hint of salt in the background. Topping it off is a cardamom and pistachio garnish, which adds even more quintessential Indian flavors.

. . . And if you want to make Guys' Night even more fun, I suggest spiking this milkshake with a shot or two of rum!

Combine the frozen mango, yogurt, milk, honey, and salt in a blender. Blend until completely smooth, about 2 minutes. Depending on the size of your blender, you may need to do this in two batches. Adjust the honey to taste.

Pour into tall glasses. Dust with a pinch of cardamom and garnish with chopped pistachios. Serve with a straw. (Alternatively, you could finely chop the pistachios, combine with the cardamom, and rim each glass with the mixture.)

DINNER

PAN-SEARED COD 113
Flaky Fillets Coated with Curry Leaves
and Spices

DONDAKAYA 114
Sautéed Ivy Gourd

CHITRANNAM 116
Lemon Rice Tossed with Lentils,
Peanuts, and Chillies

MOVIE

GURU 108
Story of a self-made billionaire and
the woman behind him

GURU

FLAVOR

Despite starring India's most famous supercouple, this rags-to-riches story is incredibly grounded and relatable—a testament to its fine filmmaking.

RECIPE

Guru is said to be loosely based on the life story of Dhirubhai Ambani, cofounder of India's second largest company, Reliance Industries. Today, the Ambanis are one of the wealthiest families in the world. (Dhirubhai's son, Mukesh Ambani, lives in a 27-story house in Mumbai worth $1 billion, the most expensive private home on Earth.)

But it didn't start out that way. Just like Dhirubhai, the title character of this film, Guru, begins his life as a big dreamer in a small town. A high school drop-out, he builds a small manufacturing company. Through hard work and duplici-tous actions, Guru and his wife transform their lives, but at the risk of losing their freedom, integrity, and each other.

THE "DISH"

Move over Brangelina, the world belongs to Abhi-Ash.

Guru stars real-life husband and wife Abhishek Bachchan and Aishwarya (Rai) Bachchan. The story of Abhi-Ash, modern-day Indian royalty, is perhaps even more interesting than the one they portray in the film.

Abhishek Bachchan is the only son of Bollywood legend Amitabh Bachchan and critically acclaimed actress Jaya (Bhaduri) Bachchan. He grew up in the spotlight, in a country where a billion people worship his father, the most famous actor in the world.

Photographs courtesy
Madras Talkies
(pages 106–109, 111)

How do you live up to that? Well . . . you don't. Abhishek, for better or for worse, chose to follow in his parents' footsteps and become an actor. When he first entered the industry, all eyes were on him, to see if he would prove himself worthy of his famous last name. Unfortunately, critics and audiences weren't impressed. For much of his career (now entering its second decade), commercial success has been elusive. Abhishek and his dad are nicknamed "Big B" and "Junior B"—which are apt descriptions for a man who may forever live in his father's shadow.

Aishwarya, on the other hand, has never lived in *anyone's* shadow. "The most beautiful woman in the world," as she's often described, burst onto the international stage when she was crowned Miss World at the age of twenty-one. She entered Bollywood shortly thereafter, and although she was criticized for her acting ability (much like Abhishek), she soon rose to international stardom, walking the red carpet at Cannes, appearing on *Oprah* and *David Letterman*, and representing L'Oreal globally.

When it came time for Junior B to pick a bride, he successfully wooed the most desirable woman in India. Although Aishwarya's popularity and success eclipsed his (see *Devdas*, page 22), in many ways it was the perfect match—he's a prince by birth, she's a princess by coronation. With the blessings of a nation, they were married a few months following the release of *Guru* (it's been reported that he proposed to her in New York, after the premiere of the film).

But *Guru* isn't only significant in terms of Abhi-Ash's relationship. More important, the film represents their finest work as actors under the direction of esteemed filmmaker Mani Ratnam (see *Dil Se*, page 192). Especially for Abhishek, *Guru* is monumental. Critics universally agree that he came into his own with this film. He finally achieved respect at the level that is usually only accorded to his parents. His performance, spanning decades in the life of the titular character, is layered, restrained, and truly commanding.

In *Guru*, there's nothing "junior" about Junior B.

INGREDIENTS

CAST: Abhishek Bachchan, Aishwarya Rai, Mithun Chakraborty
DIRECTOR: Mani Ratnam
WRITERS: Mani Ratnam, Vijay Krishna Acharya
MUSIC DIRECTOR: A. R. Rahman
RELEASE: 2007

TASTE THIS

For other noteworthy films with supercouple Abhishek and Aishwarya, check out my personal favorites:

SARKAR RAJ (2008) This gripping political drama has not one or two, but *three* Bachchans—Abhishek, Aishwarya, and the granddaddy of them all, Amitabh Bachchan. Each delivers a stellar performance in this sequel to *Sarkar*, a *Godfather*-esque crime saga (you may want to start with the first installment, though Aishwarya isn't in it).

UMRAO JAAN (2006) Granted, this remake pales in comparison to the 1981 classic, but Aishwarya looks absolutely stunning as the title character, a renowned nineteenth-century courtesan, while Abhishek plays her wealthy suitor. The story is slow-moving, but it's a visual treat to watch Aishwarya, dripping in jewels and elaborate period costumes, perform poetic classical dances.

BUNTY AUR BABLI (2005) This wacky comedy stars Abhishek and Rani Mukerji, but Aishwarya makes an appearance in an infamous "item number" (the term used to describe a musical number unrelated to the plot of the film, added for sheer audience enjoyment). The song, "Kajra Re," became one of the most popular of the decade due to Ash's on-screen seduction of *both* her future husband and future father-in-law (check out the music video on YouTube).

PAN-SEARED COD

FLAKY FILLETS COATED WITH CURRY LEAVES AND SPICES

This meal, with its distinctly South Indian flavors of curry leaves, mustard seeds, and coconut, is a tribute to the blue-eyed beauty from the South—Aishwarya Rai, who hails from the coastal state of Karnataka, known for its seafood cuisine.

To begin, we have pan-seared cod. I have to admit, I get incredibly excited when I think about this dish. It's so delicious, I can't believe how healthy and easy it is to make. That's why this meal is ideal for a Friday night date. After a long week of work, you want something special and elegant that won't take much effort to prepare—and this meal offers all of that. Paired with a nice glass of Riesling and the love story of *Guru*, this meal sets the stage for a special evening.

Now don't worry if the cod falls apart while you're cooking it. Cod is delicate, and that's part of its beauty. Of course, you could substitute any white fish in its place (in India, they often use catfish), but I love the thickness and mild flavor of a cod fillet.

SERVES 4

4 cod fillets (1½ to 2 pounds)

1 tablespoon plus 1 teaspoon canola oil, divided

1 tablespoon ground coriander

1 tablespoon garlic paste (or minced garlic)

½ tablespoon ginger paste (or minced ginger)

½ tablespoon chopped cilantro

½ teaspoon salt

¼ teaspoon Indian red chilli powder (or cayenne)

¼ teaspoon ground turmeric

1 Indian green chilli, minced

7 to 10 curry leaves, finely chopped

1 lemon, divided

Wash and pat dry the fish fillets.

In a large bowl, mix together 1 teaspoon of the oil and the coriander, garlic and ginger pastes, cilantro, salt, chilli powder, turmeric, green chilli, and curry leaves with the juice of ½ lemon to create a thick paste. Place the fish fillets in the bowl and coat well. Set aside to marinate for 15 minutes. Slice the remaining ½ lemon into wedges.

Heat a nonstick skillet over medium heat. Using ½ tablespoon oil for every 2 fillets, cook the fish for 4 minutes on the first side, then carefully flip and cook for an additional 3 to 4 minutes on the other side, until the fish is opaque and beginning to flake apart.

Serve immediately with the lemon wedges.

(Opposite, clockwise from top-left)
Chitrannam, p. 116
Pan-Seared Cod
Dondakaya, p. 114

DONDAKAYA

SAUTÉED IVY GOURD

SERVES 4

1½ pounds dondakaya (ivy gourd or tindora)

1½ tablespoons canola oil

1 teaspoon black mustard seeds

1 teaspoon cumin seeds

1 teaspoon urad dal (split black gram without skin)

5 to 7 curry leaves

1 medium onion, finely chopped

1 teaspoon garlic powder

¾ teaspoon salt

½ teaspoon ground cumin

½ teaspoon Indian red chilli powder (or cayenne)

¼ teaspoon ground turmeric

2 tablespoons coconut powder

1 teaspoon ground coriander

I know I began this book by insisting that these recipes are *accessible* and all the ingredients would be easy to find, so I struggled over whether to include this dish, which showcases a brilliant, yet obscure, Indian vegetable. In the end, I decided to find a place for it because it's just so interesting and tasty—one of my all-time favorite veggies— that I had to introduce you to it.

Dondakaya (also known as tindora) is technically a fruit, called "ivy gourd" in English. It's readily available, fresh, in Indian grocery stores. On the outside, it looks like a teeny-tiny watermelon, the size of a gherkin. When you cut into it, you reveal pale (sometimes pink) flesh and seeds. It's crunchy like cucumber and when sautéed, as in this recipe, it comes alive with the flavors of mustard and cumin seeds.

Every one of my non-Indian friends who's tried dondakaya loves it. So if you're in the mood to discover something new, I hope you'll give it a shot. It's the ultimate, fresh and crispy accompaniment for the light and healthy cod.

Wash the dondakaya and dry well on kitchen towels. Trim both tips off each dondakaya at an angle, and then cut each piece into ½-inch-thick disks on the diagonal.

Heat the oil in a large sauté pan over medium-high heat. Once the oil is shimmering hot, add the mustard and cumin seeds, urad dal, and curry leaves. As soon as the mustard seeds begin to pop, add the onion. (The urad dal can burn easily, at which point you need to discard and start over or else the entire dish will taste acrid, so keep a close eye on it.) Decrease the heat to medium and cook the onion, stirring, until golden brown, 3 to 5 minutes.

Add the garlic powder, salt, cumin, red chilli powder, and turmeric. Allow the spices to bloom for about a minute. Then add the dondakaya to the pan and increase the heat to medium-high. Cook, stirring, for a few minutes to coat the veggies well in the onion and spices.

Cover, decrease the heat, and simmer, stirring occasionally, for about 10 minutes. Add the coconut powder and coriander and stir well to combine. Cover and simmer over medium heat, stirring occasionally, for an additional

10 to 15 minutes. Check the dondakaya after 10 minutes. It should be quite tender, with just a slight bite. If it still feels crisp, continue cooking for a few minutes longer.

Adjust the seasonings to taste. You may want to add a bit more coriander and/or ground cumin for additional flavor. It's best to let the dish sit for a half hour or longer (if not a day), to allow the flavors to develop more fully. Just reheat quickly before serving alongside the cod.

CHITRANNAM

LEMON RICE TOSSED WITH LENTILS, PEANUTS, AND CHILLIES

SERVES 4

1 tablespoon chana dal (Indian split chickpeas) or 2 tablespoons chopped cashews

¾ cup basmati rice

1 teaspoon salt

¼ teaspoon ground turmeric

2 tablespoons canola oil, divided

½ cup peanuts

1 pinch of hing (asafoetida) (optional)

1 teaspoon black mustard seeds

1 teaspoon urad dal (split black gram without skin)

10 to 12 curry leaves

1-inch piece fresh ginger, peeled and thinly sliced or diced

3 Indian dried red chillies, broken in half

3 Indian green chillies, cut in half

¼ cup freshly squeezed lemon juice (2 or 3 lemons)

To round out the meal, this rice side dish echoes many of the flavors found in the entrée and veggie, while providing a nice, lemony complement to the fish. Chitrannam is tart, spicy, and salty all at the same time, with fantastic crunch from lentils and peanuts. It's a traditional South Indian recipe (often called pulihora and made with tamarind instead of lemon) that's sometimes served in Hindu temples. For me, this dish brings back fond memories of the family trips we've taken all my life to temples across the United States and India.

Chitrannam is meant to be served at room temperature. And the longer it sits (in the refrigerator if more than a few hours), the deeper its trio of flavors will develop—which is why this is a great make-ahead recipe, and leftovers are excellent as a light lunch.

A note about the rice: For this preparation, you want tender, separate grains, so I usually cook the rice like pasta. But you can make it by whichever method is most convenient to you, as long as the end result isn't sticky (chitrannam can also be made with day-old rice). The key to cooking rice like pasta is to use a big pot with plenty of water so the grains have room to move around (just like pasta). For a full discussion about cooking rice, please see page 288.

Fill a large pot with about 12 cups of water and bring to a boil over high heat. Meanwhile, place the chana dal in a small bowl with warm water and set aside to soak.

Rinse the rice well several times until the water becomes less cloudy (starchy). Once the water is boiling, add the rice along with the salt and turmeric. Cook for 8 to 10 minutes at a rolling boil. Test a few grains to see if they are done. The rice should be fully tender (not al dente), but be careful to stop cooking before the rice gets mushy. Drain the rice in a colander, letting it sit for a few minutes to lose all the excess water. Then transfer to a large serving bowl or back into the dry pot.

Drain the chana dal and dry them very well with towels.

Heat 1 tablespoon of the oil in a small skillet over medium heat. Add the peanuts (and cashews, if using instead of chana dal) to the warm oil and fry gently, reducing the heat if necessary, until the nuts turn deep brown, 2 to 3 minutes. Pour over the rice.

Heat the remaining 1 tablespoon oil in the same skillet. Add the hing, followed by the mustard seeds, chana dal, urad dal, curry leaves, ginger, and red and green chillies. As soon as the mustard seeds begin to pop, pour the contents of the skillet over the rice. Be careful not to fry too long or the lentils will burn and become too crunchy.

Pour most of the lemon juice over the rice (reserve a few spoonfuls until after you've tasted). Mix all the components gently but thoroughly so that the rice gets evenly flavored.

Add a generous amount of salt (½ to 1 teaspoon) and the remaining lemon juice, if desired. Chitrannam is meant to be spicy, so if you can handle a little more heat, add another dried red chilli (or crushed red pepper flakes). Serve at room temperature alongside the cod, informing your guests to discard the chillies and curry leaves as they eat.

LUNCH

KATI ROLLS   125
Individualized Street-Food Wraps with Choice of:

UNDA   126
Fried Egg

ALOO   127
Saucy Potatoes

CHICKEN
With Charred Onion and Peppers   128

MOVIE

KAHAANI   120
Suspenseful mystery set in the streets of Calcutta

KAHAANI

FLAVOR

If you like a good mystery, I've got the perfect film for you. Get ready to pound the pavement in Kolkata (formerly Calcutta), searching for the truth in this suspenseful drama.

RECIPE

A pregnant woman (Vidya) arrives in Kolkata from London, looking for her missing husband (Arnab Bagchi). Arnab was a software engineer who traveled to India on assignment for a company called the National Data Center, or NDC. Vidya is a stranger in Kolkata with no family or support, and when she goes to the police for assistance, they give her the runaround.

Vidya checks herself into a shabby motel and is able to persuade a sympathetic cop (Rana) to help her, sensing a cover-up. She and Rana hit the streets of Kolkata on their own, assembling clues and risking their lives to discover what happened to Vidya's husband.

THE "DISH"

I love this movie. Granted, I love all the movies in this book for one reason or another, but this film is the one in recent years that I find myself recommending time and again to people who aren't familiar with Bollywood. It demonstrates that Indian films are more than song-and-dance vehicles; they're world-class cinema, which includes all genres of storytelling. *Kahaani* (which, incidentally, means "story") is a taut, suspenseful mystery that holds its own against the best that Hollywood has to offer. Frankly, I'm surprised the film hasn't been remade in Hollywood yet.

The central role of Vidya is played by actress Vidya Balan, who carries the film on her shoulders. The award-winning actress has built her career on films with strong female protagonists like the one in *Kahaani*. Along the way, Vidya has redefined the perception of the "Bollywood heroine" by demonstrating that movies with female leads can be commercially successful. She's debunked the commonly held belief—in both Bollywood and Hollywood—that in order to draw audiences, a movie must have a marquee male star.

Hailing from South India, Vidya moved to Mumbai and pursued acting from a young age, eventually landing a breakthrough role in *Parineeta*. This intimate drama put her on the map as an actress with real chops, garnering multiple award nominations for her very first film. In the years that followed, she didn't head down the traditional path for many starlets—accepting roles as arm candy in hero-centric movies. She also didn't step into the trap of believing that actresses need to be a size zero. Instead, Vidya embraced her natural beauty, spoke openly about body image, and set about focusing on her craft.

And it worked. Beginning in 2009, Vidya landed back-to-back films like *The Dirty Picture*, *Paa*, and *Ishqiya* that scored her acting awards year after year. Moreover, these movies were box-office hits. Along with Kangana Ranaut (see *Queen*, page 266), Vidya now holds the distinction of being one of the few female actors in the world who can "open" a film *and* spark a sequel, as she did with 2016's *Kahaani 2*.

Who needs Shah Rukh Khan when you've got a superstar like Vidya Balan?

INGREDIENTS

CAST: Vidya Balan, Parambrata Chatterjee, Nawazuddin Siddiqui
DIRECTOR: Sujoy Ghosh
WRITERS: Sujoy Ghosh, Advaita Kala, Suresh Nair, Nikhil Vyas, Ritesh Shah, Sutapa Sikdar
MUSIC DIRECTOR: Vishal-Shekhar
RELEASE: 2012

TASTE THIS

In the mood for mystery? Like *Kahaani*, these suspenseful dramas will keep you guessing till the end:

A WEDNESDAY (2008) A middle-aged man calls the Mumbai police department to inform them he's placed bombs all around the city, which will detonate if his demands aren't met. But that's just the *beginning* of the story. One of the few Indian films to be remade in the West, the English-language version starred Ben Kingsley and was titled *A Common Man*.

JOHNNY GADDAAR (2007) In classic film noir style, *Johnny Gaddaar* is a twisty crime drama about a gang of five backstabbing criminals. As the men try to outwit one another, the plot takes one surprising turn after another, making for a smart and sleek ride.

DRISHYAM (2015) This compelling drama explores what happens when an average, loving family finds themselves in the middle of a brutal crime investigation . . . and *they* are the prime suspects. Based on a South Indian (Malayalam) film, the Hindi version is the fourth remake in just three years, proving that this is one killer story.

KATI ROLLS

INDIVIDUALIZED STREET-FOOD WRAPS

Kati rolls began, the story goes, on the streets of Calcutta (now known as Kolkata), where *Kahaani* takes place. Meat kebabs were wrapped in flatbread and sold as an easy, portable meal. *Kati* means "stick" and refers to the skewer on which the kebabs were cooked. Since then, kati rolls have evolved beyond kebabs to encompass hand-held wraps with any number of fillings—India's version of the burrito.

This fun concept for a lunch (or brunch) party centers around "do-it-yourself" kati rolls. Guests can individualize their rolls by mixing and matching ingredients. There's the chicken-aloo roll, the chicken-unda roll, the unda-aloo roll . . . the possibilities are numerous.

To get started, purchase a dozen or so roti (see "Breads," page 291). If you can't get to an Indian grocery store, then feel free to use whole wheat tortillas. Warm the bread one at a time on a hot griddle/skillet, or wrap the whole stack in aluminum foil and place it in the oven at 350°F for 8 to 10 minutes. In either case, you don't want to heat the bread too long or else it will become crispy and difficult to roll.

Set up a "kati roll bar" with the bread, fillings, and condiments. Your guests can begin by spreading a thin layer of mango pickle (see "Condiments," page 297) on the inside of their roti (or skip this step if they don't like it spicy); then fill with any combination of chicken, potatoes, fried egg, or onions and peppers; drizzle with mint chutney (page 43); and finally, wrap the roti into a cylinder.

Kati roll shops are popping up in major cities across the United States, and my hope is that they someday become as popular as burritos. Thank you, Calcutta, for giving us a universally appealing sandwich and a great idea for a party.

(Opposite, clockwise from top-right)
Aloo, p. 127; mango pickle, p. 297; roti, p. 291; mint chutney, p. 43;
Chicken, p. 128; (center) Unda, p. 126

UNDA KATI ROLL

FRIED EGG

PER SERVING

1 large egg

2 pinches of salt

1 pinch of ground coriander

1 pinch of Indian red chilli powder (or cayenne)

Sprinkle of chopped cilantro

½ tablespoon butter

The first component of the kati roll, if you choose, is a delicious fried egg. Lay the fried egg (*unda*) directly on top of the roti to act as a liner for the bread. It's such a simple concept, but it's really what takes the kati roll to another level. The thin layer of egg acts as a second skin in the wrap. Honestly, you may not even need any more fillings. On a Saturday morning, there's nothing better than an unda kati roll with a generous schmear of spicy mango pickle—the ultimate cure for a hangover.

To make each unda, beat 1 egg in a small bowl with the salt, coriander, red chilli powder, and chopped cilantro.

Melt the butter in a small omelet pan over medium-high heat. Once the pan is hot, add the egg. Allow the egg to begin to set for about a minute. Pull the edges toward the center of the pan with a fork, allowing uncooked egg to run to the perimeter. Once the egg is sturdy enough to flip, do so.

Cook for an additional minute or less on the other side. Remove to a serving plate and begin with the next egg. Create a stack of undas like pancakes to serve alongside the other kati roll components.

ALOO KATI ROLL

SAUCY POTATOES

As we all know, potatoes go with everything. That's why this potato (*aloo*) filling is an essential component of your kati roll bar. Pair it with the egg if you're in the mood for brunch flavors; combine it with the chicken for a lunch wrap; or choose the potatoes alone for a satisfying vegetarian option.

Better yet—don't choose—just pile everything on!

SERVES 4

1 tablespoon canola oil

1 bay leaf

1 medium onion, finely chopped

2 teaspoons garlic paste (or minced garlic)

1 teaspoon ginger paste (or minced ginger)

½ tablespoon salt

½ teaspoon Indian red chilli powder (or cayenne)

¼ teaspoon ground turmeric

8 ounces tomato sauce

½ teaspoon ground coriander

2 pounds red potatoes, peeled and diced

2 tablespoons chopped cilantro

In a medium saucepan, heat the oil over medium-high heat. Add the bay leaf and allow it to start infusing the oil for 15 seconds. Then add the onion and cook, stirring, until softened, 2 to 3 minutes.

Add the garlic and ginger pastes and cook, stirring, for a minute. Then add the salt, red chilli powder, and turmeric and allow the spices to bloom for about 30 seconds.

Add the tomato sauce and stir well. Decrease the heat, cover, and simmer for 5 minutes. Add the coriander and potatoes and stir well. Cover and simmer, stirring occasionally, until the potatoes are tender, 25 to 30 minutes.

Sprinkle with the cilantro. Adjust the salt and seasonings to taste. Transfer to a large serving bowl and serve alongside the other kati roll components.

CHICKEN KATI ROLL

WITH CHARRED ONION AND PEPPERS

SERVES 4

1 teaspoon ground coriander

1 teaspoon garlic powder

½ teaspoon ground ginger

½ teaspoon salt

½ teaspoon Indian red chilli powder (or cayenne)

¼ teaspoon ground turmeric

¼ teaspoon ground cinnamon

¼ teaspoon ground cloves

1½ pounds boneless, skinless chicken breasts

1 tablespoon canola oil

FOR THE ONION AND PEPPERS

1 tablespoon canola oil

2 green bell peppers, cored, seeded, and thinly sliced

1 medium red onion, thinly sliced

¼ teaspoon ground cumin

¼ teaspoon ground turmeric

¼ teaspoon salt

This chicken preparation is the central component of your kati roll bar. Placing the onions and peppers alongside the chicken, as opposed to stir-frying them together, allows vegetarians to enjoy them, too. If I'm pressed for time, I've been known to buy a rotisserie chicken or grilled chicken breasts at the grocery store to make this recipe even quicker on a weeknight or as a weekend lunch. Just shred the rotisserie chicken or cut the grilled breasts into strips and proceed with heating in a skillet, sprinkled with the spice blend. (I promise I won't tell anyone you took a shortcut.)

In a small bowl, combine the coriander, garlic powder, ginger, salt, red chilli powder, turmeric, cinnamon, and cloves to create a spice blend.

Cut the chicken into thin strips, similar to fajitas.

In a large skillet, heat the oil over medium-high heat. Once the pan is hot, add the chicken to get a nice sear on the meat. Sprinkle half the spice blend over the chicken. After 4 to 5 minutes, flip the chicken to sear the other side. Sprinkle with the remaining spice blend. Decrease the heat to medium and cook, stirring occasionally, until the chicken is no longer pink when you slice into it, 8 to 10 minutes.

For the onion and peppers, heat the oil in a second skillet over high heat. Once the pan is very hot, add the peppers and onion. They should sizzle on contact. Then add the cumin, turmeric, and salt and cook, stirring, until deeply charred, 5 to 7 minutes.

Remove the chicken to a platter and the onion-pepper mixture to a serving dish. Serve alongside mint chutney (page 43) and the other kati roll components.

DINNER

HIMALAYAN SHEPHERD'S PIE   137
Rustic Casserole of Ground Beef, Lentils, and Rice

BUTTERNUT SQUASH SOUP   140
Warmly Scented with Ginger, Cumin, and Coriander

MOVIE

HAIDER   132
Bollywood adaptation of *Hamlet*, set in the foothills of Kashmir

FLAVOR

A Hindi-language adaptation of *Hamlet*, this moody drama takes some of the best talent in contemporary Bollywood and matches it with Shakespeare's storytelling, like a pairing of fine wine and cheese.

RECIPE

The year is 1995 and Kashmir is plagued with political conflict when a well-meaning doctor aids an injured terrorist. As a consequence of his actions, the doctor's house is bombed by the military and he is taken away for questioning—an example of the "civilian disappearances" that were rampant in the region during that era.

The doctor's son, Haider (Hamlet), returns home from college to find his mother, Ghazala (Gertrude), laughing and singing with his uncle, Khurram (Claudius). This seeming betrayal sends Haider on a single-minded mission to avenge his father's death. Haider descends into a desperate spiral, replete with visits to graveyards and one very famous monologue on the nature of existence.

THE "DISH"

Kashmir has been an ongoing source of conflict for India. The state, snuggled in the Himalayas between India and archrival Pakistan, has been embroiled in violent unrest ever since the two countries were partitioned after British independence in 1947. India and Pakistan have fought three wars and countless skirmishes over the disputed territory, which continues to be part of India.

For Bollywood, Kashmir has served as a lush and dramatic backdrop. For decades, filmmakers have flocked to its ice-capped mountains and scenic valleys to shoot musical numbers. But beyond beautiful cinema vistas, the dispute of

Images © UTV Software
Communications
Limited and Vishal
Bhardwaj Pictures
Private Limited, 2016
(pages 130–133, 135)

Kashmir has provided rich material for a handful of bold storytellers. Films like *Mission Kashmir*, *Fanaa*, and *Henna* dramatized the conflict, always woven around an ill-fated love story, to much success.

Haider is perhaps the most studious of these films, thanks in no small part to the weighty script inspired by *Hamlet* (and, to note, the film is an *adaptation* that deviates from the original play in several instances). The picturesque drama is acclaimed writer-director Vishal Bhardwaj's third film in his Shakespeare trilogy (see the following page for the others).

Although named for Hamlet, the movie truly belongs to Gertrude, played by actress Tabu, who steals the show with her elegant yet pained portrayal of Hamlet's mother. Critical darling Tabu has made a career out of being the nontraditional Bollywood heroine, choosing complicated, realistic characters who span the range from young to old, rural to urban, docile to kick-ass. Along the way, Hollywood has noticed her talent too, casting her in films such as *The Namesake* and *Life of Pi*.

Lead actor Shahid Kapoor's career trajectory has unfortunately not been as smooth. No relation to the Bollywood Kapoor dynasty, Shahid was in some ways the underdog trying for years to make a name for himself. After an unremarkable debut, he finally found a megahit in 2007's *Jab We Met*, a romantic comedy starring his real-life girlfriend. But following their much-publicized breakup (and her ascent to superstardom), Shahid suffered from a string of failures.

Haider, however, marks a pinnacle in Shahid's career. He was awarded the Filmfare Award for Best Actor (Bollywood's version of the Oscars) for his layered performance as Hamlet. The perpetual boy next door was finally recognized for his talent and hard work, beginning a new and successful chapter of his career.

INGREDIENTS

CAST: Shahid Kapoor, Tabu, Kay Kay Menon
DIRECTOR: Vishal Bhardwaj
WRITERS: Vishal Bhardwaj, Basharat Peer
BASED ON THE PLAY *HAMLET*, BY WILLIAM SHAKESPEARE
MUSIC DIRECTOR: Vishal Bhardwaj
RELEASE: 2014

TASTE THIS

It makes a lot of sense that Shakespeare and Bollywood would be such great companions—both love sprawling story lines, surprise plot twists, and dramatic soliloquies—as evidenced by these adaptations:

MAQBOOL (2004) The first film in director Vishal Bhardwaj's Shakespeare trilogy, *Maqbool* is an interpretation of *Macbeth*, trading royal Scotland for the Mumbai underworld. The gritty crime drama (costarring Tabu as Lady Macbeth) is the film that put the director on the map and, some argue, remains his best film.

OMKARA (2006) With *Omkara*, the second and most successful film in Bhardwaj's trilogy, the director takes on *Othello*. The film is packed with brutal, stellar performances and a sexy dance number, "Beedi," which continues to be a dance club favorite (and is worth viewing on YouTube, even if you don't watch the film).

RAM-LEELA (2014) For a very different take on Shakespeare, check out Bollywood's adaptation of *Romeo and Juliet*. Unlike the bleak style of Vishal Bhardwaj, director Sanjay Leela Bhansali brings his signature lavish and opulent aesthetics to Verona via Gujarat. Never have the Montagues and Capulets looked so gorgeous, nor sung and danced so well.

HIMALAYAN SHEPHERD'S PIE

RUSTIC CASSEROLE OF GROUND BEEF, LENTILS, AND RICE

Vishal Bhardwaj isn't the only guy who can do British adaptations. While watching the scenic vistas of Kashmir, enjoy my Himalayan spin on shepherd's pie, which uses rice and lentils in place of mashed potatoes. I admit there are a lot of steps to this crowd-pleasing casserole, which is why I suggest starting the meal simply with soup—and letting your friends bring dessert. I also recommend making the ground beef ahead of time, so you can just assemble and bake before your guests arrive. If anything, the casserole will taste even better if the beef has a day or two to develop its flavors. Also, you'll notice that I instruct cooking the rice like pasta, in a large pot of boiling water. This technique is preferable because we want the grains to be separate and fluffy (see my discussion about rice on page 288).

Himalayan Shepherd's Pie is a treat to make and serve on a chilly evening, something Haider would've appreciated after traipsing through snow-covered graveyards. It's warm and comforting, and incredibly filling—the kind of meal where everyone digs in without pretense and goes back for seconds and thirds.

TO MAKE THE BEEF LAYER: Heat a very large sauté pan with high sides over medium heat. Add the ground beef and sprinkle with the turmeric. Crumble the meat with a wooden spoon and cook for 7 to 9 minutes, rendering its fat. Remove the meat using a slotted spoon or fine-mesh strainer, allowing the fat to stay in the pan. Set the meat aside.

Discard the grease and wipe the pan dry. Add the oil to the pan and heat over medium-high heat. Add the bay leaves and allow them to begin infusing the oil for 15 seconds. Add the onions, decrease the heat to medium, and cook, stirring, until they turn golden brown but do not burn, 5 to 7 minutes. Add the garlic and ginger pastes and cook, stirring, for 1 to 2 minutes. Then add the red chilli powder, cloves, salt, and cinnamon and stir the spices into the onions, allowing them to bloom for another minute.

SERVES 6 TO 8

FOR THE BEEF LAYER

2 pounds 85% lean ground beef

½ tablespoon ground turmeric

2 tablespoons canola oil

3 bay leaves

2 medium onions, finely chopped

3 tablespoons garlic paste (or minced garlic)

2 tablespoons ginger paste (or minced ginger)

½ tablespoon Indian red chilli powder (or cayenne)

½ tablespoon ground cloves

2 teaspoons salt

1 teaspoon ground cinnamon

1 medium tomato, finely chopped

2 Yukon gold potatoes (about ½ pound), washed and peeled

½ cup chopped cilantro

2 teaspoons ground coriander

FOR THE LENTIL LAYER

1 cup whole masoor dal (see Note)

1 teaspoon ground coriander

1 teaspoon salt

(CONTINUED)

¼ teaspoon ground turmeric

¼ teaspoon Indian red chilli powder (or cayenne)

FOR THE RICE LAYER

1½ cups basmati rice

2 teaspoons salt

1 teaspoon cumin seeds

½ teaspoon ground turmeric

½ cup frozen peas

FOR THE ONION TOPPING

1 medium onion, very finely sliced

¼ cup all-purpose flour

1 teaspoon salt

1 large egg, beaten

1 cup panko breadcrumbs

Canola oil

Freshly squeezed lemon juice, to taste

Greek yogurt (2% or whole), for serving

Stir in the tomatoes to create a thick paste. Cover and simmer until the tomatoes have completely broken down, 5 to 7 minutes. The sauce should start to "come together," or pull away slightly from the sides of the pan, with the oil separating to the perimeter.

Meanwhile, cut the potatoes into bite-size, ½-inch pieces.

Return the meat to the pan. Stir well, coating the meat with the spicy tomato sauce. Then add the potatoes and sprinkle them with a generous pinch or two of salt. Stir to combine. Cook over medium heat, uncovered, stirring occasionally, for about 10 minutes, until the potatoes are tender.

Remove the bay leaves. Add the cilantro and coriander. Adjust the seasonings to taste and set aside.

TO MAKE THE LENTIL LAYER: Rinse the masoor dal well several times, removing any small stones that may be mixed with the lentils. Cover with plenty of water in a medium saucepan and set aside to soak for 20 to 30 minutes.

Drain the lentils. Cover with plenty of water again and bring to a boil.

Add the coriander, salt, turmeric, and red chilli powder. Boil until the lentils are tender, 10 to 12 minutes. Drain the lentils and spread onto a plate to dry.

TO MAKE THE RICE LAYER: Rinse the rice well several times until the water becomes less cloudy (starchy). Cover with plenty of water in a large, 5-quart saucepan and bring to a boil. Add the salt, cumin seeds, and turmeric. Boil until the rice is al dente (it will finish cooking in the oven), 6 to 8 minutes.

Drain the rice. Toss the peas with the rice in the colander (no need to thaw the peas). Spread onto a plate to dry.

Preheat the oven to 350°F. Grease a 9 x 13-inch casserole dish with cooking spray.

To assemble, begin by spreading half the ground beef in the pan and patting gently to create a smooth, compact layer. Then spread half the lentils and pat smooth. Follow with half the rice. Repeat the layers one more time so you end up with rice on top, and have used all your ingredients.

FOR THE ONION TOPPING: In a medium bowl, toss the onion slices in the flour and salt. Then pour the beaten egg over and stir to combine. Follow by adding the panko and coating all the onion slices well.

Spread the breaded onions on top of the casserole. Generously spray or brush with oil. (You most likely will not need all the onions, in which case you can place the remainder on a baking sheet and throw in the oven for tasty, crispy onion rings.)

Place the casserole in the oven and bake for 25 to 30 minutes, until the top is golden brown.

Squeeze lemon over the casserole and serve with Greek yogurt on the side.

NOTE: Be sure to use whole masoor dal, which is brown in color (split masoor dal, which is pinkish, is often labeled simply as "masoor dal"—but that's not what this recipe calls for).

BUTTERNUT SQUASH SOUP

WARMLY SCENTED WITH GINGER, CUMIN, AND CORIANDER

SERVES 6 TO 8

2 tablespoons extra-virgin olive oil

1 medium onion, roughly chopped

2 teaspoons ginger paste (or minced ginger)

2 teaspoons salt

1 teaspoon ground cumin

1 teaspoon ground coriander

¼ teaspoon Indian red chilli powder (or cayenne)

¼ teaspoon ground cinnamon

4 pounds butternut squash, cut into chunks (I like to buy packaged, precut squash available in most supermarkets)

4 cups vegetable stock

Greek yogurt (2% or whole), for serving

FOR THE SPICY PUMPKIN SEEDS

½ cup pumpkin seeds

1 teaspoon extra-virgin olive oil

½ teaspoon Indian red chilli powder or cayenne (if you don't want too much heat, use ¼ teaspoon)

¼ teaspoon salt

Our cozy, cold-weather meal warms up with a big pot of butternut squash soup. I love the vibrant orange color of this dish—a visual reminder of autumn—while its aromatic spices will fill your kitchen with the scent of ginger, cumin, coriander, and cinnamon. Topped with creamy yogurt and toasted, red chilli pumpkin seeds, this comforting soup can easily feed a crowd, making it the perfect starter for our hearty casserole.

Preheat the oven to 300°F.

Heat the olive oil in a large soup pot or Dutch oven over medium heat. Add the onion and cook, stirring gently, until soft and translucent, 5 to 7 minutes, reducing the heat to medium-low if necessary. Add the ginger paste, salt, cumin, coriander, red chilli powder, and cinnamon and allow the spices to bloom for 1 to 2 minutes.

Add the butternut squash and vegetable stock and stir to combine. Cover and simmer until the squash is tender, 25 to 30 minutes.

Meanwhile, for the spicy pumpkin seeds, pour the pumpkin seeds onto a foil- or parchment-lined baking sheet. Drizzle with the olive oil and sprinkle with the red chilli powder and salt. Toss to coat. Then spread the seeds into a single layer and roast for 20 minutes. Remove to a bowl to cool.

Let the squash mixture cool partially. Working in batches, transfer the mixture to a blender and puree until smooth, being careful to leave some room at the top of the blender and cover loosely with a dish towel, allowing steam to escape. Return the soup to the pot and continue to simmer.

Taste and adjust the seasonings. Thin with a little vegetable stock, if desired. Serve with a dollop of yogurt on each bowl (or drizzle over) and garnish with the spicy pumpkin seeds.

DINNER

BEEF CURRY 149
Juicy Cubes of Steak Slowly Braised in Spicy Gravy

BELL PEPPERS WITH BESAN 151
Chunks of Pepper Coated with Chickpea Flour and Spices

MALLIKA PINNI'S BEETROOT 152
Sautéed with Curry Leaves, Cumin Seeds, and Indian Green Chillies

MOVIE

KUCH KUCH HOTA HAI 144
Iconic 1990s romance that defined an era

KUCH KUCH HOTA HAI

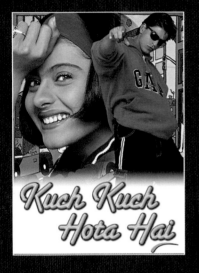

FLAVOR

Sugary sweet and achingly melodramatic, this candy-coated romance is required viewing for any fan of contemporary Indian cinema, having helped usher in a new era of Bollywood.

RECIPE

A story of interconnecting love triangles, *Kuch Kuch Hota Hai* follows bickering best friends, Rahul and Anjali, through their carefree days at a Mumbai college. Rahul is the big man on campus while Anjali is the tomboy that's always at his side. By the time Anjali realizes she's in love with Rahul, it's too late—he's already smitten with Tina, the headmaster's beautiful daughter.

Cut to ten years later. Tina has died and her young daughter takes it upon herself to reunite her widower dad with his onetime best friend and, perhaps, true love. But will Rahul and Anjali's timing be misaligned yet again?

THE "DISH"

Kuch Kuch Hota Hai is a poetic way to say "something happens," and with the release of this film, something definitely *did* happen. Bollywood broke beyond the boundaries of India and hasn't looked back since.

Although the film has an air of 1990s kitsch about it now, at the time, it was fresh and original. The visionary behind this fashionable confection is writer-director Karan Johar, who made his debut with this film at the age of twenty-six. Because of *Kuch Kuch* (and its predecessor, *Dilwale Dulhania Le Jayenge*, for which

Johar served as assistant director), the gates were thrown open to an entire new genre of filmmaking, one that could be described as "NRI films." NRI stands for "non-resident Indians," referring to Indian immigrants who live outside the motherland (like my family). Karan Johar became the poster boy for NRIs, churning out a series of films over the next two decades, as both director and producer, that appealed tremendously to expat Indians.

These NRI films were glossy and big budget, often shot in Europe or America, with stars who dressed in American clothes. But although the movies were Western in style, they were deeply Indian in ethos—which is why they worked so well. Underneath the Gap sweatshirts and stonewashed jeans, the characters espoused sentimental, Indian values of family, honor, and sacrifice, tapping into the NRI community's nostalgia and longing for their homeland. Johar's world looked modern on the outside, but was incredibly traditional on the inside—much like NRIs themselves.

Since his first film, Karan Johar has gone on to become a brand name and media mogul, building one of the most influential movie studios in Bollywood. Johar himself has turned into a talk show host and all-around style maven, setting the bar for what's on-trend in India. Many would say he is *the* center of the wheel around which Bollywood spins.

Of course, the success of *Kuch Kuch Hota Hai* had everything to do with the film's stars as well. Shah Rukh Khan and Kajol had taken the country by storm with their previous film, *Dilwale Dulhania Le Jayenge*, and with this follow-up, their position as one of Bollywood's most iconic couples was solidified. In addition, the film marks one of the few times two of the reigning Khans—Shah Rukh and Salman—have appeared on-screen together. (Salman's role was a well-kept secret; when the superstar appeared midway through the film, audiences in theaters everywhere lost their minds.)

INGREDIENTS

CAST: Shah Rukh Khan, Kajol, Rani Mukerji, Salman Khan
WRITER AND DIRECTOR: Karan Johar
MUSIC DIRECTOR: Jatin-Lalit
RELEASE: 1998

TASTE THIS

There are so many popular NRI films that you could teach a college course about them all (and, somewhere, I'm sure that's happened). Here's just a sampling:

DILWALE DULHANIA LE JAYENGE (1995) This was the movie that truly started it all. The predecessor to *Kuch Kuch*, *DDLJ* (as it's known) is iconic, 1990s Bollywood. The blockbuster musical catapulted Shah Rukh Khan and Kajol to superstardom and the film remains one of the most popular in Bollywood history—having played continuously in one Mumbai theater for over twenty years (and counting).

KABHI KHUSHI KABHIE GHAM . . . (2001) Director Karan Johar's follow-up to *Kuch Kuch* reunites his stars, Shah Rukh and Kajol, and throws in another legendary couple for good measure (Amitabh Bachchan and real-life wife Jaya Bachchan to play Shah Rukh's parents). Everything about this multigenerational tearjerker is over-the-top—with melodramatic acting, extravagant sets and costumes, and musical numbers galore.

AE DIL HAI MUSHKIL (2016) Karan Johar turns a corner with this tale of unrequited love, the best film of his career. Although the romantic drama still has all his signature elements (beautiful people dressed in beautiful clothes singing in beautiful locations), the characters display an emotional authenticity never before seen in Johar's work.

BEEF CURRY

JUICY CUBES OF STEAK SLOWLY BRAISED IN SPICY GRAVY

Just as Karan Johar mastered the art of the NRI film, Indian cooks in the United States have created a stable of popular recipes that blend Indian flavors with quintessentially American ingredients. And beef curry is a perfect example of that fusion. Traditionally, this dish would be made with lamb or mutton, but my mom (and other immigrant cooks like her) adapted it with good old American steak.

Beef curry is a favorite in my family—we make it several times a month. Its pungent aroma fills the house as the beef slowly simmers on the stove. I've tried making this dish with a "higher" cut of meat like sirloin, but honestly, I find beef chuck to be best suited for the low-and-slow cooking process. And as I recommend with other curries in this book, try to prepare this dish a day or two ahead, if you can, because the meat becomes even more delicious as it soaks up the flavors of the gravy overnight.

Kuch Kuch Hota Hai is a milestone for an entire generation of Indian-American movie-goers. In much the same way, this dish, to me, represents the best of Indian-American home cooking.

Heat 1 tablespoon of the oil in a Dutch oven or large saucepan. Pat the meat dry and season with the turmeric. Once the pan is very hot, sear the meat in multiple batches (to avoid crowding the pan). Don't turn the pieces until they naturally release from the bottom of the pan, with a dark crust all around, 2 to 3 minutes per side. Remove the meat to a bowl or plate.

Pour off the excess grease from the pan and heat the remaining 1 tablespoon oil. Add the bay leaves and allow them to begin infusing the oil for 15 seconds. Add the onion and cook, stirring and scraping up the brown bits from the bottom of the pan, for about 7 minutes. Add the garlic and ginger pastes and cook, stirring, for another 2 minutes, reducing the heat if necessary to prevent burning. Then add the salt, red chilli powder, cinnamon, and cloves and allow the spices to bloom for about a minute.

Add the tomatoes and cook, stirring well, until the tomatoes have broken down and the sauce starts to "come together" (pull away from the sides of the pan with droplets of oil separating on the perimeter), 3 to 5 minutes.

SERVES 4

2 tablespoons canola oil, divided

2 pounds stew meat (beef chuck), cut into bite-size, 1-inch cubes

½ teaspoon ground turmeric

3 bay leaves

1 large onion, finely chopped

2 tablespoons garlic paste (or minced garlic)

1 heaping tablespoon ginger paste (or minced ginger)

2 teaspoons salt

1 teaspoon Indian red chilli powder (or cayenne)

1 teaspoon ground cinnamon

1 teaspoon ground cloves

1½ medium tomatoes, finely chopped (or ¾ cup crushed tomatoes)

2 tablespoons Greek yogurt (2% or whole)

¾ cup chopped cilantro, plus extra for garnish

2 tablespoons coconut powder

1 tablespoon ground coriander

Cooked rice (any type), roti, or naan, for serving

Add the seared beef pieces to the pan and stir well to coat with the spicy tomato sauce. Stir in the yogurt. Decrease the heat, cover, and simmer gently, stirring occasionally, for 30 minutes.

Stir in the cilantro, coconut powder, and coriander. If you're making the dish a day or two ahead of time, stop at this point.

Decrease the heat to the lowest setting, cover, and finish cooking for around 15 minutes. Taste a piece of the meat. If it's still tough, continue cooking until the meat becomes tender.

Adjust the seasonings to taste. Garnish with fresh cilantro and serve with rice or roti/naan.

BELL PEPPERS WITH BESAN

CHUNKS OF PEPPER COATED WITH CHICKPEA FLOUR AND SPICES

Who doesn't love steak and peppers? That's why I've chosen to pair my beef curry with this savory bell pepper side dish. Scented with ginger and coated with chickpea flour, the thick slices of pepper taste best when scooped up with warm roti or naan.

Chickpea flour (*besan* in Hindi) is an interesting ingredient widely used in Indian cuisine. It often takes the place of eggs as a binder, since so many Indians are vegetarian and don't eat eggs. Other times, as is the case here, besan serves as a thickening agent to help create a spicy paste. Chickpea flour is much higher in protein than wheat flour, is gluten free, and crisps up nicely when fried. I prefer buying it in Indian grocery stores, which carry a slightly different variety than American chickpea flour found in the supermarket—but either works for the recipe below.

In a medium saucepan, heat the oil over medium-high heat. Once the oil is shimmering hot, add the mustard seeds. As soon as the seeds begin to pop, add the onion and cook, stirring, until softened, 2 to 3 minutes. Add the garlic and ginger pastes, decrease the heat to medium, and cook, stirring, for about a minute. Then add the cumin, salt, turmeric, and red chilli powder and allow the spices to bloom in the oil for about a minute. Add the bell peppers and stir well for a few minutes to coat the veggies with the spicy onion.

Dissolve the tamarind paste in 1 tablespoon hot water and pour into the pan. Decrease the heat and simmer with the lid slightly ajar, stirring occasionally, for 10 minutes.

Dissolve the chickpea flour in 2 tablespoons hot water. Pour into the pan, along with the coconut powder and coriander. Stir well to coat. Cook with the lid slightly ajar, stirring occasionally, for an additional 10 minutes.

Adjust the seasonings to taste. Continue cooking until the peppers have reached your desired tenderness. I prefer them to be quite soft, with just a slight bite in the center. Serve with the beef curry and roti or naan.

SERVES 4

1 tablespoon canola oil

1 teaspoon black mustard seeds

1 medium onion, finely chopped

½ tablespoon garlic paste (or minced garlic)

½ tablespoon ginger paste (or minced ginger)

1 teaspoon ground cumin

½ teaspoon salt

¼ teaspoon ground turmeric

¼ teaspoon Indian red chilli powder (or cayenne)

3 or 4 green bell peppers (2 pounds), diced into 1-inch chunks

¼ teaspoon tamarind paste*

2 tablespoons besan (chickpea flour)

1 tablespoon coconut powder

½ teaspoon ground coriander

Roti or naan, for serving

* Substitute: 2 teaspoons freshly squeezed lemon juice

(Opposite, clockwise on plate from top)
Mallika Pinni's Beetroot, p. 152
Beef Curry, p. 149
Bell Peppers with Besan

MALLIKA PINNI'S BEETROOT

SAUTÉED WITH CURRY LEAVES, CUMIN SEEDS, AND INDIAN GREEN CHILLIES

SERVES 4

1 tablespoon canola oil

1 teaspoon black mustard seeds

2 or 3 Indian green chillies, cut in half

1 teaspoon cumin seeds

1 teaspoon urad dal (split black gram without skin) (optional)

7 to 10 curry leaves

1 small onion, finely chopped

3 garlic cloves, sliced

½ teaspoon salt

¼ teaspoon ground turmeric

1½ pounds beets, peeled and cut into ½-inch pieces

1 tablespoon coconut powder

Roti or naan, for serving

To temper the bold flavor of our beef curry, I offer these sweet-and-spicy beets. I first encountered this dish on a trip to India, as I sat on the kitchen counter watching my *pinni* (or "maternal aunt" in Telugu), Mallika, quickly preparing a meal for me as I had unexpectedly decided to stay for dinner. Mallika Pinni has a razor-sharp wit, with which she kept me entertained as she whipped together this stir-fry. So much was encapsulated in that moment—the generous hospitality of Indians, who will share with you whatever they have in the kitchen; the comfort of family; and a visceral connection to my humble roots.

Whenever you're dealing with beets, be careful of the utensils and cutting boards you choose to use—the red stains are nearly impossible to get out of wood and other materials. For that reason, I use stainless steel when cooking this dish. Some people like to take the extra precaution of wearing gloves, but personally, I don't mind the beautiful red color staining my hands for a day. It's a reminder of the intimate relationship we share with food—how it comes from the ground and brings with it the rich colors of the earth.

It's also a reminder to me of that simple, wonderful evening I spent sitting on Mallika Pinni's kitchen counter.

Heat the oil in a large, wide sauté pan or wok over medium heat. Once the oil is shimmering hot, add the mustard seeds and then the green chillies, cumin seeds, urad dal, and curry leaves. As soon as the mustard seeds begin to pop, add the onion and cook, stirring, for 1 minute. Then add the garlic and cook, stirring, for another minute, reducing the heat if necessary to prevent burning. Add the salt and turmeric and cook, stirring, for about 30 seconds.

Add the beets to the pan. Increase the heat to medium-high and cook, stirring, until the beets are well coated with the onion and spices, 2 to 3 minutes.

Add ¼ cup water, cover, decrease the heat, and simmer, stirring occasionally, for 20 minutes.

Stir the coconut powder into the beets. Cover and simmer until the beets are tender, another 5 to 10 minutes.

Adjust the salt to taste. Remove the green chillies and inform your guests to discard the curry leaves while eating. Serve with the beef curry and roti or naan.

DINNER

CHICKEN KORMA — 161
Chicken Breasts Smothered in
Rich Yogurt Sauce with Almonds and Raisins

INDIAN-STYLE KALE — 163
Spicy Chopped Greens with Cherry Tomatoes

SIMPLE ZUCCHINI STIR-FRY — 165
Flavored with Mustard Seeds, Garlic, and
Black Pepper

MOVIE

BAJIRAO MASTANI — 156
Lush, epic romance set
in eighteenth-century India

BAJIRAO MASTANI

FLAVOR

It doesn't get any grander than this. With exquisite sets, gorgeous costumes, and massive battle scenes, this period epic is like the chef's fourteen-course tasting menu.

RECIPE

Based on a true story from the eighteenth century, the film focuses on Bajirao, the prime minister and fearless general of the Maratha Empire, which controls much of the Indian subcontinent. While on a military campaign, Bajirao's camp is infiltrated by Mastani, the beautiful daughter of a nearby king who demands Bajirao's assistance in defeating a Mughal invader.

Bajirao and Mastani join forces to defeat their common enemy—and in the process, fall in love. The only problem is, Bajirao is already married, to Kashibai. Bajirao is torn between his allegiance to his wife and his transcendent passion for Mastani. The royal love triangle between these three powerful players changes all of their lives and the course of history.

THE "DISH"

Director Sanjay Leela Bhansali (see *Devdas*, page 22) is at the top of his game with this film. All of his signature elements—opulent production design, meticulous cinematography, operatic music and dance—come together brilliantly in *Bajirao Mastani*, the best film of his career. It's no wonder the movie took twelve years to develop, going through several major cast changes for the title roles, until finally settling on Ranveer Singh and Deepika Padukone.

Photographs courtesy
Eros International
(pages 154–157, 159)

But it was certainly worth the wait. Ranveer and Deepika are the perfect choice for the story's tortured lovers. The actors—who have long been rumored to be in a relationship off-screen—share incredible chemistry. If you want to see even more of the sexy couple, check out their scorching hot performance as Romeo and Juliet in Bhansali's previous pairing of the duo, *Ram-Leela*.

Bajirao Mastani may be named for Ranveer and Deepika's characters, but in some ways, it's Priyanka Chopra who steals the show. Playing the jilted wife, Priyanka brings quiet strength and dignity to a role that could otherwise have been cliché. And you have to give a lot of credit to the *Quantico* star when you consider that she was simultaneously portraying an American FBI agent and an eighteenth-century Indian royal—filming in two different languages, and on two different continents.

Speaking of dancing, like all of Bhansali's films, the musical numbers in *Bajirao Mastani* were as eagerly anticipated as the movie itself. The music video for "Pinga" was released before the film and was immediately devoured and dissected all over the Internet. Although the consensus is that the dance duel between Deepika and Priyanka pales in comparison to the legendary Madhuri-Aishwarya face-off in Bhansali's other epic, *Devdas*, the song was a hit nonetheless.

As was the movie. *Bajirao Mastani* has been described by critics as a "masterpiece" and a "feverish love poem." Bhansali finally received the unadulterated accolades that had been elusive to him for most of his career—often praised for his visual aesthetic, but criticized for his lack of restraint and succumbing to melodrama. This time, not only did he win Best Film and Best Director at the Filmfare Awards (Bollywood's Oscars), but the movie also picked up another five trophies, including acting awards for Ranveer Singh and Priyanka Chopra (Deepika Padukone was nominated for Best Actress, but lost *to herself*—in the film *Piku*, see page 204).

INGREDIENTS

CAST: Ranveer Singh, Deepika Padukone, Priyanka Chopra
DIRECTOR: Sanjay Leela Bhansali
WRITERS: Prakash Kapadia, Sanjay Leela Bhansali
BASED ON THE NOVEL *RAAU,* **BY NAGNATH S. INAMDAR**
MUSIC DIRECTOR: Sanjay Leela Bhansali
RELEASE: 2015

TASTE THIS

Soldiers on horses, princesses in scrumptious costumes, royal backstabbing and intrigue . . . sometimes the occasion calls for an epic drama:

MUGHAL-E-AZAM (1960) The epic to end all epics, *Mughal-e-Azam* was the most expensive Bollywood film ever made at the time, and the first to be digitally colorized. The historical legend of a Mughal prince and his ill-fated love for a court dancer is a nostalgic favorite of all Indians and, reportedly, Sanjay Leela Bhansali's inspiration for *Bajirao Mastani*.

BAAHUBALI (2015) The highest grossing South Indian film in history, this massive two-part epic was dubbed into Hindi after being simultaneously shot in Telugu and Tamil. Filled with visual effects and enormous battle scenes, this is India's answer to *300*.

JODHAA AKBAR (2008) Hrithik Roshan and Aishwarya Rai are practically too pretty to look at in this period drama set in the Mughal Empire. Princess Jodhabai is forced to marry Emperor Akbar, but refuses to let him into her heart. Thankfully, she eventually capitulates; otherwise, they'd never have had their grandson, who built the Taj Mahal as a tribute to his own true love.

CHICKEN KORMA

CHICKEN BREASTS SMOTHERED IN RICH YOGURT SAUCE WITH ALMONDS AND RAISINS

Chicken korma is a traditional Mughal recipe, from the era of *Bajirao Mastani* (the Mughals were the Muslim invaders that Bajirao and Mastani defeat in the story). Much like the film, korma is traditionally luxurious and over the top, with meat braised in a rich sauce of yogurt, cream, and nuts. I love the flavor of korma, but have always looked for a simpler—and healthier—way to prepare it. This is my solution.

I start with thinly cut chicken pieces because they cook quickly and stay juicy the whole way through (there's nothing worse than dry chicken breast). Of course, if you're using regular chicken breast, all you need to do is place each piece between a folded sheet of plastic wrap and beat it with a rolling pin or the smooth side of a meat tenderizer until roughly ¼ inch in uniform thickness. Then, a quick yogurt marinade ensures the spices penetrate the meat to give it a faux-braised taste. And instead of simmering the gravy for an hour, I make a quick pan sauce that's poured over the breast to give it that classic korma flavor.

Think of this as twenty-first-century korma—made with simple techniques to suit our modern lifestyle, but with decadent flavors to suit the emperor inside us all.

In a large bowl, whisk together all the marinade ingredients.

Place the sliced chicken in the bowl with the marinade and stir well to coat all the pieces. Cover with plastic wrap and place in the refrigerator to marinate for 30 minutes (if you have more time, 2 to 3 hours is even better).

When you're ready to cook, heat 1 tablespoon of the oil in a large skillet over medium-high heat. Using tongs and a spatula, remove the chicken from the bowl and scrape off as much of the marinade as possible (reserving the marinade in the bowl) before placing the chicken in the skillet in multiple batches. Decrease the heat to medium and cook (replenishing with the remaining 1 tablespoon oil as needed) for 5 to 7 minutes on the first side, then flip and cook for another 5 to 7 minutes on the other side. (You could also do this on an outdoor grill for a nice charred effect.) To check if the chicken is done, cut into the thickest part of each

(Opposite, clockwise from top-left)
Chicken Korma; Indian-Style Kale, p. 163; Simple Zucchini Stir-Fry, p. 165

SERVES 4

FOR THE MARINADE

1 cup Greek yogurt (2% or whole)

1½ tablespoons garlic paste (or minced garlic)

1 tablespoon ginger paste (or minced ginger)

1 teaspoon salt

1 teaspoon Indian red chilli powder (or cayenne)

1 teaspoon ground coriander

½ teaspoon ground cinnamon

½ teaspoon ground cloves

¼ teaspoon ground turmeric

FOR THE CHICKEN

1½ pounds boneless, skinless chicken breasts, thinly cut

2 tablespoons canola oil, divided

Chopped fresh mint, for garnish

FOR THE PAN SAUCE

4 shallots, sliced (about 1 cup)

¼ cup sliced almonds, plus extra for garnish

1½ cups milk (whole or 2%)

½ cup golden raisins

Buttery naan, for serving

piece and make sure the meat is not pink. As each piece is finished, arrange on a platter.

For the pan sauce, remove any of the larger, burned remnants from the pan (but don't clean it out completely because the brown bits have tons of flavor). Decrease the heat to medium-low and add a touch of oil to the skillet if needed. Add the shallots and almonds and cook, stirring, until the shallots have softened, about a minute. Then add the marinade from the bowl, along with the milk. Whisk well. As soon as the sauce comes up to a bubble, decrease the heat, stir in the raisins, cover, and simmer, allowing the raw spices to be cooked, for 3 to 5 minutes.

Taste the sauce. If it's too intense or too thick, simply add more milk to thin it out.

Pour the sauce over the chicken breasts on the platter. Garnish with chopped mint and serve with buttery naan.

INDIAN-STYLE KALE

SPICY CHOPPED GREENS WITH CHERRY TOMATOES

Here's a perfect example of what I mean by "Indian-American cuisine." Kale is not native to India, but given its prevalence in the United States, it seemed to me like there must be a way to throw some Indian spices on it to make it more flavorful. As my mom has always said, "Bring me a vegetable, and I can make a curry out of it."

And she was right. I developed this recipe by treating kale similar to spinach and other greens in an Indian kitchen—by sautéing with onions and tomatoes to soften the leaf, and flavoring with go-to Indian spices such as garlic, ginger, cumin, and coriander. You could even add chickpeas to this dish for a hit of protein, which would make for a nice, simple lunch.

The transformation is astounding. Indian-style kale is just as healthy as its Western counterparts, but with *tons* more flavor. And it provides a fresh pop of green to the plate, counterbalancing the creamy richness of the chicken korma.

SERVES 4

1 pound curly kale

1 tablespoon canola oil

1 teaspoon black mustard seeds

1 teaspoon cumin seeds

1 medium onion, finely chopped

½ tablespoon garlic paste (or minced garlic)

½ teaspoon salt

¼ teaspoon ground turmeric

¼ teaspoon Indian red chilli powder (or cayenne)

½ pint cherry tomatoes, cut in half

½ teaspoon ground coriander

Rinse and dry the kale. Remove the stems and finely chop the leaves. There will be quite a bit of kale, so you'll need a large colander or very large bowl to accommodate it all.

In a large saucepan or wok, heat the oil over medium-high heat. Once the oil is shimmering hot, add the mustard and cumin seeds. As soon as the mustard seeds begin to pop, add the onion, decrease the heat to medium, and cook, stirring, until softened, about 3 minutes.

Add the garlic paste and cook, stirring, for another minute. Then add the salt, turmeric, and red chilli powder and allow the spices to bloom for about a minute.

Add the tomatoes and stir well to combine with the onion. Then pile in the kale. It might seem like your pan is going to overflow, but don't worry—the kale will wilt down to become more manageable. Cover the pan tightly, decrease the heat, and simmer for 7 to 10 minutes.

Remove the lid, being sure to pour back into the pan any water that accumulated in the lid. Use tongs to mix the wilted kale with the onion and tomatoes buried underneath. This takes a little bit of patience, so continue gently combining the contents of the pan for a few minutes until everything is well incorporated.

Add the coriander. Adjust the seasonings to taste. You may want a bit more salt, or if you're looking for more "flavor," add ½ teaspoon of ground cumin and perhaps another ½ teaspoon of ground coriander. Transfer to a platter or bowl and serve.

SIMPLE ZUCCHINI STIR-FRY

FLAVORED WITH MUSTARD SEEDS, GARLIC, AND BLACK PEPPER

Our royal dinner is complete with this refreshing side of zucchini. Crisp chunks of zucchini are quickly stir-fried with gentle shallots spiced with mustard seeds, garlic, and black pepper. The flavors are clean and simple, exactly what you're looking for in a healthy meal.

Heat the oil in a large sauté pan over medium-high heat. Once the oil is shimmering hot, add the mustard seeds. As soon as the seeds begin to pop, decrease the heat to medium, add the shallots, and cook, stirring, for about 2 minutes.

Add the cumin, garlic powder, ginger, black pepper, turmeric, and red chilli powder. Stir the spices into the shallots, allowing them to bloom for about a minute. Then add the zucchini, turn up the heat to medium-high, and cook, tossing the zucchini in the spices so the veggies become well coated and begin to soften, about 5 minutes.

Sprinkle with the coriander and salt and stir to combine. Decrease the heat, cover, and simmer for just a minute, so that the zucchini softens but retains its crispness.

Adjust the seasonings to taste and serve.

SERVES 4

1 tablespoon canola oil

1 teaspoon black mustard seeds

1 cup chopped shallots (about 4 shallots)

1 teaspoon ground cumin

1 teaspoon garlic powder

½ teaspoon ground ginger

½ teaspoon freshly ground black pepper

¼ teaspoon ground turmeric

¼ teaspoon Indian red chilli powder (or cayenne)

2 pounds zucchini (3 or 4), cut into ½-inch-thick wedges

½ teaspoon ground coriander

½ teaspoon salt

DINNER

KEEMA PAV
(AKA SLOPPY JAI)   173
Indian Sloppy Joe with Ground Turkey

PAN-ROASTED ALOO   174
Charred Baby Potatoes

NIMBU PAANI   175
Sweet and Salty Lemon-Lime Spritzer

MOVIE

3 IDIOTS   168
Wholesome, slapstick comedy with lots of heart

3 IDIOTS

FLAVOR

This broad comedy about three buddies navigating the stress of college while getting into slapstick mayhem is like a food fight in your dining hall during finals week.

RECIPE

At a competitive engineering university, three guys meet as roommates, each from a different walk of life—Farhan, secretly harboring artistic dreams, is forced to be here by his parents; Raju is here out of desperation to better his family's future; and Rancho seems to be here just to have a good time, living by his motto, "All is well." Together, the threesome gets into a ton of mischief under the ire of their tyrannical headmaster.

Ten years later, Farhan and Raju come back to campus for a reunion—but there's no sign of Rancho, who disappeared after graduation. So the friends set off on a journey to discover whatever happened to their inspiring ringleader.

THE "DISH"

3 Idiots is one of the most successful Bollywood comedies of all time. The film appeals to the entire family, with physical comedy to make the kids laugh, along with a "carpe diem" theme to resonate with adults. The three guys who struck this perfect balance—director Rajkumar Hirani, writer Abhijat Joshi, and producer Vidhu Vinod Chopra—aren't idiots at all. They're laughing all the way to the bank.

The creative threesome has built a distinctive comedy brand in Bollywood, beginning with the *Munna Bhai* movies prior to *3 Idiots*, and continuing with *PK* as its successor. You can recognize their films immediately for their unique tone,

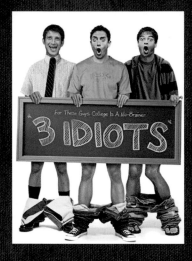

blending heartfelt emotions amid the laughs and embedding important social messages within the story line.

The social commentary in *3 Idiots* concerns the unrelenting pressure that Indian youth face in regard to academic performance. Even in America, those of us with Indian parents can relate to the stress that the characters in this film experience, to be model students bringing home stellar grades. But in India, the pressure sometimes reaches hysterical levels. The suicide rate among kids during exam periods is alarmingly significant. It's not uncommon to read stories in the newspaper about young people hanging themselves because they failed to get admission to a prestigious college or didn't score high marks on their report card.

As crazy as it sounds, there's a rationale behind these tragedies. Parents in India are desperate for their children to have a life of opportunity—which isn't easy in a country with over one billion people competing for finite resources. So they sometimes become overbearing in their kids' education, "for their own good." But when a young person then underperforms, he or she feels like not only a personal failure, but also a disgrace to the entire family, who often have sacrificed greatly so the child can obtain an education. It's a vicious cycle. And it's not exclusive to India. *3 Idiots* performed particularly well in East Asian countries like South Korea, China, and Taiwan, perhaps because audiences there could relate to the same societal pressures.

At the end of the day, though, *3 Idiots* is simply a wholesome comedy. It's the perfect movie to expose your middle- and high-school-aged kids to the world of Bollywood because they'll be able to enjoy the humor while relating to the characters' dilemmas. And it might remind you of the youthful exuberance and wide-eyed dreams of your own college days.

INGREDIENTS

CAST: Aamir Khan, R. Madhavan, Sharman Joshi, Kareena Kapoor, Boman Irani
DIRECTOR: Rajkumar Hirani
WRITERS: Abhijat Joshi, Rajkumar Hirani, Vidhu Vinod Chopra
MUSIC DIRECTOR: Shantanu Moitra
RELEASE: 2009

TASTE THIS

The creative forces behind *3 Idiots* are the kings of feel-good Bollywood comedy, as demonstrated by their string of megahits:

PK (2014) The highest grossing Bollywood film in history (as of 2016), *PK* tells the story of an alien who lands on Earth (played by a super buff and naked Aamir Khan). The alien is here to conduct research on human civilization, but is perplexed by our conflicting ideas of religion—providing an incisive and satirical commentary on religious intolerance.

MUNNA BHAI MBBS (2003) Similar to the Robin Williams film *Patch Adams*, this comedy is about a Mumbai gangster named Munna Bhai who enrolls in medical school to appease his parents who are ashamed of their son's illegal profession. Although a horrible med student, he brings his unique brand of humor and compassion to transform the uncaring medical institution.

LAGE RAHO MUNNA BHAI (2006) In this sequel to *Munna Bhai MBBS*, the gangster takes a job as a radio DJ to get closer to a girl he loves. When he starts having visions of Mahatma Gandhi, he uses Gandhi's teachings of truth and nonviolence to help listeners solve their life problems.

KEEMA PAV
(AKA SLOPPY JAI)

INDIAN SLOPPY JOE WITH GROUND TURKEY

Watching this movie takes me back to my own school days. And there is one thing for which I often feel nostalgic: school cafeteria lunches. I know it's odd, but it's true. Maybe it was because the food we ate at school was so different from what my mom cooked at home. Or maybe it was the allure of those polycarbonate lunch trays.

Reading the monthly lunch menu—which we kept on our refrigerator door—I would always look forward to Sloppy Joes. There was something comforting about the warm, messy sandwiches, rich with tomato sauce and ground beef. I later came to learn that there's a similar Indian street-side sandwich called keema pav, which is equally delicious. Traditionally, a keema pav is made with minced mutton, but I like to use ground turkey for a healthier (and more accessible) alternative.

The secret to this recipe is the ground cloves, which give a sharp bite to what otherwise could be bland turkey. Combined with spicy tomato sauce, this Sloppy Jai takes my beloved school lunch to a whole other level.

In a medium saucepan, heat the oil over medium-high heat. Add the bay leaf and allow it to begin infusing the oil for 15 seconds. Add the onion and bell pepper and cook, stirring, until the onion has turned golden, about 5 minutes.

Add the garlic and ginger pastes and cook, stirring, reducing the heat if necessary to prevent burning, for another 2 minutes. Add the salt, cloves, red chilli powder, cinnamon, and turmeric and allow the spices to bloom for about a minute.

Increase the heat and add the turkey. Crumble the meat as you combine it with the spicy onion and cook until browned, 5 to 7 minutes. Add the tomato sauce and stir well. Decrease the heat, cover, and simmer, stirring occasionally, for 15 minutes.

Add the peas (no need to thaw in advance) and coriander and continue simmering, uncovered, to thicken, about 5 minutes.

Adjust the seasonings to taste. Street vendors in India sell these sandwiches on something similar to sweet Hawaiian buns, but I prefer whole wheat buns.

SERVES 4

1 tablespoon canola oil

1 bay leaf

1 medium onion, finely chopped

½ bell pepper, finely chopped

1 tablespoon garlic paste (or minced garlic)

½ tablespoon ginger paste (or minced ginger)

½ teaspoon salt

½ teaspoon ground cloves

½ teaspoon Indian red chilli powder (or cayenne)

¼ teaspoon ground cinnamon

¼ teaspoon ground turmeric

1 pound 93% lean ground turkey

One 15-ounce can tomato sauce

¼ cup frozen peas

½ teaspoon ground coriander

Buns (whole wheat or Hawaiian), for serving

(Opposite)
Keema Pav
Pan-Roasted Aloo, p. 174

PAN-ROASTED ALOO

CHARRED BABY POTATOES

SERVES 4

2 pounds baby potatoes (any variety), washed and cut into halves or quarters (unpeeled)

2 tablespoons canola oil

1 teaspoon black mustard seeds

1 teaspoon cumin seeds

3 Indian green chillies, cut in half

1 large onion, finely chopped

1 tablespoon garlic paste (or minced garlic)

1 tablespoon ginger paste (or minced ginger)

½ tablespoon salt

1 teaspoon freshly ground black pepper

¼ teaspoon ground turmeric

¼ cup chopped cilantro, plus extra for serving

Continuing our tribute to school lunches, my favorite single item was—by far—tater tots. I still adore those bite-size, fried delights as an adult. Dipped in ketchup, they're a throwback to childhood every time I have a chance to eat them.

Granted, these pan-roasted aloo ("potatoes" in Hindi) aren't tater tots per se, but consider them a slightly more adult iteration. Doused with spices and charred until crispy, they're just as addictive as the tots, but with a lot more flavor. Although pan-roasted aloo are a great side dish for Sloppy Jais, you could also serve them for brunch, to accompany a "masala frittata," or Indian-style omelet.

Place the potatoes in a pot of salted water and bring to a boil over high heat. Parboil until the potatoes are tender when stabbed with a fork, but still firm in the center, about 7 minutes. Drain.

Heat the oil in a very wide sauté pan or cast-iron skillet over medium-high heat. Once the oil is shimmering, add the mustard seeds, cumin seeds, and green chillies. As soon as the mustard seeds begin to pop, add the onion and cook, stirring, for 2 minutes. Add the garlic and ginger pastes, salt, pepper, and turmeric and cook, stirring, for another minute.

Add the potatoes to the pan and stir well to coat with the spicy onion. Cook, uncovered, for about 10 minutes over medium-high heat so the potatoes get a nice char on them.

Stir in the cilantro. Decrease the heat to medium-low, cover, and finish cooking until the potatoes reach the desired firmness (my personal preference is to cook for another 5 minutes).

Adjust the salt to taste. Be sure to remove the chillies, or else someone might chomp down on a bite that could ruin their whole dinner! Serve alongside the Sloppy Jais.

NIMBU PAANI

SWEET AND SALTY LEMON-LIME SPRITZER

Every time I visit India, my mouth waters at the sight of vendors selling this refreshing, sparkling lemonade on the side of the street. There is nothing I would love more than to guzzle a tall glass of nimbu paani to rescue me from the sweltering heat. But, alas, I likely would "pay the price" for drinking street water, so I just sweat through it, envious.

Luckily, I can make this recipe at home. Now if the idea of adding spices to your lemonade seems strange—*trust me*—this drink is fantastic. A touch of salt is what makes it so special. The sparkling lemon is an excellent thirst-quencher, but the salt leaves you wanting to drink more. You just can't stop! Add a couple of shots of vodka to this concoction and it'll take you straight back to your college days.

SERVES 4

½ cup sugar

¼ cup fresh mint leaves

5 cups seltzer (1 liter)

½ cup freshly squeezed lemon juice, plus lemon slices for garnish

¼ cup freshly squeezed lime juice, plus lime slices for garnish

¼ teaspoon ground cumin

¼ teaspoon salt

¼ teaspoon freshly ground black pepper

In a small saucepan over medium heat, dissolve the sugar in ½ cup water, stirring, to create a simple syrup.

Add the mint to the simple syrup. Remove from the heat and allow to steep as the syrup cools.

In a pitcher, combine the seltzer, lemon juice, lime juice, simple syrup (with mint leaves), cumin, salt, and pepper and stir. Place in the refrigerator to chill for a few hours.

Serve in tall glass tumblers filled with lots of ice. Garnish with slices of lemon and lime.

DINNER

SRI'S SIGNATURE CHICKEN 183
Juicy Chunks of Boneless Chicken
Simmered in Aromatic Spices

CUCUMBER RAITA 185
Cooling Yogurt Accompaniment

STRING BEANS
WITH PEANUTS 187
Crunchy Stir-Fry with Indian Dried Red Chillies

CHOCOLATE CHAI AFFOGATO 188
Spicy Tea and Hot Cocoa Over Ice Cream

MOVIE

ENGLISH VINGLISH 178
Subtle character drama and Bollywood
icon's comeback

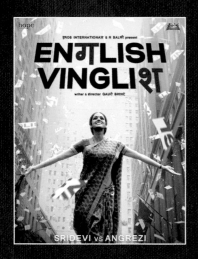

FLAVOR

Like the recipes in this book, *English Vinglish* is a story about the immigrant experience, melding traditional Indian culture with an American sensibility.

RECIPE

This subtle drama follows the journey of Shashi, a middle-class housewife in India who deftly takes care of her husband and children while running the household. But like millions of other women, Shashi lacks the respect from her family that she deserves, especially from her daughter, who's embarrassed that her mom can't speak English.

When Shashi's niece announces she's getting married in New York, Shashi travels to America on her own. A stranger in a foreign city, she's overwhelmed and lonely, but once she decides to learn English, she embarks on an education about her own self-worth.

THE "DISH"

English Vinglish is all about its star, Sridevi. In order to fully appreciate the film, it's important to know a little backstory about its leading lady.

Sridevi is an icon. She started her career as a child actor in South Indian movies, but rose to stratospheric fame in Bollywood in the 1980s with films like *Mr. India*, *Chandni*, and *Lamhe*. For over a decade, she mesmerized audiences with her doe eyes, curvaceous figure, and sultry dance moves. Sridevi is the queen of delightfully kitschy musical numbers. In fact, I urge you to stop reading right now and watch a song on YouTube titled "Naino Mein Sapna" in order to truly understand the magic of Sridevi. Go ahead, I'll wait.

Photographs courtesy
Eros International
(pages 176–179, 181)

That song was *the* anthem of my childhood.

At the height of her career, Sridevi got married and retired. She was almost entirely absent from the spotlight for fifteen years—until *English Vinglish*. When it was announced that she'd be making a comeback with this film, her legions of fans were wracked with anticipation. And they weren't disappointed. With *English Vinglish*, Sridevi astutely chose a mature, delicate film that showcased her acting talent. It was exactly *not* the kind of movie that made her famous. As a wife and mother in real life, she returned to the screen with more life experience, which elevated her performance and her overall esteem as an actor.

This is a movie about language (the title is a playful expression, the way we might say, *English Schminglish*). For all immigrants, the process of assimilation is closely tied to language. And it can be a hard road for many. People who don't speak English well are mistakenly seen as unintelligent—an arbitrary association, if you think about it. But the discrimination isn't just from the outside. Even within immigrant families and communities, those who can speak English fluently are placed higher on the social ladder—and those who can speak without an accent are the cream of the crop.

I'll be the first to admit that I carry this prejudice myself. Growing up, it was really difficult to have a mom who speaks broken English. *English Vinglish* director Gauri Shinde has said that she, too, felt embarrassed by her mom, which was the inspiration for this film. As an adult, I'm now incredibly proud of everything my parents accomplished to make a successful life in this country. But at the same time, when I see other immigrants not at least *trying* to speak English, it angers me as an American. Does that contradict my liberal identity? I don't know.

It's complicated. Immigration, assimilation . . . these are issues that are ingrained in our DNA, given the history of our nation. *English Vinglish* is one intimate, personal, and touching perspective on this important subject.

INGREDIENTS

CAST: Sridevi

WRITER AND DIRECTOR: Gauri Shinde

MUSIC DIRECTOR: Amit Trivedi

RELEASE: 2012

THE NAMESAKE (2006) Although the novel by Pulitzer winner Jhumpa Lahiri is far superior, this is one of the only major Hollywood films to explore the Indian-American immigrant experience. A first-generation-American young man grapples with his identity and comes to learn the story behind his peculiar name.

SWADES (2004) In an uncharacteristically subdued performance, Shah Rukh Khan plays an immigrant who feels incomplete despite his successful life as a NASA engineer. He returns to a small village in India and discovers what he's been missing all along.

MY NAME IS KHAN (2010) Another immigrant drama starring Shah Rukh Khan (the poster boy for expat Indians), this teary melodrama depicts the plight of an Indian family in post-9/11 America. In a *Forrest Gump*-esque story line, an autistic man travels across the country to meet the president and seek redemption for his son, a victim of Islamophobia.

SRI'S SIGNATURE CHICKEN

JUICY CHUNKS OF BONELESS CHICKEN SIMMERED IN AROMATIC SPICES

I can't decide if I have a *favorite* movie in this book, but *English Vinglish* is certainly near the top. Likewise, if there's only one recipe you take with you from this book, my signature chicken curry should be it. Every home has a go-to chicken dish—the one that you make more than any other, that pleases everyone in the family, and that you're proud to serve to guests. This is that dish in my house.

I'm incredibly satisfied with this recipe just as it is, rich with spice and flavor, but you can also view it as a base from which to create slightly different curries. For a creamy variation, swap the coconut powder for 2 tablespoons of Greek yogurt. Or for a saucier version, add one finely chopped tomato after you've sautéed the onion (and skip the coconut). In fact, if you choose to cook with chicken breasts instead of thighs, I recommend opting for one of these variations because they'll provide more moisture for the lean meat. (I also suggest reducing the amount of time you cook the chicken by about 10 minutes.)

This recipe, like all curries, is inevitably better the day after you've cooked it, once the spices have had a chance to soak even deeper into the meat. So make it a day ahead if you can. Once you get the hang of it, you could easily be cooking Sri's Signature Chicken every week . . . at which point, you're welcome to call it *your* signature chicken.

Heat 1 tablespoon of the oil in a Dutch oven or heavy saucepan over medium to medium-high heat. Season the chicken pieces with the turmeric. In multiple batches (to prevent crowding the pan), lightly brown the chicken on all sides. Remove to a plate.

Heat the remaining 1 tablespoon oil in the pan and add the bay leaves, allowing them to begin infusing the oil for 15 seconds. Add the onion and cook, stirring, until golden brown, reducing the heat if necessary to prevent burning, 7 to 10 minutes.

Add the garlic and ginger pastes and cook, stirring, for 2 minutes. Then add the salt, red chilli powder, cinnamon, and cloves. Stir the spices into the onion, allowing them to bloom for another minute.

SERVES 4 TO 6

2 tablespoons canola oil, divided

2 pounds boneless, skinless chicken thighs, cut into 1½-inch chunks

1 teaspoon ground turmeric

2 bay leaves

1 large onion, finely chopped

2 tablespoons garlic paste (or minced garlic)

1 heaping tablespoon ginger paste (or minced ginger)

½ tablespoon salt

1 teaspoon Indian red chilli powder (or cayenne)

¾ teaspoon ground cinnamon

¾ teaspoon ground cloves

½ cup chopped cilantro

½ cup coconut powder

½ tablespoon ground coriander

Lemon wedges, for garnish

Onion slices, for garnish

Cooked rice (any type), for serving

(Opposite, clockwise from top-right)
Sri's Signature Chicken
String Beans with Peanuts, p. 187
Cucumber Raita, p. 185

Return the chicken to the pan. Stir well to coat all the pieces evenly with the spice paste. Decrease the heat, cover, and simmer, stirring occasionally while scraping up the brown bits from the bottom of the pan, for 15 minutes.

Remove the bay leaves. Stir in the cilantro, coconut powder, and coriander. If you're making the dish a day ahead, turn off the heat at this point. Cool before refrigerating and then finish cooking before you serve.

Decrease the heat to the lowest setting, cover, and continue cooking for another 15 minutes.

Stir well. Adjust the seasonings to taste. Turn off the heat and allow the meat to rest for 10 minutes. Garnish with the lemon wedges and slices of onion. Serve with rice.

CUCUMBER RAITA

COOLING YOGURT ACCOMPANIMENT

Yogurt is a staple at every Indian dinner table because nothing tames heat better than dairy (not even water). Cucumber raita is the quintessential companion to chicken curry—they go together like meat and potatoes. Raita is a "dressed up" yogurt dish that's incredibly quick and easy to make. It's so versatile—doubling as a dip or refreshing snack—that you may just end up keeping a bowl in the refrigerator at all times.

I always have homemade yogurt on hand because it's surprisingly simple to prepare (see page 296), but you can just as well use store-bought Greek yogurt. Cucumber raita is the classic version, but there are many interesting variations you can try in place of cucumber: add pomegranate seeds and mint for a tart crunch; roasted sweet potatoes or beets for a sweeter taste; baby spinach for a fresh twist; or pineapple and mango for a fruity variation.

SERVES 4

1 medium cucumber

16 ounces plain Greek yogurt (2% or whole)

½ small red onion, finely chopped

1 teaspoon salt

½ teaspoon ground cumin, plus more for serving

¼ teaspoon Indian red chilli powder (or cayenne), plus more for serving

Peel the cucumber, slice it lengthwise, and scrape out the seeds using a small spoon. Grate the cucumber and place it in a mixing bowl.

Add the yogurt and onion and stir well. Add the salt, cumin, and red chilli powder and stir, adding a tablespoon or two of water to thin the mixture. Cover and store in the refrigerator for a few hours (ideally) to allow the flavors to combine.

Prior to serving, adjust the seasonings to taste. Transfer to a serving bowl. Sprinkle some additional ground cumin and chilli powder on top to garnish (in a pattern, if you desire, or simply dusted). Raita can be stored in the refrigerator for about a week.

STRING BEANS WITH PEANUTS

CRUNCHY STIR-FRY WITH INDIAN DRIED RED CHILLIES

To pair with the rich and thick chicken curry, you need something bright and simple. These string beans add color and crispness to the meal. For that reason, I always prefer using fresh beans, but frozen will work in a pinch. Peanuts add to the crunch, while dried red chillies bring a different kind of heat than that found in the chicken.

The ingredient that really makes these beans come alive is tamarind paste. Made from the pulp of a podlike fruit, tamarind paste is highly concentrated and deliciously sour. A quarter teaspoon may not seem like a lot, but I've tried making this dish without it, and it's just not the same. If you don't have tamarind paste, you can try substituting lemon juice to taste. But I strongly recommend buying a small jar online or at an Indian grocery store—it will keep in your refrigerator for months.

Cut the beans into uniform pieces of any size (or leave them whole if you prefer).

Heat the oil in a large sauté pan or wok. Once the oil is shimmering hot, add the mustard seeds and then the dried red chillies and curry leaves. As soon as the mustard seeds begin to pop, add the onion and cook, stirring, for 2 minutes. Add the garlic powder, ginger, cumin, salt, and turmeric and cook, stirring, for another minute.

Add the beans and peanuts. Cook, stirring frequently, over high heat, coating the beans with the spices, for 3 to 5 minutes. Add the coriander. Dissolve the tamarind paste in 2 tablespoons warm water and pour into the pan. Decrease the heat, cover tightly, and finish cooking the beans, 5 to 10 minutes depending on the size of the cut. Adjust the seasoning, serve, and warn your guests not to eat the chillies.

SERVES 4

1 pound green beans, washed and trimmed

1 tablespoon canola oil

1 teaspoon black mustard seeds

2 or 3 Indian dried red chillies, broken in half

7 to 10 curry leaves

1 small onion, roughly chopped

2 teaspoons garlic powder

2 teaspoons ground ginger

1 teaspoon ground cumin

1 teaspoon salt

¼ teaspoon ground turmeric

½ cup roasted, salted peanuts

½ teaspoon ground coriander

¼ teaspoon tamarind paste

(Opposite)
Cucumber Raita, p. 185; String Beans with Peanuts

CHOCOLATE CHAI AFFOGATO

SPICY TEA AND HOT COCOA OVER ICE CREAM

SERVES 4

3 black tea bags

3 green cardamom pods, bruised with the back of a spoon

2-inch piece fresh ginger, cut into chunks

2-inch cinnamon stick

⅛ teaspoon whole black peppercorns

1 cup whole milk

½ cup unsweetened cocoa powder

Vanilla ice cream

4 cinnamon sticks or 4 star anise, for garnish

I have to give credit where credit is due. This dreamy creation was the brainchild of my partner, Jason, and it may very well be the best idea he's ever had. Vanilla ice cream is drowned in homemade chai infused with warm spices and chocolate. What could be better?

There are a million different recipes for chai, and every household has its own. The base is almost always black tea, ginger, and green cardamom, but where you go from there is entirely up to personal preference. I like the combination of flavors in this recipe because it's potent but not overwhelming. You should feel free to play with it, though. The fun is in creating your own personal chai recipe. Start with mine, but then try varying the quantity of spices while experimenting with other ingredients that I don't use, such as cloves, fennel, star anise, nutmeg, and red chilli. You also can allow the chai to steep after it's boiled, if you prefer stronger tea.

However you choose to make it, this creamy, spicy, and chocolaty concoction is the ultimate way to end your dinner.

Pour 4 cups water into a saucepan. Add the tea bags, cardamom, ginger, cinnamon, and black peppercorns and bring to a boil.

After about 30 seconds of boiling, add the milk. Bring back up to a boil.

Turn off the heat and remove the tea bags. Whisk in the cocoa powder until completely dissolved. Strain the chai into a decanter or teapot.

Place two scoops of ice cream into each individual glass serving bowl, mug, or martini glass with a spoon for serving. At the table, pour the chai over each dish of ice cream. Garnish with a cinnamon stick or star anise.

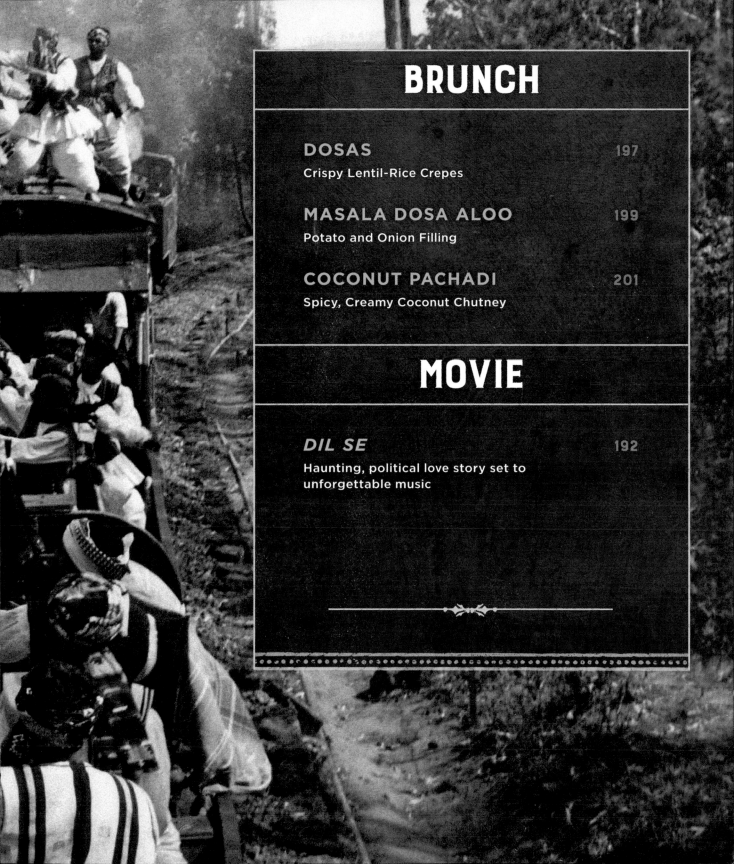

BRUNCH

DOSAS   197
Crispy Lentil-Rice Crepes

MASALA DOSA ALOO   199
Potato and Onion Filling

COCONUT PACHADI   201
Spicy, Creamy Coconut Chutney

MOVIE

DIL SE   192
Haunting, political love story set to
unforgettable music

DIL SE

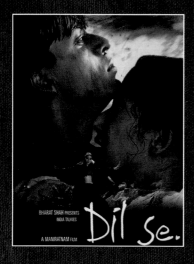

FLAVOR

With a blockbuster soundtrack, this haunting love story framed by a violent political conflict is classic '90s Bollywood.

RECIPE

An employee of All India Radio (Amar) travels on assignment to the remote Indian state of Assam in the foothills of the Himalayas. En route he meets a mysterious woman (Meghna) in a train station and is immediately smitten with her.

When their paths cross again, Amar becomes determined to find out her identity, but Meghna is reclusive, hiding a dangerous secret. As Amar's love for Meghna grows, he falls deeper into a spiral of violence that reflects the real-life atrocities and complicated roots of terrorism.

THE "DISH"

Dil Se (which means "from the heart") was a much bigger hit outside of India than it was within. This success abroad can be attributed to the international-caliber direction of Mani Ratnam and indelible music of A. R. Rahman (not to mention, of course, Shah Rukh Khan's fervent fan base). *Dil Se* marked the first Hindi film from Mani Ratnam, who had been a successful director of Tamil-language films. Over the course of his thirty-five-year career, he has undoubtedly become one of the most well-respected Indian directors of all time. With a long list of critically acclaimed movies, including *Roja*, *Bombay*, *Nayakan*, *Anjali*, and *Guru* (see page 108), Mani Ratnam's work could be studied by film students and audiences alike for his poetic style and stories of substance that tackle controversial political topics. He's also regarded as a humble, down-to-earth guy whom actors dream to work with.

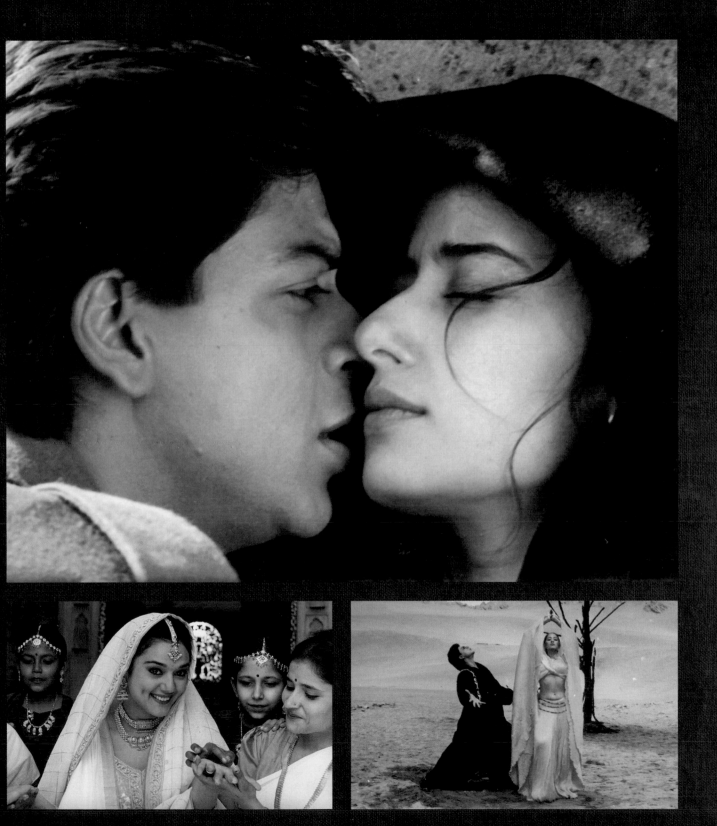

An incredibly significant contribution Mani Ratnam made—not just to Indian cinema, but to the world—was his discovery of composer A. R. Rahman. Rahman was hired by Ratnam to work on his first film score for *Roja*, and since then has written the music for all of the director's films. Rahman's signature sound blends classical Indian compositions with electronic, Western, and global influences. His music was truly revolutionary when it first appeared in Bollywood with the soundtrack for *Bombay*, breaking all sorts of records.

A. R. Rahman is probably best known in the West for his Oscar-winning music in *Slumdog Millionaire*, including the song "Jai Ho." He also collaborated with producer Andrew Lloyd Webber on the Broadway musical *Bombay Dreams*, which features the song "Chaiyya Chaiyya" from *Dil Se*.

With *Dil Se*, the duo of Mani Ratnam and A. R. Rahman come together to create an unforgettable film. In many ways, this is Bollywood at its best. The film uses music as a tool to convey heightened emotions—with full-on music videos nestled in the narrative. The production values are at an international standard, but the overall effect is uniquely Indian. Where else could serious actors lip-synch amid slow-motion explosions and dance with a herd of elephants? But the thing is—*it works*.

Some of the songs from this film are truly iconic. Shah Rukh's opening number on top of a train ("Chaiyya Chaiyya") will go down in history among the most memorable Bollywood songs ever. Meanwhile, "Jiya Jale," set in the lush backwaters of Kerala, is one of the last film songs that the renowned singer Lata Mangeshkar recorded. Her classic voice set against A. R. Rahman's fusion instrumentals was a symbolic passing of the torch from one musical legend to the next.

INGREDIENTS

CAST: Shah Rukh Khan, Manisha Koirala, Preity Zinta
DIRECTOR: Mani Ratnam
WRITERS: Mani Ratnam, Tigmanshu Dhulia
MUSIC DIRECTOR: A. R. Rahman
RELEASE: 1998

TASTE THIS

The intersection of politics, terrorism, and love has proven to be fertile ground for Bollywood, as demonstrated by these dramatic films:

BOMBAY (1995) Originally shot in Tamil but dubbed into Hindi, this is the film that put Mani Ratnam and A. R. Rahman on the map in Bollywood. *Bombay* features *Dil Se* heroine Manisha Koirala, with her beguiling and enigmatic expressions, in a story of star-crossed lovers caught in Hindu-Muslim violence. It's a must-see for any fan of Mani Ratnam or A. R. Rahman.

FANAA (2005) The undeniable chemistry and acting talent of superstars Aamir Khan and Kajol in this romantic drama makes you wonder why *Fanaa* is the only film to have ever featured the pair. Kajol plays a blind woman and Aamir her loving tour guide in a film with sweeping ballads and Bollywood-style plot twists.

NEW YORK (2009) I admit I'm biased because I produced this film and spent a year of my life working on it. This suspenseful thriller from award-winning director Kabir Khan is set in post–September 11 America (we actually shot it in Philly to double for NYC). It explores collateral damage from the war on terror, as an innocent Indian-American man is persecuted for being in the wrong place at the wrong time.

DOSAS

CRISPY LENTIL-RICE CREPES

Mani Ratnam and A. R. Rahman are the two most influential South Indian creative forces in contemporary Bollywood. Their distinctly South Indian aesthetic—from music to costumes to locations—has created indelible images in recent years (like the song "Jiya Jale," set in Kerala with Malayalam lyrics). So in tribute to Mr. Ratnam and Mr. Rahman, we prepare a quintessential South Indian meal.

Although dosas hail from the South, they're loved by Indians all over the world. In restaurants, these tangy breakfast crepes are paper-thin and rolled into cylinders that can be two feet long, spreading across your entire table. At home, they're less dramatic, but equally delicious. We make them the size of a dinner plate and fill them with savory potato stuffing, along with a side of spicy coconut chutney.

Admittedly, dosas can be a little tricky to master, but it just takes some practice. That's why I think this is a great activity for brunch. Invite a few friends over and have some fun with it. The secret to a perfectly browned, crispy dosa is to start with a screaming hot griddle and then spread the batter super thin (you should be able to see the griddle through it).

Even though the batter requires a bit of prep work the day before your brunch, it's worth it. And this recipe will give you plenty of leftover batter, which you can keep refrigerated for up to a week. It only gets better as it ferments (just thin the batter with a little water each time).

THE DAY BEFORE YOUR BRUNCH, mix the urad dal and fenugreek seeds in a large bowl. Rinse well. Cover with plenty of water and soak for at least 6 hours.

THE NIGHT BEFORE YOUR BRUNCH, drain the dal. Grind in a blender on the highest speed, gradually adding 1 cup warm water to create a thin batter. Feel the batter between your fingers—it should be totally smooth, not gritty. The process of grinding does require some patience (about 5 to 10 minutes), stopping the blender frequently to scrape down the sides and mixing with a spoon to help the blades along.

In a large mixing bowl, whisk the rice flour with 2 to 2½ cups warm water to create a smooth batter with no lumps. Pour the rice flour batter into the blender and blend until well incorporated with the dal.

SERVES 4 TO 6

1 cup urad dal (split black gram without skin)

½ teaspoon fenugreek seeds

3 cups rice flour

2 teaspoons salt

Canola oil

Coconut Pachadi (page 201), for serving

(Opposite, clockwise from top-right)
Masala Dosa Aloo, p. 199
Coconut Pachadi, p. 201
Dosa

Pour the batter back into the bowl, cover, and store in a warm place (such as your oven) overnight to ferment.

THE MORNING OF YOUR BRUNCH, check the batter. The surface should be bubbly. Stir in the salt. You may also want to thin the batter with water if it thickened overnight (it should be thinner than pancake batter, like crepe batter).

Begin making the dosas by heating a nonstick griddle or skillet over medium-high heat. Wait until the pan is sizzling hot and then drizzle a teaspoon of oil over the surface. Pour a ladleful of batter (about ⅛ cup) into the center of the griddle. Using the back of your ladle in a concentric, circular motion, spread the batter on the griddle to form a roughly 6-inch circle. The batter should be see-through thin. It might even have a few holes in it—that's okay. You can add a drop of batter to patch any large holes.

Drizzle a few droplets of oil around the perimeter of the dosa and allow it to cook until the edges are brown. Lift a small corner to check the underside. It should be deep brown in color. Dosas are meant to be thinner and crispier than French crepes. The thinner you can spread the batter, and the longer you cook it (without burning!), the better your dosa will taste.

Most people don't flip their dosas, but I like to do so, allowing the other side to cook for 30 seconds or so.

Plate the dosa, brown side down. Spoon some warm potato filling onto one half of the dosa, then fold it over gently. Serve with coconut chutney.

Continue with your next dosa. After every 2 or 3, add a few more drops of oil to the griddle to keep things running smoothly.

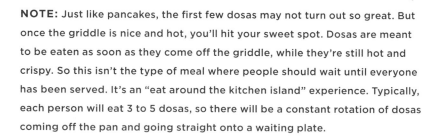

NOTE: Just like pancakes, the first few dosas may not turn out so great. But once the griddle is nice and hot, you'll hit your sweet spot. Dosas are meant to be eaten as soon as they come off the griddle, while they're still hot and crispy. So this isn't the type of meal where people should wait until everyone has been served. It's an "eat around the kitchen island" experience. Typically, each person will eat 3 to 5 dosas, so there will be a constant rotation of dosas coming off the pan and going straight onto a waiting plate.

MASALA DOSA ALOO

POTATO AND ONION FILLING

In India (and increasingly in America as well), there are restaurants that specialize in serving dosas. And they're hugely popular—particularly crowded during breakfast and lunch. If you peruse the menu at one of these establishments, you'll discover over a dozen different varieties of dosas—like the exhaustive list of pancakes at IHOP.

Paper dosas are delightfully crispy (they get their name because they're paper-thin). Mysore dosas (named for a city in South India) have a spicy schmear of chutney on the inside of the crepe. And rava dosas are made with semolina in the batter, which gives them a hearty texture.

The most common type of dosa, however, is the masala dosa, which comes stuffed with onions and potatoes (*aloo* in Hindi). The filling is so addictively tasty that you'll want to serve it as a side dish on many occasions, casting the dosa aside. It goes great with eggs for breakfast or alongside beef for dinner. I suggest making this stuffing the day before your brunch, which will not only cut down on your work the morning of, but also will allow time for the potatoes to fully absorb the spices in this recipe.

And there's no reason you need to limit yourself to a traditional stuffing like this one. Dosas are wonderfully versatile. Try experimenting with different, creative fillings, such as ham and cheese, scrambled eggs, or grilled chicken and vegetables. Think of dosas as an alternative to sandwiches; this is great if you have a wheat sensitivity, because dosas are gluten free. You could even venture into gluten-free desserts with fillings like mangoes and berries.

SERVES 4 TO 6

2 pounds Yukon gold potatoes, peeled and cut into roughly 1-inch pieces

2 tablespoons canola oil

4 Indian green chillies, cut in half

1 teaspoon black mustard seeds

1 teaspoon cumin seeds

10 to 12 curry leaves

3 medium onions, sliced into ¼-inch-thick half-moons

½ teaspoon ground turmeric

1 teaspoon salt

½ cup frozen peas (optional)

Indian red chilli powder, to taste (or cayenne)

Freshly squeezed lemon juice, to taste (optional)

Chopped cilantro, for garnish

Place the cut potatoes in a large pot of salted water. Bring to a boil and cook until tender, 15 to 20 minutes. Remove from the heat and reserve the cooking water.

Meanwhile, heat the oil in a large sauté pan. Once the oil is shimmering hot, add the chillies, mustard and cumin seeds, and curry leaves. As soon as the mustard seeds begin to pop, add the onions. Decrease the heat to medium and sprinkle with the turmeric and salt. Cook, stirring, until the onions have softened but have not become charred, 3 to 5 minutes.

Add the potatoes, along with a ladleful of the cooking water. Stir the potatoes into the onions well. As you stir, use your spoon to break up the potato pieces,

199

so the dish starts to resemble smashed potatoes with bite-size chunks of potato peeking through. If it gets too dry, feel free to add more of the starchy potato cooking water.

Mix in the frozen peas. Decrease the heat, cover, and simmer until the potatoes are quite tender (again, like smashed potatoes), about 5 minutes.

Adjust the salt to taste. You may like to sprinkle a few pinches of red chilli powder over the top, as I do. This will give the potatoes an added hit of flavor, a top note of heat. Add a squeeze of lemon juice, if desired, and garnish with cilantro.

Serve by folding a generous portion into the middle of each dosa. (But make sure you don't serve anyone the green chillies!)

COCONUT PACHADI

SPICY, CREAMY COCONUT CHUTNEY

Dosas can't be served without coconut pachadi (it's like ketchup to French fries). You can make this chutney as spicy as you like by adding another green chilli (or two, if you're daring). I would describe my version as "medium hot." But it's not really about the heat—it's about the unexpected and brilliant taste of coconut mixed with mustard seeds, curry leaves, and a host of other flavor components. If you love it, as I think you will, you can make a larger batch to keep in your fridge or freezer and use as a condiment for all sorts of things (it goes particularly well with fried foods).

The second step of this recipe involves tempering the chutney with an infused oil. This process, called *tadka*, is a traditional Indian cooking technique that adds a final burst of flavor to a dish immediately before serving.

For the chutney base, in a blender, combine the chana dal with the coconut powder, cilantro, yogurt, ginger paste, cumin, salt, and chilli, adding up to 1¼ cups water as needed and scraping down the sides, until you achieve a coarse puree. Transfer to a serving bowl.

Finishing the chutney requires a *tadka*, or infused oil. For the *tadka*, heat the oil in a very small pan over medium-high heat. Once the oil is shimmering hot, add the mustard seeds and then the urad dal, cumin seeds, hing, curry leaves, and red chilli and cook, stirring, until the mustard seeds begin to pop, about 30 seconds. Be careful because there will be a lot of spluttering!

For the dramatic finish, immediately pour the hot oil and spices on top of the chutney. Stir to combine and serve as a condiment to the dosas.

NOTE: You can purchase husked, roasted chana dal, often called chana dalia, in Indian grocery stores or online. Otherwise, simply roast regular chana dal in a dry skillet over medium heat for 3 to 5 minutes.

SERVES 4 TO 6

**FOR THE
CHUTNEY BASE**

¼ cup roasted chana dal (Indian split chickpeas) or cashews (see Note)

1 cup coconut powder

½ cup chopped cilantro

3 tablespoons Greek yogurt (2%)

1 tablespoon ginger paste (or minced ginger)

1 teaspoon ground cumin

1 teaspoon salt

1 Indian green chilli

**FOR THE TADKA
(TO TEMPER)**

2 tablespoons canola oil

1 teaspoon black mustard seeds

1 teaspoon urad dal (split black gram without skin)

½ teaspoon cumin seeds

2 pinches of hing (asafoetida) (optional)

7 to 10 curry leaves

1 Indian dried red chilli

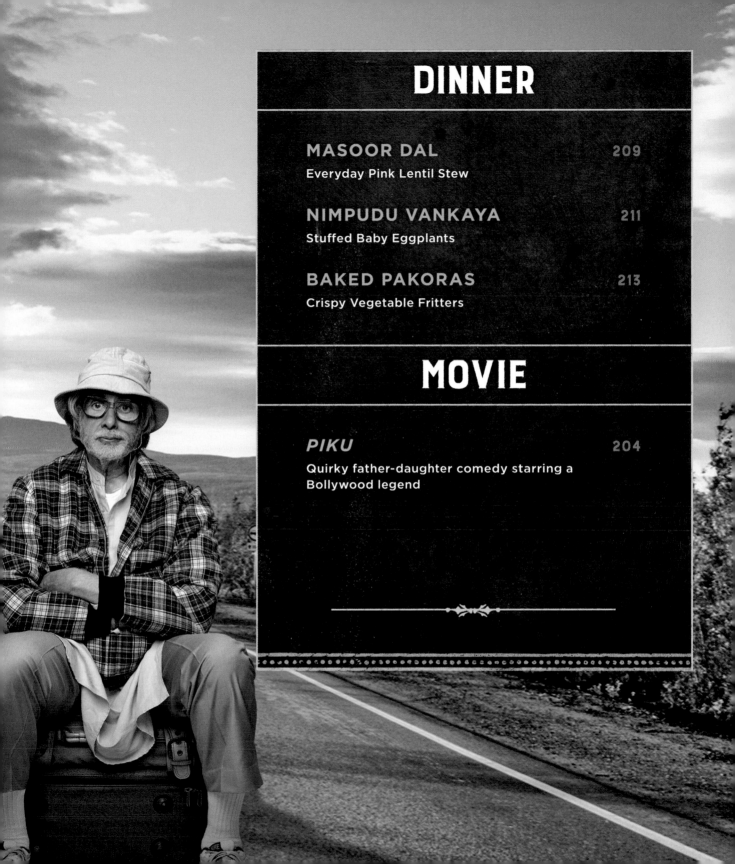

DINNER

MASOOR DAL   209
Everyday Pink Lentil Stew

NIMPUDU VANKAYA   211
Stuffed Baby Eggplants

BAKED PAKORAS   213
Crispy Vegetable Fritters

MOVIE

PIKU   204
Quirky father-daughter comedy starring a
Bollywood legend

PIKU

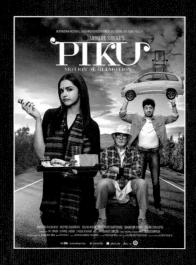

FLAVOR

I'm not quite sure how to say this tastefully, so I'll just blurt it out: This is a movie about constipation.

RECIPE

Bhaskhor Banerjee is obsessed with his bowel movements. The eccentric seventy-year-old charts every detail of his GI health daily to share with his adult daughter, Piku, much to her dismay. Piku takes care of her widowed dad as best she can, while juggling a career as a New Delhi architect and trying (unsuccessfully) to maintain a personal life.

When Piku decides she wants to sell the family home in Kolkata, her father insists on coming with her. The only problem is—Bhaskhor is constipated. He demands they travel by car so he can make frequent stops to use the facilities. Piku wrangles a begrudging driver named Rana to take them on the journey, resulting in a quirky road trip reminiscent of *Little Miss Sunshine*.

THE "DISH"

I acknowledge it may be in poor taste to include a film about constipation in a cookbook. But if you look at it another way, there could be nothing more appropriate for a book about food. Being married to a gastroenterologist, I can attest that there are few topics people love discussing more than their "GI issues" (though they would never admit it). Every dinner party that Jason and I have attended eventually devolves into perfect strangers sharing the intimate details of their bowel movements with him. And all I can do is smile through gritted teeth.

Joking aside, the real reason I've included *Piku* in this book is because it's a delightful little film about the relationship between adult children and their parents. The comedy, as endearing as it is, doesn't sugarcoat the truth—sometimes our parents drive us crazy (and vice versa, I'm sure). The thing I love most about *Piku* is that it never resorts to melodramatic tropes—there are no heartfelt monologues and tearful confessions. Like most families, the love is unstated, but real nonetheless.

The other reason *Piku* is a must-see is because of its costar, Mr. Amitabh Bachchan. It's hard to describe the significance of this man in a few paragraphs. Bachchan is a living god in India, revered by people of every age, social status, and religion. With close to 200 films to his credit, he is the embodiment of Bollywood itself, the only actor to have maintained his superstar stature for four decades and counting.

Bachchan shot to fame in the late '70s, playing the "angry young man"—a new brand of hero who rebelled against social injustice in the country. He then transitioned to a romantic heartthrob in the '80s. In 1982, he suffered an accident while shooting a fight scene in the film *Coolie*. Bachchan was hospitalized for months, at times near death, throwing the entire country into hysteria. Millions of fans prayed for him around the clock, performing elaborate rituals and offering to sacrifice their own body parts for his recovery.

Bachchan survived and continued to build his career, ultimately transitioning gracefully into character roles such as the one in *Piku*. As legendary as he may be, he has never hidden behind his movie star image, embracing unglamorous and complex roles with the fervor of a true actor. Even when it involves constipation.

INGREDIENTS

CAST: Amitabh Bachchan, Deepika Padukone, Irrfan Khan
DIRECTOR: Shoojit Sircar
WRITER: Juhi Chaturvedi
MUSIC DIRECTOR: Anupam Roy
RELEASE: 2015

TASTE THIS

Amitabh Bachchan's career has spanned generations and continents, but it all started with a handful of films that solidified his status as a superstar:

SHOLAY (1975) Perhaps the most iconic Bollywood film in history, *Sholay* revolutionized Indian cinema with its story of two petty thieves who are hired to take down a notorious bandit. Inspired by Hollywood Westerns, the dialogue, music, and rugged, cowboy aesthetic of *Sholay* are as cool today as they were forty years ago.

DEEWAAR (1975) This family/crime drama is a hard-hitting story about two brothers on opposite sides of the law. Along with *Zanjeer*, this film molded Bachchan's image as "the angry young man," with iconic lines of dialogue that every Indian can recite by heart.

SILSILA (1981) In a case of art imitating life, this romance features Bachchan as a married man who can't quit the passion he feels for another woman—with Bachchan's real-life wife and real-life mistress playing their respective roles in the film! Bachchan's relationship with Rekha, his ravishing costar in numerous movies, is a legendary Bollywood love affair. How the director convinced Bachchan's wife, Jaya, to be in this movie will never be known. Perhaps not by coincidence, *Silsila* was the last film in which Bachchan and Rekha appeared together.

MASOOR DAL

EVERYDAY PINK LENTIL STEW

I'm not going to belabor this point, other than to say: for a movie about struggling to cure constipation, I offer a fiber-rich, vegetarian meal featuring this soothing lentil stew.

Now, I promise you won't miss the meat for a second in this dinner because masoor dal is just as satisfying. Tomatoes, onions, and *tons* of garlic (practically an entire head) simmer with split pink/red lentils to create a thick and rich stew. Unlike a lot of vegetarian food in the West that's trying to *imitate* meat—and falling short of the real thing—masoor dal is a star unto itself.

Usually, dal (lentils) take a long time to boil and require soaking overnight. But the great thing about masoor dal is that it's quick-cooking. It's the one variety of dal that can be made into a fast, weeknight meal, which is why it's a great addition to your pantry. Better yet, I've seen split red lentils carried in many supermarkets (look for it in the health food section).

And let's not forget about the nutritional value. Lentils are a brilliant way for vegetarians and vegans to get their protein without relying on soy or fatty cheeses. Served with rice or roti to create a complete protein, masoor dal is so tasty that even the carnivores will come clamoring.

SERVES 4 TO 6

1 cup split masoor dal
(split pink/red lentils)

2 teaspoons salt

½ teaspoon ground turmeric

½ teaspoon tamarind paste

1 tablespoon canola oil

1 teaspoon black mustard
seeds

1 teaspoon cumin seeds

12 curry leaves

2 Indian green chillies,
cut in half

2 pinches of hing (asafoetida) (optional)

10 garlic cloves, whole

1 medium onion, roughly
chopped

1 medium tomato, roughly
chopped

1 teaspoon ground coriander

¼ cup chopped cilantro

Melted butter or ghee
(page 298), for serving

Cooked rice or roti,
for serving

Rinse the dal well. Add to a pot, cover with 3 cups water, and bring to a boil over high heat. A thick foam will form on top of the water—skim this off. Decrease the heat to a gentle boil and cook the lentils with the lid slightly ajar for 10 to 15 minutes.

Once the lentils are soft, add the salt, turmeric, and tamarind paste. Decrease the heat and simmer. If at any point the pot starts to run dry, feel free to add more water.

Meanwhile, heat the oil in a sauté pan over medium-high heat. Once the oil is shimmering hot, add the mustard and cumin seeds, curry leaves, chillies, and hing. As soon as the mustard seeds begin to pop, add the whole garlic cloves and onion and cook, stirring, to give the garlic a golden hue, 3 to 5 minutes, reducing the heat if necessary.

(Opposite, from top)
Masoor Dal
Nimpudu Vankaya,
p. 211

Add the tomato and continue cooking, stirring occasionally, until the tomato has broken down, 2 to 3 minutes.

Pour the contents of the sauté pan into the pot of lentils and stir well. Add the coriander. Cover, decrease the heat, and simmer for 10 to 15 minutes.

Stir in the cilantro. Adjust the seasonings to taste and transfer to a serving bowl. Inform your guests to avoid eating the green chillies and curry leaves. Just before serving, drizzle with melted butter. Serve with rice or roti.

NIMPUDU VANKAYA

STUFFED BABY EGGPLANTS

Our vegetarian feast continues with luscious, savory, and decadent baby eggplants. Forgive me for the superfluous adjectives, but my mouth waters just thinking about these little gems. Stuffed with a sublime paste made of sesame seeds, peanuts, and coconut, this is eggplant as you've never tasted it before.

Baby eggplants (sometimes called Indian eggplants) can be found in some supermarkets these days. If they're not in yours, you'll have to make a trip to an Indian grocery store—but it'll be worth it. This is another one of those dishes you'll rarely encounter in an Indian restaurant. It's a traditional South Indian preparation that's a real treat (*nimpudu* means "stuffed" and *vankaya* means "eggplant" in Telugu). Typically made with a lot of oil, my recipe has been tailored to be healthier, without sacrificing any of the taste.

When you're shopping for baby eggplants, be sure to pick the smallest ones in the lot. Which brings me to the other thing I love about this dish—the eggplants are *so cute!* I like to keep the stems intact because that offers a fun way to pick them up (like shrimp tails). Nimpudu vankaya are tiny, aubergine packages stuffed with incredible flavor.

Wash the eggplants. Cut a deep "X" into the base of each (the end without the stem), going about three-fourths of the way down, creating an opening for the stuffing. Place the eggplants in a large bowl of salted water.

In a dry skillet, toast the sesame seeds, coconut powder, and peanuts over medium heat until fragrant and golden, about 3 minutes. Then transfer to a spice mill and grind to a fine powder.

In a small mixing bowl, stir together the sesame powder mixture, garlic and ginger pastes, cumin, coriander, salt, red chilli powder, cinnamon, and cloves with 2 to 3 tablespoons warm water to create a thick paste.

Stuff each eggplant with about 1 teaspoon of the spicy paste (more or less depending on the size of each eggplant). The easiest way to do this is to use your fingers, separating the pocket gently with one hand, while stuffing it with the other. Set the stuffed eggplants aside on a plate. There should be a good amount of paste remaining—keep this for later.

In a large, wide sauté pan (wide enough to fit all the eggplants in a single layer), heat the oil over medium-high heat. Once the oil is shimmering hot, add

SERVES 4

1½ pounds baby eggplants

3 tablespoons sesame seeds

3 tablespoons coconut powder

3 tablespoons peanuts

½ tablespoon garlic paste (or minced garlic)

½ tablespoon ginger paste (or minced ginger)

½ tablespoon ground cumin

1 teaspoon ground coriander

1 teaspoon salt

¾ teaspoon Indian red chilli powder (or cayenne)

½ teaspoon ground cinnamon

½ teaspoon ground cloves

3 tablespoons canola oil

1 teaspoon black mustard seeds

10 to 12 curry leaves

1 medium onion, finely chopped

¼ teaspoon ground turmeric

¼ teaspoon tamarind paste

2 tablespoons chopped cilantro, plus extra for garnish

Roti or naan, for serving

the mustard seeds and curry leaves. As soon as the mustard seeds begin to pop, add the onion and cook, stirring, until softened, about 3 minutes, sprinkling with the turmeric along the way.

Arrange the eggplants in the pan by placing them horizontally in a single layer. Cover and simmer over gentle heat for 15 minutes; use tongs to flip the eggplants halfway through.

Flip the eggplants again. Add the remaining paste to the pan, spooning it in between the eggplants. Dissolve the tamarind paste in 1 cup warm water and pour into the pan. Increase the heat slightly and bring the liquid to a bubble.

Cover, decrease the heat, and simmer, rotating the eggplants occasionally, for 15 minutes. Continue simmering until the oil separates and floats to the surface (this indicates that the sauce is well cooked). If the sauce has dried up, simply add more water.

Add the cilantro. Check the eggplants. They should be melt-in-your-mouth tender. Depending on the size of your eggplants, you may need to simmer for up to 10 more minutes until they're done.

Adjust the seasonings to taste. This dish is meant to be spicy, so add more red chilli if you are so inclined. Turn off the heat and let the dish sit, covered. The longer it sits, the more the eggplants will soak up the flavorful sauce. Spoon gently into a large serving bowl and garnish with chopped cilantro. Serve with roti or naan.

BAKED PAKORAS

CRISPY VEGETABLE FRITTERS

Pakoras are popular fried snacks that can be eaten on their own (sometimes with chai) or as part of a larger meal. In this case, I've come up with a baked version to serve alongside the dal and eggplant, as a nice way to add some crunch to our vegetarian dinner. But since they're baked and not fried, they need to be eaten as soon as they come out of the oven.

The fritters are coated in besan, or Indian chickpea flour, which is seasoned with cumin, coriander, and red chilli powder. This recipe calls for potatoes and broccoli, but you can use any number of chopped/shredded vegetables combined with onions. Spinach, cauliflower, carrots, and corn all work very well in pakoras.

Preheat the oven to 450°F. Line a baking sheet with aluminum foil and spray well with cooking spray or coat with vegetable oil.

In a large mixing bowl, whisk together the besan, cumin, coriander, salt, and red chilli powder. Then add the potato, onion, broccoli, and cilantro. Toss well to coat the veggies evenly with the flour mixture. Add ¼ cup plus 1 or 2 tablespoons water, stirring to create a thick batter, like lumpy cookie dough.

Drop the batter by spoonfuls onto the baking sheet (you should end up with 16 pakoras). Flatten them gently with the back of your spoon (the flatter, the crispier the pakora).

Bake for 25 minutes, flipping the pakoras halfway through the baking time, until the pakoras are dark brown and crispy. Remove from the oven.

Sprinkle with sea salt. Serve immediately with tamarind chutney or ketchup.

SERVES 4

¾ cup besan (chickpea flour)

1¼ teaspoons ground cumin

1¼ teaspoons ground coriander

1 teaspoon salt

¾ teaspoon Indian red chilli powder (or cayenne)

¾ cup shredded potato (any variety)

¾ cup thinly sliced red onion, in quarter moons

¾ cup chopped broccoli

½ cup chopped cilantro

Sea salt

Tamarind chutney (a sweet-and-tart bottled condiment available in Indian grocery stores) or ketchup

(Opposite)
Baked Pakoras

DINNER

BBQ CHICKEN DRUMSTICKS 221
Fall-Off-the-Bone Tender Chicken Legs
Braised in Spicy BBQ Sauce

BAINGAN BHARTA 223
Smoky Eggplant Puree

VEGETABLE PULAO 226
Colorful Veggie Fried Rice

PERUGU PACHADI 227
Creamy, Chunky, Hot Salsa

MOVIE

MARY KOM 216
Priyanka Chopra's award-winning boxing biopic

MARY KOM

VIACOM18 MOTION PICTURES AND
BHANSALI PRODUCTIONS PRESENT

PRIYANKA CHOPRA IN AND AS

DIRECTED BY OMUNG KUMAR
PRODUCED BY VIACOM18 MOTION PICTURES & SANJAY LEELA BHANSALI

FLAVOR

It's Fight Night with Priyanka Chopra in this biopic about a scrappy, amateur boxer who claws her way to glory, like Bollywood's *Million Dollar Baby*.

RECIPE

Mary Kom is a five-time World Amateur Boxing champion and the first female fighter to represent India at the Olympics. The film inspired by her life story doesn't delve into her Olympics victory, but instead charts her early days, struggling for opportunity in a community and a sport that don't believe women can be boxers.

   The film is set in Mary's home state of Manipur, a remote region of northeast India along the border with Myanmar (Burma) that's been mired with insurgencies for the past fifty years. As a school kid, Mary stumbles into the local gym and encounters a champion coach who's training guys to box. Mary convinces the coach to take her on, despite hiding her newfound passion from her disapproving dad. As Mary embarks on her journey as a fighter—full of sacrifice and failure, along with success—she faces just as many obstacles outside the ring as she does within.

THE "DISH"

This film is really a matchup of two all-stars: Mary Kom and Priyanka Chopra.

   Mary was a little-known athlete at the time the film began development, prior to her win at the 2012 Summer Games. Female boxing wasn't even an *event* at the Olympics until Mary's year. So when she came home from London with one of India's only six medals, it was a huge honor for the nation. But for Mary, the Olympic bronze only added to her already impressive list of titles.

Priyanka Chopra has a similar, though certainly more privileged, story of international success. Growing up as an Army brat in India, and later spending a few teenage years in America, Priyanka stepped into the global spotlight when she was crowned Miss World in 2000. As impressive as this may be, she was the *sixth* Indian girl to win Miss World/Miss Universe in the previous seven years (the '90s were a big decade for Indian beauty).

So when Priyanka made the transition to films after conquering the pageant circuit, she didn't particularly make a huge splash—at the time, it seemed like Bollywood was littered with former beauty queens. After a promising start, she was relegated to a string of unmemorable roles and ensemble films where she played the pretty girl.

But Priyanka persevered. And she finally made her mark by starring in the gritty art house film *Fashion*, in which she played a troubled supermodel. Audiences and critics sat up and noticed. Since then, Priyanka has astutely managed to balance critically acclaimed films like *Bajirao Mastani* and *Barfi!* (see pages 156 and 278) with popular box office hits like the *Don* and *Krrish* franchises, making her one of the most bankable actresses in India today.

And she didn't stop there. Priyanka set her sights on Hollywood, signing with the powerhouse talent agency CAA. But her first venture in the United States— an attempt to launch a music career—found her the target of vicious, racist attacks from NFL viewers who called her a "terrorist" when she performed the theme song for "Thursday Night Football." Just like Mary Kom, though, Priyanka didn't let the haters win. She landed the coveted role of an FBI agent in ABC's *Quantico* (a role, incidentally, that was written for a white girl). She has since become, without question, the first Bollywood star to successfully cross over into American pop culture.

INGREDIENTS

CAST: Priyanka Chopra, Darshan Kumar
DIRECTOR: Omung Kumar
WRITERS: Saiwyn Quadras, Karan Singh Rathore, Ramendra Vashishth
MUSIC DIRECTOR: Shashi-Shivamm
RELEASE: 2014

TASTE THIS

India is a country full of injustice toward women, so like Mary Kom, the lead characters in these dramas learned how to punch back:

CHANDNI BAR (2001) Acclaimed actress Tabu (see *Haider*, page 132) stars as a bar dancer in this exposé of Mumbai's seedy nightlife. The film is unrelenting in its dark realism and won a slew of major awards for presenting a world of sex-for-sale that is rarely brought to light.

BANDIT QUEEN (1994) Based on the life of Phoolan Devi, this biopic is about a lower-caste woman who overcomes heinous sexual assaults to become a notorious bandit imparting justice on her own terms. Director Shekhar Kapur went on to make an Academy Award–nominated film about another powerful woman, *Elizabeth*.

PARCHED (2015) If Sarah Jessica Parker had starred in this movie, it could've been called *Sex and the Desert*. A group of four women in a desert village tackle love, sexuality, and friendship with humor and strength in this beautiful indie film.

BBQ CHICKEN DRUMSTICKS

FALL-OFF-THE-BONE TENDER CHICKEN LEGS BRAISED IN SPICY BBQ SAUCE

These chicken drumsticks, dripping with sticky, faux barbecue sauce, are the perfect centerpiece for Fight Night. Spread them out on a platter on the coffee table and let everyone help themselves as they watch the film. The secret to these chicken legs is to braise them for a solid hour. You could do this in a slow cooker, but I like to start the flavor base by sautéing the onions and spices really well on the stovetop, then transferring to the oven. The result is chicken legs that are meltingly tender. You can make the sauce as spicy as your guests can handle by adding more red chilli powder (I would describe the recipe below as safely "medium"). And I'll be the first to place bets that your friends will be wiping extra sauce off their plates with pieces of warm naan.

SERVES 4 TO 6

12 small chicken drumsticks
(about 4 pounds) (see Note)

1½ teaspoons salt, divided

½ teaspoon ground turmeric

3 tablespoons canola oil,
divided

2 bay leaves

2 medium onions, roughly
chopped

2 tablespoons garlic paste
(or minced garlic)

1 heaping tablespoon ginger
paste (or minced ginger)

½ teaspoon Indian red chilli
powder (or cayenne)

½ teaspoon ground
cinnamon

½ teaspoon ground cloves

8 ounces tomato sauce

½ tablespoon ground
coriander

Chopped cilantro, for garnish

Preheat the oven to 375°F.

You can certainly make this dish leaving the skin on the drumsticks, but I prefer to remove it because the skin acts as a barrier, preventing the spices from sinking into the meat. In order to remove the skin easily, use paper towels or latex gloves because the meat is too slippery to handle with your bare hands. Grasp the meaty end of the leg with a paper towel in one hand. With another paper towel in the other hand, grasp the skin and forcefully pull it in the opposite direction, yanking the skin off in one piece.

Once all the legs have been skinned, season them with ½ teaspoon of the salt and the turmeric.

In a Dutch oven or very wide, oven-safe sauté pan with a lid, heat 1 tablespoon of the oil over medium-high heat. Once the pan is hot, place the first batch of drumsticks in a single layer. Sear the meat for 5 minutes on the first side, then flip with tongs and sear on the other side until the chicken is deeply brown all around, an additional 5 minutes. Remove the drumsticks to a plate, replenish with another tablespoon of the oil, and repeat the process for the remaining pieces. Set all the chicken aside.

Heat the remaining 1 tablespoon oil in the pan and add the bay leaves, allowing them to begin infusing the oil, about 15 seconds. Then add the onions and cook, stirring, until softened, 3 to 5 minutes, reducing the heat if necessary.

(Opposite, clockwise
from top-left)
BBQ Chicken Drumsticks,
Vegetable Pulao, p. 226
Perugu Pachadi, p. 227
Baingan Bharta, p. 223

MARY KOM

Add the garlic and ginger pastes and cook, stirring, for 2 minutes. Then add the red chilli powder, cinnamon, cloves, and remaining 1 teaspoon salt. Stir the spices into the onions, allowing them to bloom for another minute. Add the tomato sauce and stir well, scraping up the brown bits from the bottom of the pan. Decrease the heat and simmer, stirring regularly, for 3 to 5 minutes.

Add the coriander and remove the bay leaves. Return the chicken to the pan, nestling the drumsticks snugly to fit as many as possible into a single layer, with any smaller drumsticks on top as a second layer. Add ¾ cup water and bring to a gentle boil.

Cover the pan and place it in the oven. Braise for 30 minutes. Use tongs to turn and reposition the drumsticks to ensure that all the meat gets some contact with the sauce. Continue braising for another 15 minutes.

Check the chicken. It should be extremely tender and nearly falling off the bone. If the drumsticks seem like they need deeper color, take off the lid and continue cooking for a final 5 to 10 minutes.

Remove the pan from the oven. Transfer the drumsticks to a serving platter. Spoon over some of the sauce. Garnish with the cilantro. Transfer the remaining sauce to a small bowl and serve alongside the chicken, allowing your guests to pour this thick and spicy "BBQ sauce" over their meat.

NOTE: These days, chicken legs are enormous. Try to find drumsticks that are as small as possible, or maneuvering them in the pan will be cumbersome.

BAINGAN BHARTA

SMOKY EGGPLANT PUREE

This quintessentially Punjabi dish has become a favorite among so many of my American friends. And it's easy to understand why. Eggplant (*baingan*) is roasted and smashed into a rich, flavorful puree, infused with warm cumin and ginger. It's amazing that one simple vegetable can taste this good.

The distinctive feature of baingan bharta is its smoky flavor. There are a couple of ways to accomplish this. If you have an outdoor grill—perfect. Throw the eggplant on the grill and soak up the wonderful charcoal aroma. If, like me, you're working indoors, the easiest technique is to broil the eggplant in the oven, as I've described below. But if you want even more authentic, smoky flavor—and don't mind cleaning up a bit of a mess—you should roast the eggplant over a gas flame on the stovetop until the skin gets nice and charred.

Baingan bharta is a great addition to our Fight Night spread. Place it in bowls alongside warm, buttery naan and invite your guests to dip the bread into the eggplant, like baba ghanoush. (By the way, I intentionally increased the quantities in this recipe because baingan bharta tastes even better the day after the main event.)

Turn your oven to broil at the highest setting. Place a rack on the level closest to the top. Line a baking sheet with aluminum foil.

Cut the eggplants in half lengthwise. Rub 1 tablespoon of the oil all over the eggplants and place them on the baking sheet, skin side up.

Broil the eggplants for about 30 minutes. Depending on the type of broiler you have, you may need to reposition the eggplants during this time to make sure all 4 pieces get equal exposure to the direct heat source. The eggplants are done when they are extremely soft and their skins are charred. A butter knife should easily pierce the skin and sink into the tender interior. Place the eggplants in a large bowl to cool.

Meanwhile, heat the remaining 2 tablespoons oil in a medium saucepan over medium-high heat. Add the cumin seeds and green chillies and cook for about

2 large eggplants (about 2½ pounds)

3 tablespoons canola oil, divided

1 teaspoon cumin seeds

2 Indian green chillies, minced

1 large onion, finely chopped

1 tablespoon ginger paste (or minced ginger)

½ tablespoon garlic paste (or minced garlic)

1 teaspoon salt

½ teaspoon ground cumin

¼ teaspoon ground turmeric

2 medium tomatoes, finely chopped

½ teaspoon ground coriander

¼ cup chopped cilantro, plus extra for garnish

Buttery naan, for serving

20 seconds. Add the onion, decrease the heat to medium, and cook, stirring, until golden, about 5 minutes.

Add the ginger and garlic pastes and cook, stirring, for 1 to 2 minutes. Then add the salt, cumin, and turmeric and allow the spices to bloom for 30 seconds. Add the tomatoes and stir well. Cover, decrease the heat, and simmer, stirring occasionally, until the tomatoes have broken down to create a thick sauce, about 10 minutes.

Once the eggplants are cool, remove the skin, which should peel off easily. If some charred remnants of skin remain, that's okay—they will only add to the dish's smoky flavor. Mash the eggplants with a fork to create a puree.

Add the mashed eggplants along with any juices that have accumulated in the bowl to the sauce. Stir well. Sprinkle with the coriander and cook, uncovered, stirring occasionally, for 10 minutes.

Add the cilantro. Check and adjust the seasonings. Continue simmering over very low heat until you're ready to serve. The longer the dish simmers, the more deeply its flavors will develop.

Garnish with fresh cilantro and serve with warm, buttered naan.

VEGETABLE PULAO

COLORFUL VEGGIE FRIED RICE

SERVES 4 TO 6

2 cups basmati rice

2 tablespoons canola oil

6 cloves

2 bay leaves

3-inch cinnamon stick

2 Indian green chillies,
cut in half

½ tablespoon cumin seeds

¼ teaspoon black
peppercorns

1 medium onion, roughly
chopped

1 tablespoon garlic paste
(or minced garlic)

1 tablespoon ginger paste
(or minced ginger)

1 teaspoon ground coriander

½ cup cut green beans
(1-inch pieces)

½ cup peeled and diced
red potatoes

½ cup peeled and diced
carrots

½ cup cauliflower florets
(tiny, bite-size pieces)

½ cup fresh or frozen peas

2 teaspoons salt, divided

2 tablespoons chopped
cilantro

10 fresh mint leaves

Freshly squeezed lemon
juice (optional)

Pulao (which is a root word for "pilaf") is made by toasting rice and mixing it with any combination of spices, meats, vegetables, fruits, and nuts. In this case, I've chosen to keep it clean and fresh with vibrant veggies and subtle flavors to accompany your Fight Night spread. But feel free to use any vegetables you have in your fridge (for example, green bell peppers would be a nice addition). Throw in some golden raisins for sweetness, cashews or peanuts for protein, and you've got a complete, one-pot meal.

Rinse the rice well several times until the water starts to become less cloudy (starchy). Cover with water in a bowl and set aside to soak.

In a large, wide saucepan (preferably nonstick), heat the oil over medium-high heat. Add the cloves, bay leaves, cinnamon stick, chillies, cumin seeds, and peppercorns and fry in the hot oil for less than a minute. Add the onion and cook, stirring, until softened, about 3 minutes. Add the garlic and ginger pastes and cook, stirring, for about a minute, reducing the heat if necessary to prevent burning. Then add the coriander and stir into the onion for 30 seconds.

Add the green beans, potatoes, carrots, cauliflower, and peas to the pan. Season with 1 teaspoon of the salt and cook over medium heat, stirring frequently, until they turn bright in color, 2 to 3 minutes.

Drain the rice well and add it to the pan. Season with the remaining 1 teaspoon salt. Cook, stirring, until the rice becomes toasted, 2 to 3 minutes.

Pour 4 cups hot water into the pan and stir well. Add the cilantro and mint and bring to a boil. Then decrease heat to the lowest setting, cover tightly, and cook undisturbed for 30 minutes.

Fluff the rice with a fork. Bite on a few grains to see if they are fully cooked. If it's still al dente, cover and continue to cook for a few more minutes. If the rice is cooked, but soggy, continue to cook uncovered until the excess water has evaporated. Adjust the salt to taste. Tumble the rice onto a serving platter. Remove the bay leaves and chillies. Finish with a squeeze of lemon, if desired, and serve. Inform your guests to avoid eating the cloves (and the black peppercorns if they're sensitive to heat).

PERUGU PACHADI

CREAMY, CHUNKY, HOT SALSA

Perugu means "yogurt," and *pachadi* means "chutney" or "pickle" in Telugu. This yogurt salsa is an excellent condiment for the BBQ drumsticks, something like blue cheese dressing to chicken wings. Unlike the more popular yogurt dish, raita, which is meant to have a cooling effect, perugu pachadi is supposed to be *spicy*. I've suggested mincing two green chillies in the recipe below, but you're welcome to decrease that to one and add another after you've taste-tested. Don't be too intimidated, though, because the heat is enveloped in a creamy base that counters its effects.

You will likely have plenty left over from this recipe. Keep it in the fridge for up to 5 days and use it as a dip for veggies. But keep in mind that the longer perugu pachadi sits, the spicier it will become!

In a mixing bowl, whisk together the sour cream, yogurt, chillies, salt, and cumin.

Peel the cucumber, slice it lengthwise, and scoop out the seeds using a small spoon. Then dice it into pieces roughly the same size as the quartered tomatoes. Add the cucumber, tomatoes, onion, and cilantro to the mixing bowl. Stir well.

Adjust the seasonings to taste. Transfer to a serving bowl. Sprinkle paprika on top for presentation (in a pattern or simply dusted). Garnish with a whole green chilli, to let people know that this dish is spicy!

SERVES 4 TO 6

8 ounces sour cream

4 ounces Greek yogurt (2% or whole)

2 Indian green chillies, minced (if you prefer less heat, start with 1 chilli and add another or ½ after you taste), plus extra for garnish

½ teaspoon salt

½ teaspoon ground cumin

½ small cucumber

¼ cup quartered grape tomatoes

½ small red onion, chopped same size as tomatoes

2 tablespoons roughly chopped fresh cilantro

Paprika, for garnish

COCKTAIL PARTY

COCKTAIL KOFTA   235
Mini Meatballs in Creamy Cashew Sauce

BAKED SAMOSAS   236
Easy Potato Turnovers

CHANA CHAAT   239
Spicy Roasted Chickpeas

MUMBAI MULE   241
Refreshing Ginger Cocktail

MOVIE

DABANGG   230
Action-packed entertainment for the masses

DABANGG

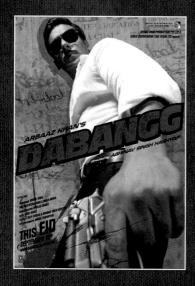

FLAVOR

This is what's called a "masala film"—a spicy blend of action, romance, comedy, and music—with no brains, but a lot of brawn.

RECIPE

The plotline for this movie is entirely too convoluted to summarize. There's no actual "recipe"—instead, the filmmakers just opened their refrigerator, threw a little bit of everything into a pot, and called it a day. But admittedly, sometimes that's the way you end up with the tastiest dish.

Generally, though, the film revolves around a cop in a small town who considers himself Robin Hood. Macho beyond belief, the cop beats bad guys to a pulp, romances the girl, loves his momma, and vows to take down the corrupt local politician. And he does it all while flexing his enormous muscles, glaring into the camera, and delivering the hammiest lines of dialogue ever written for the screen.

THE "DISH"

I'm gonna be straight with you: You need to be drinking to watch this movie.

Dabangg is the most mindless piece of entertainment I've seen in a really long time. So why did I choose it for this book? Because it's quintessential Bollywood. It's cheesy, ridiculously melodramatic, and laugh-out-loud funny (not always intentionally). It's the perfect movie for a cocktail party because there are great, colorful visuals to have playing in the background, including intense fight scenes and sexy dance numbers. Best of all, your guests can tune in and out as they choose because there's no logical plot to follow anyway.

Dabangg is a throwback, retro cool. This is what Bollywood *used to be* all about—when men were men, and movies were made exclusively for them. In the '70s and '80s, the most successful films were ones like *Dabangg*—full of fistfights, cops and gangsters, and damsels in distress. The business was built on working-class guys who watched movies in small-town theater halls, whistling at the screen and dancing in the aisles. But then the '90s came along. Filmmakers took a turn toward sweeping romances (see *Kuch Kuch Hota Hai*, page 144), catering to educated audiences in cities, watching movies in modern multiplexes. Bollywood got soft, some might say.

Well, Salman Khan is here to change all that. The testosterone-laden super-star (think of him as Bollywood's Sylvester Stallone) shot to fame in the '90s as a young, lanky romantic hero. After twenty years of successfully playing the heart-throb, he was pushing forty-five and needed to reinvent himself. *Dabangg* started a whole new chapter in his career. Now, as a man in his fifties, he's become India's most bankable action star. Working-class audiences worship him—literally—making him a veritable industry unto himself, untouchable by actors half his age.

Although I'm not a fan of masala films, there is one thing about them I abso-lutely love—the "item number." This is a dance number placed in the middle of the movie, with no particular relation to the narrative. Its lyrics are tawdry and it features a scantily clad woman surrounded by leering men. I know it sounds bad, but the songs are so much fun to dance to at clubs (or in your living room). In *Dabangg*, the scantily clad starlet is Salman Khan's former sister-in-law (and one of the film's producers), Malaika Arora Khan, whom you might recognize from her other iconic item number on top of a train in the film *Dil Se* (see page 192).

INGREDIENTS

CAST: Salman Khan, Sonakshi Sinha, Sonu Sood, Arbaaz Khan, Dimple Kapadia, Vinod Khanna
DIRECTOR: Abhinav Kashyap
WRITER: Dilip Shukla, Abhinav Kashyap
MUSIC DIRECTOR: Sajid-Wajid, Lalit Pandit
RELEASE: 2010

TASTE THIS

If you're having a bout of 'roid rage, look no further than the action, comedy, and romance in these testosterone-fueled "masala films":

DON (1978) Bollywood's answer to James Bond (or is it Austin Powers?), this pulp crime drama stars Amitabh Bachchan in an iconic role as a stylish gangster. The franchise was rebooted with Shah Rukh Khan in the 2000s, but there's nothing like the original, with its polyester fashions and sultry dance numbers.

DHOOM 2 (2006) The second installment in Bollywood's most successful action franchise is pure eye candy. This buddy cop comedy is sparse on logic, but packed to the rafters with glistening bodies, beautiful locations, and hard-core stunts.

CHENNAI EXPRESS (2013) Shah Rukh Khan unwittingly steps into trouble when he comes to the aid of a beautiful young woman (Deepika Padukone) while riding the express train to Chennai. The twist is, she's no damsel in distress but actually a mobster's daughter who takes him on the ride of his life.

COCKTAIL KOFTA

MINI MEATBALLS IN CREAMY CASHEW SAUCE

These mouthwatering meatballs will surely be the star of your cocktail party. Smothered in a piquant cashew sauce, their decadent taste harkens to the Mughal era, while the presentation is modern. Their two-bite size makes them ideal for serving on small plates, feeding a crowd on just one pound of ground meat. I've chosen to use beef in this recipe, but you could just as well make them with lamb.

MAKES ABOUT 25

2 tablespoons canola oil, divided

1 bay leaf

1 medium onion, finely chopped

2 tablespoons garlic paste (or minced garlic)

1 heaping tablespoon ginger paste (or minced ginger)

½ tablespoon plus ½ teaspoon salt, divided

1 teaspoon ground coriander

1 teaspoon Indian red chilli powder (or cayenne), divided

½ teaspoon ground cinnamon

½ teaspoon ground cloves

¼ teaspoon ground turmeric

1 pound 85% lean ground beef

1 large egg, beaten

½ cup plain breadcrumbs

½ cup chopped cilantro, plus extra for garnish

1 cup milk

½ cup Greek yogurt (2%)

¼ cup cashews, ground to a powder

Butterey naan, for serving

In a sauté pan, heat 1 tablespoon of the canola oil over medium-high heat. Add the bay leaf and allow it to begin infusing the oil for 15 seconds. Add the onion and cook, stirring, until golden, 5 to 7 minutes, reducing the heat if necessary.

Add the garlic and ginger pastes and cook, stirring, for 1 to 2 minutes. Then add ½ tablespoon of the salt, the coriander, ½ teaspoon of the red chilli powder, the cinnamon, cloves, and turmeric and allow the spices to bloom for about a minute. Remove the pan from the heat while you prepare the meatballs.

In a mixing bowl, combine the ground beef, egg, breadcrumbs, cilantro, 2 tablespoons of the onion mixture, the remaining ½ teaspoon salt, and the remaining ½ teaspoon red chilli powder. Use your hands to combine the ingredients well.

Using a melon baller or mini ice cream scoop, roll the mixture into small meatballs and place on a baking sheet or platter. Put the platter in the refrigerator while you make the sauce.

Return the sauté pan with the onion mixture to the stove over medium heat. Whisk in the milk, yogurt, and ground cashews. Decrease the heat, cover, and allow the sauce to simmer gently while you brown the meatballs. Feel free to add more milk if the sauce gets too thick.

In a second large sauté pan, heat the remaining 1 tablespoon oil over medium-high heat. Brown a batch of the meatballs for 3 minutes on the first side, then flip and brown for another 3 minutes on the other side. As the meatballs are done browning, drop them into the sauce and continue with the next batch.

Turn the meatballs gently to coat with the sauce. Cover and simmer for 15 to 20 minutes. Garnish with fresh cilantro and serve with small pieces of warm, buttered naan.

BAKED SAMOSAS

EASY POTATO TURNOVERS

MAKES 50 TO 60

2 pounds Yukon gold pota-
toes, peeled and quartered

1 tablespoon canola oil

1 teaspoon cumin seeds

2 Indian green chillies, cut
in half

½ tablespoon ginger paste
(or minced ginger)

½ teaspoon ground cumin

¼ teaspoon ground turmeric

1 teaspoon salt

½ cup frozen peas

¼ cup chopped cilantro

Freshly squeezed lemon
juice

Pinch of Indian red chilli
powder (or cayenne)

One 12-ounce package
wonton wrappers (quantity
50 to 60)

Tamarind chutney or
ketchup, for serving

No Indian party would be complete without samosas, the country's most popular snack. These triangular pastries are incredibly versatile because they can be stuffed with many different types of vegetables, minced meat, or lentils. In this recipe, I'm keeping it classic with a traditional filling of potatoes and peas, but with a modern twist. Samosas are typically fried, with a dough that's made from scratch. I don't personally like the idea of deep-frying, nor do I want your house to smell like hot oil during your party, so my solution is to use wonton wrappers. The result is crispy packets that are easy to throw in the oven, and even easier to pick up and nibble while watching the movie.

Preheat the oven to 375°F.

Place the potatoes in a pot and cover with plenty of water. Bring to a boil and continue boiling, with the lid slightly ajar, until the potatoes are tender, about 15 minutes. Drain the potatoes and dice them into small pieces. (The potatoes will be mushy, so this will be a rough dice.)

Heat the oil in a large, wide sauté pan over medium-high heat. Once the oil is shimmering hot, add the cumin seeds and chillies and cook, stirring, for about 20 seconds. Add the ginger paste, ground cumin, and turmeric and allow the spices to bloom for about a minute, adding a little bit of water, if needed, to prevent the spices from burning.

Add the potatoes to the pan and stir well to coat with the spices. Cook, stirring, until the potatoes have browned slightly, 2 to 3 minutes. Sprinkle with the salt. Since the samosas are so small, you want to crumble the potatoes with the back of your spoon so there are no large chunks.

Add the peas (no need to thaw), cilantro, and a squeeze of lemon. Decrease the heat to medium and continue cooking until the peas have cooked through, about 5 minutes. Taste and adjust the seasonings (especially the salt). The filling should be tasty enough to eat on its own. I usually like to add a pinch or two of red chilli powder. Set aside to cool.

Meanwhile, line a baking sheet with aluminum foil and spray well with

(Opposite, clockwise
from top-left)
Mumbai Mule, p. 241
Chana Chaat, p. 239
Baked Samosas
Cocktail Kofta, p. 235

cooking spray or coat with vegetable oil. Place the first batch of wonton wrappers on the baking sheet. Drop ½ tablespoon of the potato filling onto the center of each wrapper. (Be sure to discard the green chillies as you encounter them.)

Set yourself up with a small bowl of water on the side. Dip your finger into the water and rub it along the four edges of the wonton wrapper (to act as a sealant). Fold the wrapper diagonally, to create a triangle. Press down the edges to form a tight seal. Flatten the filling gently so it squeezes toward the corners.

Bake for 10 to 12 minutes, until the edges are brown and crispy.

Serve with tamarind chutney (a sweet-and-tart bottled condiment available in Indian grocery stores and online). If you don't have tamarind chutney, ketchup is equally tasty and, believe it or not, enjoyed with samosas in most Indian households!

CHANA CHAAT

SPICY ROASTED CHICKPEAS

Chana chaat is a fun street food that's sold in newspaper cones by roadside vendors all over India. Salty, spicy, and tangy, these crispy chickpeas (*chana*) are totally addictive. Put them by the bar and your guests will devour them with cocktails.

Typically, chana chaat is made with black chickpeas (*kala chana*), but regular white chickpeas (garbanzo beans) are more readily available and work just as well. If you happen to be at the Indian grocery store, pick up a box of chaat masala—a blend of spices with a unique flavor profile that's used on street-side snacks such as this one. In lieu of that specialty spice blend, I've created a simple, homemade mix that packs a similar burst of flavors. And if you want even more authentic taste, add a generous pinch of dried mango powder (for tartness) and black salt—two specialty spices that are hallmarks of chaat.

This recipe is for one batch. The chickpeas only stay crisp for a short while after they come out of the oven, so this is a dish you want to make just as your guests arrive—and perhaps have a few more batches ready to go into the oven throughout the party. You can also play with different variations on chana chaat by adding diced tomatoes, potatoes, and/or mangoes.

Dry the chickpeas by spreading them onto kitchen towels and blotting/rolling with a second layer of towels. Discard any skins that may peel off. Leave to air-dry for about 20 minutes.

Meanwhile, preheat the oven to 400°F.

Transfer the dried chickpeas to a mixing bowl and toss with the olive oil. Spread onto a baking sheet lined with aluminum foil. Roast for about 40 minutes, shaking the pan at the 20-minute and 30-minute marks. The chickpeas are done when they've turned deep brown and crispy.

Pour the warm chickpeas back into the mixing bowl. Sprinkle with the salt, garlic, cumin, coriander, ginger, red chilli powder, and fennel and toss well. Then add the onion, cilantro, lemon zest, and lemon juice. Toss well again.

SERVES 8 TO 10

Two 15.5-ounce cans chickpeas, rinsed and drained

2 tablespoons extra-virgin olive oil

½ tablespoon sea salt

1 teaspoon garlic powder

1 teaspoon ground cumin

½ teaspoon ground coriander

½ teaspoon ground ginger

¼ teaspoon Indian red chilli powder (or cayenne)

¼ teaspoon ground fennel seed or 1 tablespoon finely chopped fresh mint

½ cup finely chopped red onion

2 tablespoons chopped cilantro

Grated zest of 1 lemon plus juice of ½ lemon

Taste and adjust the seasonings (if you want more of a kick, sprinkle over some additional red chilli powder). Transfer to a serving bowl. Or for something more festive, serve the way they do on the street in India—in a newspaper cone. Roll a folded page of newspaper into a cone, tape the seam, fill the cone with chana chaat, and either stand it upright in a glass or lay it on its side (like a cornucopia) along the bar.

MUMBAI MULE

REFRESHING GINGER COCKTAIL

I've always had an affinity for Moscow Mules and I think part of the reason—aside from the refreshing flavor—is because they're served in copper mugs. In India, copper drinkware is ancient and traditional due to its natural ability to keep water cool in a country where ice is rarely used.

I always like to have a "signature drink" at every party, and this is my favorite. It's festive, has a nice kick, but is mellow enough for everyone to enjoy. Spicy ginger mixed with zesty lime is the perfect flavor complement to Indian snacks.

But the best part about a Mumbai Mule is that it's the kind of cocktail you can sip all night long without realizing how many you've had. And *that* makes for my kind of party!

SERVES 4

1 cup vodka

2 limes

½ teaspoon ground coriander

½ teaspoon ground cumin

Two 12-ounce bottles ginger beer (nonalcoholic)

Fresh mint, for garnish

Fill 4 copper mugs or copper tumblers with ice.

Pour the vodka into a cocktail shaker. Squeeze in the juice of 2 limes (about ¼ cup lime juice). Add the coriander and cumin. Fill with ice and shake well.

Strain the vodka into the mugs, filling each about a third full (or a quarter for those who like their drinks on the weaker side).

Top off the mugs with ginger beer. Stir gently. Garnish with mint and serve.

DINNER

COCONUT SALMON STICKS   249
Crunchy Baked Fish Tenders

CRISPY BROCCOLI FLORETS   250
Roasted with Garlic and Lemon

**CORN AND
CAPSICUM RELISH**   251
Sweet Corn Sautéed with Red Bell Pepper

MOVIE

CHILLAR PARTY   244
Raucous kids' movie
with a family-friendly message

CHILLAR PARTY

FLAVOR

Break out the popcorn and candy for this fun, mischievous kids' film that's whole-some entertainment for the entire family.

RECIPE

The Chillar Party is a ragtag group of miniature menaces who live in—and rule over—a middle-class apartment complex. Think of them as Bollywood's "Little Rascals," each with a nickname to match his personality. Much to their dismay, these munchkins are perpetual losers on the cricket field, always getting clobbered by the boys from the next neighborhood.

But the Chillar Party discovers a much bigger battle to fight when a local, corrupt politician declares that dogs—such as the boys' mascot—will no longer be allowed to roam free in residential communities. The dogs are declared a nuisance to public safety and are threatened to be locked up. That's when the Chillar Party swings into action, taking on politicians, the media, and the entire city of Mumbai to save their canine friends.

THE "DISH"

Surprisingly, Bollywood doesn't produce many children's movies. It's particularly confounding when you realize that India has 480 *million* children, more than the population of the entire United States! It's hard to verify the rationale for this severely untapped market, but one theory is that the vast majority of Indian kids have limited buying power and get a ton of entertainment from inexpensive satellite TV. And the kids who are affluent enough to go to the multiplex are of a

social class that would much rather watch the latest Disney or Pixar movie from America than a Hindi-language film.

In any case, there have been a few standouts through the years, *Chillar Party* among them. I wanted to include this film in the book because it's a great introduction to world cinema for the kids in your family. Granted, they need to be old enough to read the subtitles, but *Chillar Party* is perfect entertainment for elementary and middle school children. After all, who wouldn't love a story about a bunch of rowdy kids who strip down to their undies and march through town to teach stupid grown-ups a lesson about taking care of their pets?

Shenanigans aside, I also think there's deeper value in introducing young people to films from other countries. When I was growing up in a small town in Pennsylvania, Bollywood exposed me to life outside the pristine confines of suburban America. Even though I was only eight or nine, these films opened my horizons to the way people live in other parts of the world—and, specifically, to the problems with which they grapple.

For example, depending on the age of your children, you may encounter some questions regarding the young, homeless boy in the film who earns a living by washing cars. As I watched the movie recently, I was struck by the callous attitude with which the adults in the film treat this boy (who's no older than ten) and use him for child labor. But that's a reality in India. Even among educated families, it's not uncommon to see children working in homes as servants. It's heartbreaking. But hopefully it can spur some meaningful conversation with your own kids. If Bollywood can serve as a way to open their eyes to the fact that not all children have an iPad, iPhone, and Xbox at their disposal, then that's a productive way to spend an evening with the family, in my opinion.

INGREDIENTS

CAST: Chinmay Chandraunshuh, Vedant Desai, Rohan Grover, Divji Handa, Naman Jain, Aarav Khanna, Sanath Menon, Raju, Vishesh Tiwari, Shriya Sharma
DIRECTORS: Nitesh Tiwari, Vikas Bahl
WRITERS: Nitesh Tiwari, Vikas Bahl, Vijay Maurya
MUSIC DIRECTOR: Amit Trivedi
RELEASE: 2011

TASTE THIS

In addition to popular favorites *Iqbal* and *Taare Zameen Par* (see page 281), here are some family-friendly films with a Bollywood flair:

CHAK DE! INDIA (2007) In a plot line reminiscent of Hollywood underdog stories, a down-and-out field hockey coach (Shah Rukh Khan) trains a group of girls for the World Cup. Split by religious and regional differences, the girls learn to work together, uniting not just their team but all of India.

BAJRANGI BHAIJAAN (2015) Directed by my friend Kabir Khan, this feel-good movie is the story of a young Pakistani girl who gets lost in India. Action hero Salman Khan plays a devout Hindu who embarks on a journey to return the Muslim girl to her family behind enemy lines.

UDAAN (2010) This coming-of-age drama about a teenage boy who gets expelled from boarding school and returns home to a violent dad, offers an anti-Bollywood portrayal of adolescence. It was one of the few Indian films ever selected to compete at Cannes.

COCONUT SALMON STICKS

CRUNCHY BAKED FISH TENDERS

What kid doesn't love fish sticks? And I don't think I'm alone when I say I love them as a grown-up, too. Jason and I like these fish sticks so much that I make them a couple of times a month—and we don't even *have* kids. The crunchy, coconut coating plays wonderfully against the buttery salmon tenders. And the best part of all—there's no guilt in enjoying them because they're baked and healthy. I like serving them with Coconut Pachadi (page 201), a spicy and creamy dipping sauce, but you could also opt for tartar sauce or Greek yogurt mixed with a little dill.

Coconut salmon sticks are a great way to begin introducing your kids to Indian flavors. Before you know it, they'll be asking for chicken curry.

SERVES 4 TO 6

2 pounds salmon, skinned

½ cup all-purpose or whole wheat flour

1 teaspoon salt

½ teaspoon freshly ground black pepper

4 large egg whites

1 cup panko breadcrumbs (I prefer whole wheat)

1 cup coconut powder

1 tablespoon paprika

Extra-virgin olive oil

Sea salt, to taste

Freshly squeezed lemon juice, to taste

Coconut Pachadi (page 201)

Preheat the oven to 450°F. Line 2 baking sheets with aluminum foil and spray them generously with cooking spray or coat with vegetable oil.

Wash the salmon and pat dry with paper towels. Cut the fish into 1-inch-wide sticks, each about 4 to 5 inches in length.

Set up your dredging station with 3 bowls or plates: In the first bowl, place the flour and season with the salt and pepper. In the second bowl, beat the egg whites until frothy. And in the third bowl, combine the panko, coconut powder, and paprika with a fork or whisk.

Dredge each fish stick by first turning it in the flour for a light dusting on all sides. Then dip it into the egg. Finish by rolling it in the panko-coconut mixture and pressing the coating gently into the fish. Then place the fish stick on the prepared baking sheets.

Once all the fish sticks are on the baking sheets, brush them lightly with olive oil (or use an oil mister if you have one). Bake for 20 minutes, flipping halfway through the cooking time.

Plate the fish sticks, sprinkle with sea salt, and finish with a squeeze of lemon. Serve with individual dipping bowls of Coconut Pachadi.

(Opposite, clockwise from top-left)
Coconut Salmon Sticks
Coconut Pachadi, p. 201
Crispy Broccoli Florets, p. 250

CRISPY BROCCOLI FLORETS

ROASTED WITH GARLIC AND LEMON

SERVES 4

1½ pounds broccoli
(1 to 2 heads)

3 tablespoons extra-virgin olive oil, plus more for brushing

1 teaspoon ground cumin

1 teaspoon ground coriander

½ teaspoon ground ginger

½ teaspoon salt

¼ teaspoon Indian red chilli powder (or cayenne)

¼ teaspoon ground turmeric

1 head garlic, separated into cloves and peeled

1 lemon

Sea salt, to taste

Since you already have the oven on for the fish sticks, let's throw in some broccoli and have it do double duty. These crispy florets are seasoned with just the right amount of spice—not overpowering for the kids, but interesting enough for the adults. Meanwhile, roasting the broccoli with a whole head of garlic and a sliced lemon infuses it with subtle flavor and wonderful aroma. I know the cliché is that kids won't eat their veggies, but when it's playful finger food like this, even broccoli becomes hard to resist.

Preheat the oven to 450°F. Line a baking sheet with aluminum foil.

Cut the broccoli into small-medium florets with short stalks. Wash the florets and dry well on towels. Place in a large bowl.

In a small mason jar, combine the oil, cumin, coriander, ginger, salt, red chilli powder, and turmeric. Drop in the garlic cloves. Close the lid and shake vigorously. Pour this mixture over the broccoli and use your hands to toss the broccoli in the oil, coating all the florets evenly with the spices.

Cut the lemon into slices and brush with olive oil. Arrange the broccoli, lemon slices, and garlic cloves in a single layer on the baking sheet. Roast for 20 to 25 minutes, until the edges of the broccoli florets are blackened and crispy.

Arrange on a platter. Sprinkle with sea salt and serve.

CORN AND CAPSICUM RELISH

SWEET CORN SAUTÉED WITH RED BELL PEPPER

Our family-friendly meal concludes with my favorite vegetable as a kid: corn. When I was growing up in central Pennsylvania, summertime meant lots of corn on the cob. My sister and I had the unenviable job of shucking the ears, while my mom did the cooking, and my dad would deftly shave off the kernels for anyone who didn't want to get corn stuck in his or her teeth. This recipe melds those very American childhood memories with the distinctly Indian flavors of mustard seeds, cumin, and coriander.

I use frozen corn, unapologetically, for this dish because it's available year-round. Granted, these days you can buy corn on the cob all year too, but I find the taste to be disappointing during the off-season. That being said, during summer and fall, by all means use the fresh stuff (3 or 4 ears should be sufficient).

Heat the oil in a large sauté pan over medium-high heat. Once the oil is shimmering hot, add the mustard seeds. As soon as the seeds start to pop, add the shallots, decrease the heat to medium, and cook, stirring, for 1 to 2 minutes.

Add the salt, cumin, garlic powder, ginger, black pepper, and turmeric. Stir the spices into the shallots, allowing them to bloom for about a minute. Add the bell pepper and cook, stirring, until the pepper has begun to soften, about 2 minutes.

Pour the corn kernels into the pan and fold all the ingredients together, continually combining for a few minutes until the corn is well incorporated with the spices. Cover, decrease the heat, and simmer for 5 minutes.

Add the cilantro, coriander, and the juice of half the lime. Stir to combine, just until the cilantro starts to wilt, another minute or two. Cut the remaining lime half into wedges. Adjust the seasonings to taste. Serve, garnished with lime wedges.

SERVES 4

1 tablespoon canola oil

1 teaspoon black mustard seeds

1 cup sliced shallots (about 4 shallots)

1 teaspoon salt

1 teaspoon ground cumin

1 teaspoon garlic powder

½ teaspoon ground ginger

¼ teaspoon black pepper (if you're making this for grown-ups, feel free to add an additional ¼ teaspoon of Indian red chilli powder or cayenne at the same time)

¼ teaspoon ground turmeric

1 red bell pepper, cored, seeded, and diced

16 ounces frozen corn

¼ cup chopped cilantro

½ teaspoon ground coriander

1 lime, cut in half, divided

LUNCH

TIFFIN EGG CURRY   259
Hard-Boiled Eggs in Nutty Tomato Sauce

UPMA   261
Savory Cream of Wheat

MIXED VEGETABLE KURA   262
Colorful Veggie Stir-Fry

MOVIE

THE LUNCHBOX   254
Art house drama about love through food
and letters

THE LUNCHBOX

IRRFAN KHAN   NIMRAT KAUR

*Lunch*BOX

Eine kleine
Prise *Glück*
kann dein Leben
verändern

Ein Film von RITESH BATRA

FLAVOR

This gentle, unique love story is the kind of meal you just don't want to end, the memories of which you'll carry with you fondly.

RECIPE

One of the Seven Wonders of the World should be the *dabbawala* lunch delivery system of Mumbai. In a city of 20 million people, a network of deliverymen called *dabbawalas* seamlessly transport home-cooked lunches from people's apartments to their offices every day. Traveling on bikes, trains, and foot to remote buildings in all corners of the city, the lunch arrives, warm and delicious, in a hand-packed *dabba* (meaning "box," while *wala* loosely means "vendor").

The *dabbawalas* are notorious for their pinpoint accuracy *without* the use of GPS. But in the story of this film, one *dabba* is mistakenly delivered to a middle-aged widower with a boring job as an accountant. After eating the tasty lunch, he returns the *dabba* with a letter explaining the mix-up—which is received by the lonely housewife who prepared the meal. They then begin corresponding to each other every day through letters and food, sparking an unusual love between strangers.

THE "DISH"

This isn't a Bollywood movie per se. It has no musical numbers and it's actually an international coproduction involving French and German producers alongside traditional Indian studios. But I chose to include it in this book anyway because it's such an incredibly sweet and touching film. It was also was one of the highest grossing foreign-language films of the year in America. The fact that India didn't

choose to submit *The Lunchbox* as its entry for the Oscars is really a travesty (and an indication of the country's mind-boggling political bureaucracy).

The Lunchbox represents a rare genre of Indian cinema that has the ability to transcend international borders. Mainstream Bollywood has always had a problem "crossing over." There is yet to be a Bollywood film that breaks through in the way that *Crouching Tiger, Hidden Dragon* did for Chinese cinema. Theories abound as to why this is—perhaps it's the lengthy running times, or the injection of musical numbers, or maybe it's just that the emotional tenor of most Bollywood films doesn't resonate for audiences outside India.

The Lunchbox, however, breaks these barriers. The film's style and tone are subtle and authentic, unlike Bollywood's typical vocabulary. The setting transports us to a place that's unfamiliar, in an alluring way, while the emotions underneath are deeply universal. Basically, the film has all the elements that art house audiences enjoy.

Most of the credit for this can be attributed to the writer-director, Ritesh Batra. It's remarkable to note that *The Lunchbox* is Batra's first feature film. It screened at Cannes, where it won an audience award and Sony Pictures Classics picked up the North American distribution rights. That's the kind of Cinderella story that all filmmakers dream of.

In addition to the writer-director, the film owes its success to its lead actors. You may recognize Irrfan Khan, who plays the widower accountant. Irrfan has become something of the go-to Indian guy in Hollywood. His long list of credits include *Slumdog Millionaire*, *Life of Pi*, *In Treatment*, *Jurassic World*, and *The Amazing Spiderman*. Newcomer Nimrat Kaur, who plays the understated housewife, could well be on her way to an international career herself, having followed up *The Lunchbox* with a major arc on TV's *Homeland*.

INGREDIENTS

CAST: Irrfan Khan, Nimrat Kaur, Nawazuddin Siddiqui
WRITER AND DIRECTOR: Ritesh Batra
RELEASE: 2013

TASTE THIS

A select number of Indian films, usually with some foreign backing, have made notable contributions to the international independent film scene. These beautiful, small films are perfect for the art house crowd:

WATER (2005) This is one of my favorite movies of all time. Directed by Indo-Canadian filmmaker Deepa Mehta (see *Fire*, page 75), this haunting drama tells the story of outcast widows in traditional Hindu society, from the point of view of a cherubic eight-year-old girl who herself has recently been widowed. If you only watch one movie from this book—*Water* should be it.

MONSOON WEDDING (2001) The first Indian movie to cross over in a meaningful way, *Monsoon Wedding* holds the record as the highest grossing film outside India. The family drama about secrets revealed during a wedding weekend launched the career of director Mira Nair in Hollywood.

DHOBI GHAT (2011) The title of this film refers to a massive outdoor area where *dhobis* (traditional dry cleaners) bring the city's laundry to wash and pound against stones. This drama explores unseen sides of Mumbai through four interconnecting stories, one of which features Aamir Khan (his wife, Kiran Rao, directed the film).

TIFFIN EGG CURRY

HARD-BOILED EGGS IN NUTTY TOMATO SAUCE

Tiffin is an Indian word used to describe lunch or a midday meal. As depicted in the film, people in cities pack their tiffin in *dabbas* (sometimes called "tiffin carriers"), which are then delivered to them at the office.

Typically, tiffin is a light meal, since you don't want to fall asleep at your desk after a heavy lunch. The main course of our tiffin is this delightful egg curry. Boiled eggs are submerged in a tart and nutty tomato sauce, full of robust spices. Poured over rice or with a side of roti/naan, egg curry makes for a great midday meal.

And if you're feeling creative, why not get yourself a tiffin carrier to serve your meal? You can buy them online or at Indian grocery stores. The tiffin carrier is a stainless steel tower made of interlocking compartments, each carrying a different dish. They're a fun way to transport food, keeping the contents warm for two to three hours. My mom used to pack a large tiffin carrier every summer when we'd go on family road trips. We'd park the car at a rest stop and have fresh curries sitting around a picnic table on the side of the Pennsylvania Turnpike. Now if that isn't a picture of American assimilation, I don't know what is!

SERVES 4 TO 6

12 large eggs

¼ cup chana dal (Indian split chickpeas) or ½ cup cashews

1 medium onion, roughly chopped

2 tablespoons coconut powder

1 tablespoon garlic paste (or minced garlic)

1 tablespoon ginger paste (or minced ginger)

1 tablespoon canola oil

2 bay leaves

1 teaspoon salt

½ teaspoon ground turmeric

½ teaspoon Indian red chilli powder (or cayenne)

¼ teaspoon ground cinnamon

¼ teaspoon ground cloves

8 ounces tomato sauce

1 tablespoon ground coriander

1 tablespoon soy sauce

Chopped cilantro, for garnish

Place the eggs in a large saucepan of water and bring to a boil. Once the water is boiling, turn off the heat, cover the pot tightly, and let sit for 8 minutes. Drain and set the eggs aside.

Meanwhile, gently toast the chana dal in a dry skillet over medium heat until fragrant, 3 to 5 minutes.

Combine the onion, chana dal, coconut powder, and garlic and ginger pastes in a blender or food processor. Blend, adding a little bit of water as necessary, to create a thick puree.

Wipe the saucepan dry and heat the oil over medium-high heat. Add the bay leaves and allow them to begin infusing the oil for 15 seconds. Add the onion puree, cover, decrease the heat, and simmer, stirring occasionally, until the onion starts to pull away from the edges of the pan and a few drops of oil begin separating around the perimeter (this is your indication that the onion is well cooked), 7 to 10 minutes.

Add the salt, turmeric, red chilli powder, cinnamon, and cloves. Stir the spices into the onion, allowing them to bloom for about a minute. Then stir in the tomato sauce. Cover and simmer, stirring occasionally, for 5 minutes.

Meanwhile, peel the eggs. Cut half of the eggs lengthwise. For the remaining eggs, leave them whole, but score them on one end with a deep "X" (cutting about halfway down the length of the egg). This will allow the curry to seep into the eggs.

Add 3 cups hot water to the saucepan along with the coriander and soy sauce. Drop in the eggs and bring to a gentle bubble. Decrease the heat, cover, and simmer for about 5 minutes. Some of the yolks from the sliced eggs will crumble away, thereby thickening the sauce and adding rich flavor. The longer you allow the eggs to sit in the sauce (with the heat off), the more they will absorb its flavor.

Adjust the salt and red chilli powder to taste. Garnish with freshly chopped cilantro.

UPMA

SAVORY CREAM OF WHEAT

In my family, upma is the perfect lunch. My mom serves this Indian version of cream of wheat on most weekends, and now I carry on the tradition to pass along to you. Infused with warm ginger, upma might be described as something similar to grits, minus the cheese. Cumin and mustard seeds add earthy notes, while cashews offer sweetness to balance the hot chillies. For Indians, upma would be the entrée of this morning or midday meal—with the egg curry on the side—but I imagine many Americans might be inclined to do the reverse.

A quick note: When you combine the boiling water with the toasted wheat grains, be sure to pour all the water in at once—and stir immediately—otherwise, the upma will become lumpy.

2 tablespoons canola oil

⅓ cup cashews

1 teaspoon black mustard seeds

1 teaspoon cumin seeds

1 teaspoon urad dal (split black gram without skin)

10 to 12 curry leaves

3 Indian green chillies, cut in half

1 small onion, roughly chopped

3-inch piece fresh ginger, peeled and cut into 4 or 5 thick slices

½ tablespoon salt

½ teaspoon cumin powder

1½ cups cream of wheat (2½-minute variety)

Freshly squeezed lemon juice, to taste

Mango pickle (see page 297), for serving

Melted butter or ghee (page 298), for serving

Bring 5½ cups water to a boil in a saucepan over high heat.

Meanwhile, in a medium nonstick saucepan, heat the oil over medium-high heat. Add the cashews and fry for 2 to 3 minutes, until they begin to turn golden brown.

Add the mustard and cumin seeds, urad dal, curry leaves, and chillies and stir to combine. As soon as the mustard seeds begin to pop, add the onion, ginger, salt, and cumin powder, decrease the heat to medium, and cook, stirring, for 2 to 3 minutes.

Add the cream of wheat to the onion mixture and stir, toasting the grains until they begin to turn light golden brown, about 2 minutes.

Add all of the boiling water at once, stirring continuously to avoid lumps. Continue stirring until the upma comes together as a smooth, thick porridge. Decrease the heat, cover, and simmer for 5 minutes.

Stir the upma well with a squeeze or two of lemon. Turn off the heat and let sit for a few minutes to allow the cream of wheat to absorb more flavor.

Adjust the salt to taste (you'll probably want to add another ½ teaspoon or so). Give the upma another stir to keep it smooth. Serve hot, accompanied by mango pickle (a spicy chutney available online or at Indian grocery stores). Drizzle with melted butter for extra richness. Inform your guests to remove the ginger, green chillies, and curry leaves while eating.

MIXED VEGETABLE KURA

COLORFUL VEGGIE STIR-FRY

SERVES 4

1 tablespoon canola oil

1 teaspoon black mustard seeds

1 medium onion, finely chopped

1 teaspoon ground cumin

1 teaspoon garlic powder

½ teaspoon ground ginger

½ teaspoon salt

¼ teaspoon ground turmeric

¼ teaspoon Indian red chilli powder (or cayenne)

16 ounces frozen mixed vegetables (such as green beans, carrots, lima beans, and corn)

¼ teaspoon tamarind paste*

½ tablespoon coconut powder

½ teaspoon ground coriander

* Substitute: juice of ½ lemon + ½ tablespoon soy sauce

To add a splash of Bollywood color to our meal, this simple vegetable stir-fry earns its place in our tiffin carrier. A mix of veggies comes alive with the flavors of cumin, coriander, and mustard seeds, which meld harmoniously with the upma (in fact, some people choose to add the veggies directly into their upma preparation). Although food snobs may turn up their nose at the idea of using frozen, packaged vegetables, I find that frozen veggies soften easily and absorb flavors in a way that fresh vegetables do not. Not to mention, tiffin is a daytime meal, so any shortcuts to ease your morning prep should be wholly embraced, in my opinion.

Heat the oil over medium-high heat in a large sauté pan. Once the oil is shimmering hot, add the mustard seeds. As soon as the seeds start to pop, add the onion and cook, stirring, for about 2 minutes.

Add the cumin, garlic powder, ginger, salt, turmeric, and red chilli powder. Stir the spices into the onion, allowing them to bloom for about a minute. Add the mixed vegetables (straight from the freezer) and cook, stirring and tossing the vegetables in the spices so they become evenly coated and fragrant, for about 3 minutes.

Dissolve the tamarind paste in 1 tablespoon hot water and pour over the vegetables. Decrease the heat, cover, and simmer for 5 minutes. Sprinkle with the coconut powder and coriander and stir to combine. Cook for an additional minute, or until the desired tenderness.

Adjust the seasonings to taste.

(Opposite, clockwise from top-left)
Mixed Vegetable Kura
Tiffin Egg Curry, p. 259
Upma, p. 261

DINNER

VEGETABLE HAKKA NOODLES
271

Indo-Chinese Veggie Lo Mein

CRAB CAKES WITH TAMARIND MAYO
272

Crab and Corn Seasoned
with Curry Leaves and Mustard Seeds

HYDERABADI CHAARU
274

Sweet-and-Sour Lentil Soup

MOVIE

QUEEN
266

Bollywood's contemporary feminist anthem

QUEEN

DIRECTED BY VIKAS BAHL
PRODUCED BY VIACOM18 MOTION PICTURES, VIKRAMADITYA MOTWANE & ANURAG KASHYAP

FLAVOR

Invite over your girlfriends and uncork the wine—this is the perfect romantic comedy for Girls' Night.

RECIPE

Rani (whose name means "queen") is a shy, mild-mannered girl who lives at home with her parents. She meets a sweet boy in town (Vijay) who woos her and proposes marriage. But hours before the wedding, Vijay gets cold feet and calls off the engagement. Devastated, Rani locks herself in her room as her family deals with the fallout and embarrassment.

After some soul searching, Rani makes a declaration: She's going on her honeymoon. By herself. She boards a flight to Paris, determined to make the best of her predicament. Alone in the City of Lights, she embarks on a journey to grapple with her grief, push beyond her boundaries, and discover the queen that she really is.

THE "DISH"

This film always puts a smile on my face. It's a delightful joy ride with great music, touching emotions, and an unforgettable character at the center who's going to steal your heart.

Queen is truly revolutionary for Bollywood. A modern feminist film, it portrays a young woman like millions of others in India—middle class, polite, sheltered from the world. Her biggest dilemma is finding a man to love who will meet her parents' approval. We've seen her countless times in Bollywood films before, and usually, that's the end of her story. But in this unique film, we watch Rani go through a metamorphosis—from naive girl to self-assured young woman. All the

Photographs courtesy
Phantom Films
(pages 264–267, 269)

while, the film never casts aspersions on her traditional values, nor does it pass judgment on her newly discovered, modern freedoms. It presents the audacious proposition that a woman can be both conservative and liberated, family-oriented and independent, romantic and pragmatic.

The star of the film, Kangana Ranaut, is the embodiment of all this and more. From Kangana's very first role as the alcoholic girlfriend of a mob boss in *Gangster*, she's been the It Girl for raw, unflinching performances, winning major accolades for her work, including a National Film Award for *Queen*. Today, she's one of Bollywood's biggest celebrities.

But it's Kangana's nontraditional behavior *off-screen* that has made her a lightning rod for controversy. The actress is bravely outspoken, frankly discussing topics like sexism and nepotism in the industry. Such honest and straight-shooting conversation is far from the norm in India, and it has made Kangana a role model for young women eager to elevate their own voices in a changing society.

But her outspokenness has also come with some backlash. Kangana was involved in a bizarre media frenzy with superstar Hrithik Roshan, who took legal action against her for insinuating they had an affair while he was married. He claims Kangana imagined the whole relationship, sending him fifty emails a day with delusional rants about her love (emails that were splashed all over the tabloids). Kangana counter-filed for criminal intimidation, but only before an ex-boyfriend added fuel to the fire by proclaiming that Kangana does black magic and physically abused him.

It's crazy, even by Bollywood standards. Whatever the truth may be, to me, Kangana is a rock star. She's a fiercely unapologetic woman and a captivating actress. This is one queen who deserves to be lauded.

INGREDIENTS

CAST: Kangana Ranaut, Rajkummar Rao, Lisa Haydon
DIRECTOR: Vikas Bahl
WRITERS: Parveez Shaikh, Chaitally Parmar, Vikas Bahl, Anvita Dutt, Kangana Ranaut
MUSIC DIRECTOR: Amit Trivedi
RELEASE: 2014

Nobody does weddings bigger than Indians. Like *Queen*, these boisterous films celebrate love with tons of color, music, and revelry—perfect for another Girls' Night:

TANU WEDS MANU RETURNS (2015) If you become a fan of Kangana Ranaut after watching *Queen*, then check her out in this romantic comedy where she plays *two* roles and steals the show with her charm. Although it's a follow-up to 2011's *Tanu Weds Manu*, this is one instance where the sequel is better than the original.

BAND BAAJA BAARAAT (2010) A Bollywood film about wedding planners—what could be more perfect? With witty banter and fiery chemistry between its leads (who were a couple off-screen as well), *Band Baaja Baaraat* is one of the best romantic comedies of the decade.

DUM LAGA KE HAISHA (2015) Breaking the mold for Bollywood romances, this touching comedy stars newcomer Bhumi Pednekar as an overweight young woman who gets married to a man who doesn't see her beauty. The film explores romance in the context of arranged marriages, when love must be discovered *after* the wedding.

VEGETABLE HAKKA NOODLES

INDO-CHINESE VEGGIE LO MEIN

Rani and Vijay's endearing first date in a Chinese restaurant reminded me of something. I realize I may offend over a billion people when I say this, but I have to confess: the most delicious Chinese food I've ever eaten has been in India.

It may come as a surprise to a lot of people, but *India has amazing Chinese food.* The two ancient cultures have shared centuries of trade (and conflict) due to their close proximity, so it makes sense that there has been significant culinary crossover as well. Today, Chinese food is incredibly popular in India, enjoyed by middle-class families and couples on date nights, just like Rani and Vijay.

But Indians' version of Chinese food is different from what we have in America (or, for that matter, authentic Chinese food in China). Indo-Chinese cuisine melds Chinese cooking techniques with Indian spices to create dishes that I absolutely adore, like Chilli Chicken, Gobi Manchurian, and this dish—Vegetable Hakka Noodles.

This simple veggie lo mein can be made with any combination of vegetables that you have on hand. Just make sure they're thinly sliced to make for quick cooking. You'll find that the spices in this dish are bolder than your traditional American lo mein. Garlic, ginger, and red chillies create a flavor profile that's reminiscent of takeout Chinese, but with a fiery, Indian twist.

8 to 10 ounces lo mein (or spaghetti) noodles

Extra-virgin olive oil

2 tablespoons canola oil

2 or 3 Indian dried red chillies

2-inch piece fresh ginger, thinly sliced

½ tablespoon garlic paste (or minced garlic)

½ cup sliced scallions (white and green parts, about 4 scallions), plus extra for garnish

½ cup thinly sliced bell pepper (about ½ pepper)

½ cup peeled and thinly sliced carrot (about 1 large carrot)

½ cup chopped green beans

½ cup sliced mushrooms

½ cup lima beans or edamame

2 tablespoons soy sauce

½ tablespoon rice vinegar

1 teaspoon sesame seeds

¼ teaspoon freshly ground black pepper

Pinch of sugar

Bring a large pot of salted water to a boil. Add the noodles and cook until al dente, following the instructions on the packet. Drain well and rinse briefly under cold tap water. Then drizzle with a bit of olive oil to keep from sticking.

Heat the canola oil in a wok over medium-high heat. Add the red chillies, ginger, and garlic paste and cook, stirring, for about 30 seconds. Then add the scallions, bell pepper, carrot, green beans, mushrooms, and lima beans. Cook over high heat, stirring, until the carrot is tender, 3 to 5 minutes.

Add the pasta to the wok along with the soy sauce and vinegar. Using tongs or two spoons, toss the pasta with the veggies for a few minutes, until well incorporated. Sprinkle with the sesame seeds, black pepper, and sugar along the way.

Adjust the seasonings to taste. Transfer to a serving platter or bowl. Garnish with chopped scallions. Be sure to warn your guests about the chillies!

CRAB CAKES WITH TAMARIND MAYO

CRAB AND CORN SEASONED WITH CURRY LEAVES AND MUSTARD SEEDS

SERVES 4

2 tablespoons canola oil, divided

1 teaspoon black mustard seeds

1 cup finely chopped scallions (white and green parts)

5 to 7 curry leaves, chopped

½ tablespoon garlic paste (or minced garlic)

1 teaspoon ginger paste (or minced ginger)

½ teaspoon ground coriander

½ teaspoon salt

¼ teaspoon Indian red chilli powder (or cayenne)

¼ teaspoon ground turmeric

1 pound fresh crabmeat

¾ cup panko breadcrumbs

2 large eggs, beaten

½ cup uncooked corn kernels

½ cup chopped cilantro

¼ cup coconut powder

2 tablespoons mayonnaise

1 lemon

FOR THE TAMARIND MAYO

1 cup mayonnaise

2 teaspoons tamarind paste

½ teaspoon salt

½ teaspoon light brown sugar

¼ teaspoon Indian red chilli powder (or cayenne)

I'm a fan of crab cakes of all varieties, but once you elevate the flavor with Indian herbs and spices, you may never go back. Starting with a base of scallions sautéed with curry leaves and mustard seeds, then adding corn and crispy panko, these crab cakes are deeply flavorful in every bite. And to finish it off, a remoulade of tamarind and mayonnaise provides a burst of sweet, tart, and spice. These crab cakes are the kind of elegant dish you could imagine Rani ordering while traveling abroad—and unlike her experience in the film, I'm sure she would be pleased with the taste of home.

In a large sauté pan, heat 1 tablespoon of the oil over medium-high heat. Once the oil is shimmering hot, add the mustard seeds. As soon as the seeds start to pop, add the scallions and curry leaves, decrease the heat to medium, and cook, stirring, for 2 to 3 minutes.

Add the garlic and ginger pastes and cook, stirring, for another minute. Then add the coriander, salt, red chilli powder, and turmeric and allow the spices to bloom for about 30 seconds. Remove the pan from the heat and set aside to cool.

In a large mixing bowl, combine the crabmeat, panko, eggs, corn, cilantro, coconut powder, and mayonnaise, along with the cooled onion mixture and a squeeze of lemon juice. Use your hands to mix all the components together well.

Return the pan to the stove and heat the remaining 1 tablespoon oil over medium heat. Form the crab cakes using a ½-cup measure. Tightly pack the crabmeat to form a patty. Don't be afraid of squeezing them firmly—you really need to pack them well so they don't fall apart (you should have 8 in total).

Place the crab cakes in the hot pan. Cook for 4 minutes on the first side, until deeply brown. Then flip and cook for an additional 3 to 4 minutes on the other side.

Meanwhile, to make the tamarind mayo, combine all the ingredients in a small mixing bowl. Adjust the seasonings to taste.

Serve the crab cakes by spreading some mayo on the plate and then placing the crab cakes on top. Finish with a squeeze of lemon.

HYDERABADI CHAARU

SWEET-AND-SOUR LENTIL SOUP

½ cup toor dal (split pigeon peas)

½ tablespoon salt

¼ teaspoon ground turmeric

1 tablespoon canola oil

1 teaspoon cumin seeds

½ teaspoon black mustard seeds

¼ teaspoon fenugreek seeds

4 or 5 whole garlic cloves, trimmed

2 pinches of hing (asafoetida) (optional)

7 to 10 curry leaves

2 to 3 Indian dried red chillies, broken in half (or ½ teaspoon Indian red chilli powder or cayenne)

1 small onion, roughly chopped

1 tablespoon tamarind paste

2 tablespoons light brown sugar

¼ cup chopped cilantro

Cooked rice, for serving (optional)

This unique lentil broth is like an Indian version of sweet-and-sour soup. There are many different types of chaaru (and its tomato-based cousin, rasam), but this one is a specialty of my dad's hometown, Hyderabad. It's a symphony of four flavors: tangy, sweet, salty, and spicy. Everyone has his or her own preference as to which of these tastes should be dominant, and part of the fun is experimenting for your own creation.

The distinctive tang in this soup comes from tamarind, a pod-like fruit that's popular in Indian cuisine. As I discuss in "Ingredients" (see page 301), I find it easiest to use concentrated tamarind paste because I can keep it for a long time in my fridge alongside soy sauce, Worcestershire, and other condiments. You can purchase tamarind paste in a jar or packet at Indian and other ethnic grocery stores, as well as online (just be sure to buy the concentrated paste, not the dried fruit). And you'll notice it's doing double duty in this menu, featuring prominently in the remoulade for the crab cakes.

Typically, Hyderabadi chaaru would be served over rice as a final course. But you could also choose to begin your meal with it, as an enlivening soup to wake up the palette.

Measure the dal into a medium saucepan and rinse well. Soak in very hot water for 1 hour.

Drain the dal. Cover with 5 cups water and bring to a boil. Skim off any foam that may appear on the surface. Decrease the heat to a rolling boil and cook with the lid slightly ajar until the dal is tender, 30 minutes. If the pan starts to run dry, feel free to add more water.

Pour the dal and cooking water into a blender. Add the salt and turmeric. Let cool partially, cover the top of the blender with a dish towel (to allow steam to escape), and blend for 15 seconds, until most of the lentils have been pureed.

Wipe the saucepan dry. Heat the oil over medium-high heat. Once the oil is shimmering hot, add the cumin, mustard, and fenugreek seeds, garlic cloves, hing, curry leaves, and red chillies. As soon as the mustard seeds begin to pop, add the onion, decrease the heat to medium, and cook, stirring, until the onion and garlic turn lightly golden, 2 to 3 minutes.

Pour the contents of the blender into the pan. Add 4 cups hot water and bring to a boil. Dissolve the tamarind paste into the soup. Then add the brown sugar and cilantro and stir well. Continue to cook at a gentle boil, stirring occasionally, for 15 to 20 minutes.

Adjust the seasonings to taste. Play around by adding a touch more salt, tamarind (tangy), chillies/chilli powder (spicy), or brown sugar (sweet), until you achieve the right balance of flavors for your personal liking. Remove the red chillies and serve in soup bowls over rice (or without).

DINNER

DALCHA   283
Comforting Lentil-Beef Stew

SPINACH-PAPAYA SALAD   285
Dotted with Pomegranate and Pumpkin Seeds

BURFI   286
Indian Fudge

MOVIE

BARFI!   278
Heartwarming love story about a deaf man
and an autistic woman

BARFI!

FLAVOR

Granted, it may have an unfortunate title (especially to be included in a cookbook), but this touching comedic drama is as delicately sweet as the confection for which it's named.

RECIPE

Barfi (pronounced "bur-fee") is like Indian fudge—a dessert made with milk and sugar, in a variety of flavors such as pistachio and almond. In this film, it's also the endearing nickname of the main character, a young man who is deaf and living in 1970s Darjeeling.

Barfi falls in love with Shruti, a beautiful young woman new to town, and sets out to woo her with his unique charm. But he's oblivious to the affection of his childhood friend, Jhilmil, a sheltered young woman with autism. The unusual love triangle between these three individuals unfolds over the rest of their lives in a heartfelt and surprising way.

THE "DISH"

Bollywood hasn't produced many films about people with disabilities, perhaps reflecting the reality that in India, although things are slowly changing, disabled people are often treated as outcasts. So a film like *Barfi!* is a significant step. It begins to lift the veil of shame by casting two hugely popular, A-list actors—Ranbir Kapoor and Priyanka Chopra—as people living with disabilities, and doing so with dignity.

However, some have criticized the film as sugarcoated and unrealistic. It's easy to embrace a woman with severe autism when she's as beautiful as Priyanka Chopra.

And the title character, deaf with absolutely no resources available to him (not even sign language), miraculously gets by on nothing more than sheer charisma.

Because of this critique, I didn't see the film when it was first released. I had no interest in watching another Bollywood-ized, patronizing portrayal of people on the margins of Indian society. It took me close to four years until I decided to give *Barfi!* a shot—and that too, begrudgingly.

I have to say—I was pleasantly surprised. The film wrapped me in its magical spell and took me on a gentle ride. I still maintain that some of the criticism is valid, but I found the film's interpretation of disability to be in sync with its overall whimsical tone. Set in the foothills of the Himalayas, *Barfi!* transports us to a picturesque place and time. It's the kind of movie that has its own language (apropos when your main characters don't speak), reminiscent of European films like *Amélie* and *Life Is Beautiful*.

Which brings us to the *other* controversy. *Barfi!* has been criticized for plagiarism. There are moments in the movie that appear to be directly lifted from Buster Keaton, Charlie Chaplin, and Gene Kelly. In addition, the score from the film bears more than a striking resemblance to the music in *Amélie*.

The film's director, Anurag Basu, has defended his choices by asserting that he was "inspired" by these classics, not ripping them off. He says he was paying homage, in the way *The Artist* paid tribute to silent films. (As a side note, it's interesting that Ranbir Kapoor's grandfather, the legendary Raj Kapoor, became famous seventy years ago for unapologetically imitating Charlie Chaplin in films like *Awaara* and *Shree 420*.)

Despite these controversies, *Barfi!* ended up capturing the hearts of millions and winning seven Filmfare Awards (Bollywood's Oscars), including Best Film and Best Actor. Whatever your personal perspective on the critiques, it's hard to argue that this is a sweet film with beautiful cinematography, an engaging story, and heartwarming performances.

INGREDIENTS

CAST: Ranbir Kapoor, Priyanka Chopra, Ileana D'Cruz

WRITER AND DIRECTOR: Anurag Basu

MUSIC DIRECTOR: Pritam

RELEASE: 2012

TASTE THIS

Although films about people with disabilities have been few and far between in Bollywood, here are a few notable exceptions:

TAARE ZAMEEN PAR (2007) Directed by superstar actor Aamir Khan, this family drama is about an eight-year-old boy with dyslexia and his relationship with his art teacher (played by Khan). The hugely popular film sparked a national dialogue about caring for children with learning disabilities.

MARGARITA WITH A STRAW (2014) This remarkably heartfelt indie depicts the rarely explored topic of sexuality among people with disabilities. An adventurous college girl with cerebral palsy tries, with humor and hormones, to find love and ends up discovering it in the most unexpected ways.

IQBAL (2005) Iqbal is the name of a village boy who is deaf and, like many young people his age, obsessed with cricket. A feel-good sports drama, the film follows Iqbal's relentless pursuit to fulfill his dream of playing for the Indian national cricket team.

DALCHA

COMFORTING LENTIL-BEEF STEW

Get ready for a big serving of hearty stew. No matter what your country or culture, everybody has his or her own version of comfort in a bowl. And dalcha is exactly that. This dish is particularly special to my family because it hails from my dad's hometown of Hyderabad.

Although traditionally made with bone-in mutton, I find beef chuck to be better suited to our American palate. And if you're thinking that you don't typically like lentil stew—please erase from your mind all your preconceived notions of tepid, tasteless lentil soup. The "lentils" in this case are actually split Indian chickpeas, and by the time you're done simmering them for hours in a multitude of spices, you're left with a pot of thick, rich stew that's steeped with incredible beef flavor.

Admittedly, dalcha takes a bit of time to cook (and requires soaking lentils overnight), but you'll love curling up with a big bowl in front of the TV. Keep the pot on a low flame and everyone can go back for extra helpings as the movie unfolds. With the length of this movie, that pot will be empty by the time the end credits roll!

Rinse the dal thoroughly and cover with water to soak overnight (or at least 6 hours) in a large pot.

When ready to start cooking, drain the dal and then cover with 10 cups water. Bring to a boil. A foam will appear on top of the water—skim this off. Maintain the heat at a rolling boil and cook with the lid slightly ajar for 45 minutes.

Meanwhile, heat 1 tablespoon of the oil in a large Dutch oven or heavy soup pot over medium-high heat. Pat the beef pieces dry and season with the turmeric. In multiple batches (to prevent crowding the pan), sear the meat on all sides, using tongs to turn the pieces when they release from the bottom of the pan. Remove the meat to a large plate.

Heat the remaining 1 tablespoon oil in the pan, add the bay leaves, and allow them to begin infusing the oil for 15 seconds. Add the onions and cook, stirring and scraping up the brown bits from the bottom of the pan, for 3 minutes. Add the garlic and ginger pastes and cook, reducing the heat if necessary to prevent burning, for 2 minutes. Add 2 teaspoons of the salt and the red chilli powder,

SERVES 8 TO 10

2 cups chana dal (Indian split chickpeas)

2 tablespoons canola oil, divided

2 pounds stew meat (beef chuck), cut into 1½-inch pieces

1 teaspoon ground turmeric

2 bay leaves

2 medium onions, roughly chopped

2 tablespoons garlic paste (or minced garlic)

1 heaping tablespoon ginger paste (or minced ginger)

3 teaspoons salt, divided

½ tablespoon Indian red chilli powder (or cayenne)

1 teaspoon ground cinnamon

1 teaspoon ground cloves

2 medium tomatoes, roughly chopped

1 teaspoon tamarind paste

2 medium red potatoes, peeled and cut into roughly 1-inch pieces

½ cup chopped cilantro

½ tablespoon ground coriander

Cooked basmati rice, for serving

Greek yogurt or sour cream, for serving

(Opposite, clockwise from top-right) Dalcha; Spinach-Papaya Salad, p. 285

cinnamon, and cloves. Stir the spices into the onions, and allow them to bloom for another minute. Add the tomatoes and cook, stirring, for 2 to 3 minutes or until the tomatoes have started to break down and create a thick sauce.

Return the beef to the pot and stir well to coat all the pieces. Cover, decrease the heat, and simmer for 5 minutes.

Meanwhile, check the dal by pressing it between your fingers. It should be cooked fully through, turning to mush when you squeeze it. Once it's done, add the remaining 1 teaspoon salt and dissolve the tamarind paste into the pot.

Remove the bay leaves from the beef. Combine the contents of both pots by pouring the dal into the beef. Bring to a boil while stirring.

Decrease the heat to low, cover, and cook at a very low simmer, stirring occasionally to prevent the dal from sticking to the bottom of the pot, for 1½ hours. (Alternatively, you could transfer the pot to a preheated 325°F oven.)

Add the potatoes, cilantro, and coriander. Add a cup or 2 of boiling water. Traditionally, dalcha is fairly liquid, like soup, but Americans may prefer it thicker, like the beef stews to which we are accustomed. In any case, simmer until the potatoes are very soft and the meat is fork tender, another 45 minutes. If the meat remains tough, simply continue simmering on low heat until it softens.

Adjust the salt and seasonings to taste. Serve in a wide bowl over basmati rice, with a dollop of Greek yogurt or sour cream.

SPINACH-PAPAYA SALAD

DOTTED WITH POMEGRANATE AND PUMPKIN SEEDS

With a meal as hearty as beef stew, you want to start with something light and refreshing. Papaya is considered a "warming" fruit in Ayurvedic medicine, which aids in digestion and pairs nicely with red meat. Just be sure to use ripened papaya, which has sweet, orange flesh (not the green, raw fruit you find in Thai papaya salad). And you're welcome to toss the salad in a bowl, but I prefer a slightly more refined, yet just as easy, presentation of arranging the components on a platter or individual salad plates.

Cut the ends off each papaya, then cut in half vertically and remove the seeds and fibers. Cut each half horizontally so you can stand each quarter flat on one end and cut away the skin. Finally, dice into 1-inch cubes.

Arrange the spinach on a large platter and scatter the papaya over the bed of spinach. Then layer on the red onion and sprinkle over the pumpkin and pomegranate seeds. Season with salt and pepper to taste.

For the dressing, in a mixing bowl, whisk the yogurt with the cumin, salt, black pepper, ground ginger, chilli powder, cilantro, olive oil, and ¼ cup water. Adjust the seasonings to taste.

Prior to serving, drizzle some of the dressing over the salad, but reserve most of it in a serving bowl so your guests can help themselves.

NOTE: Papayas are ripe when their skin turns from green to yellow (place in a paper bag to hasten the process).

SERVES 8 TO 10

2 ripe papayas (see Note)

8 ounces baby spinach leaves, washed and dried

½ red onion, sliced

½ cup pumpkin seeds

½ cup pomegranate seeds

Salt

Freshly ground black pepper

FOR THE DRESSING

1 cup Greek yogurt (2%)

½ teaspoon ground cumin

½ teaspoon salt

½ teaspoon black pepper

2 pinches of ground ginger

2 pinches of Indian red chilli powder (or cayenne)

1 tablespoon chopped fresh cilantro

2 tablespoons extra-virgin olive oil

BURFI

INDIAN FUDGE

32 ounces full-fat ricotta
cheese

3 cups sugar

Burfi (which I choose to spell differently than the filmmakers, for obvious reasons) is like Indian fudge, and there are as many varieties as there are for fudge: cashew burfi, almond burfi, and pistachio burfi, to name a few. This version is a type of milk burfi made with ricotta cheese, which was discovered by Indian-Americans as a shortcut to the traditional method of continuously stirring whole milk on the stove for hours. Although this particular variety of burfi is not common, I'm excited to share it with you because it was my mom's signature dessert when I was growing up, and the taste always takes me back to childhood. It took me a lot of trial and error to learn how to make it just like she did. It was one of my proudest cooking accomplishments when I finally achieved the coveted, deep brown color and luscious caramel flavor—*shockingly*, to my mom's approval.

The key is to keep a close eye on the pan as it slowly bubbles away in the oven. At first, it may look like nothing is happening ("It's just a pan full of melted cheese!"). But be patient. The transformation will take place before your eyes. Just make sure you don't leave it unattended in the end, or the burfi will burn in the final few moments.

Sure, it may seem odd to be eating nothing more than ricotta cheese and sugar. But believe me—something magical happens to these two simple ingredients after they've been baking for hours. The dessert transforms from simple cheese into a decadent, caramel delight.

Preheat the oven to 350°F. Grease a nonstick, 9 x 9-inch brownie pan very well with butter or cooking spray. Cut 2 pieces of parchment paper 9 inches in width. Lay the first piece into the pan and crease it to fit snugly. Grease the exposed parchment and then lay the second piece perpendicularly on top. Crease it to fit snugly. Grease all the exposed parchment paper generously (this dessert is *very* sticky!).

In a large mixing bowl, combine the ricotta cheese and sugar until smooth and evenly incorporated. Pour the mixture into the pan.

Bake on the middle rack for 1 hour and 45 minutes, until caramel brown.

Begin reducing the heat so the burfi gets fully cooked and brown all over, without burning, as follows: Decrease the heat to 300°F and bake for 15 minutes. Then decrease to 250°F and bake for an additional 10 to 15 minutes, until dark brown. Keep a close eye on it in this final stage. You want to keep baking until the surface becomes dark and porous like a sponge.

Remove the pan from the oven. Once it's cool to the touch, lift the parchment paper out of the pan to remove the burfi in one piece. Place on a cutting board to cool completely.

Wet or butter a very large, sharp knife to slice the burfi into squares. Start by cutting away and discarding the edges, which will likely be too crisp. Then press your knife down in one stroke (don't drag your knife) to make the horizontal and vertical cuts to create 16 squares.

Arrange the squares on a platter (you may need to gently pack the edges if they're crumbling). Enjoy warm or refrigerate and serve cold. Burfi will keep in the fridge for 5 to 7 days.

THE BASICS

Whether you're new to Indian cooking or have been eating it for years, there are a few basics that are helpful to review before getting started. In line with my overall philosophy in writing this book, the guidelines presented below are practical, accessible, and "real." This is how I do it in my house. Sure, if you're a die-hard foodie and love the idea of building your own tandoor oven in your backyard or scouring the Internet for obscure spices—by all means, go for it. There are numerous resources available online to help you on such a journey. But here, what you'll find are the bare essentials—and all you *truly* need, in my opinion—to enjoy authentic Indian food in your own home.

RICE

Rice is—hands down—the single most important component of any Indian meal. It's the first thing I taste when I'm served dinner. It is the foundation upon which your meal rests, and a bad batch of rice can ruin an entire culinary experience.

Luckily, it's perhaps the simplest food you can make. Cooking rice is the only thing my mother ever permitted me to do in the kitchen because, even at the age of twelve, I couldn't mess it up. So I'm continually surprised by how often I have conversations with people about their "rice issues." There's endless debate about sticky vs. fluffy, trepidation about burning or undercooking it, and lots of chatter about all the different varieties that are currently available. But the only *real* issue is—we're overthinking it.

There are three foolproof ways to make rice. The first is simply to use a rice cooker. Some people (including my mom) swear by this method. But to me, a rice cooker seems like another unnecessary appliance to take up valuable counter space in my kitchen—especially when it's so easy to make do with a regular old saucepan.

Which brings us to the second way to cook rice, my preferred method:

SIMPLE, EVERYDAY RICE

In a nonstick saucepan, rinse the rice very well several times until the water starts to become less cloudy (starchy). Choose a saucepan that will be snug instead of shallow (i.e., the water and rice should come about three-fourths of the way to the top).

Cover the rice with 2 parts water to 1 part rice. If you're cooking brown rice, you can add a touch more water (roughly 2¼ parts). Bring the pan to a boil over high heat. Once you've achieved a rolling boil, turn the heat down to the lowest setting and cover. Leave the pan undisturbed for 20 minutes if you're cooking 1 to 2 cups of rice, or 30 minutes if you're cooking a larger quantity.

Remove the cover and check the rice. If it's still moist on top, continue cooking, uncovered, on the same heat for a few more minutes until the moisture has evaporated and the rice is dry. If the rice instead is dry on top but soggy underneath (use a fork to check beneath the top layer), continue cooking, covered, for a few more minutes until dry throughout.

To prevent sticking to the pan, transfer the rice to a serving bowl or platter while it's still hot. Use a large fork to tumble the rice out and fluff.

1 part rice, any variety (estimate ½ cup/person)

2 parts water

NOTE: Some people opt to soak their rice before cooking, but I feel it complicates matters because the simple 1:2 ratio of rice to water no longer works as well, and I don't find that soaking improves the final outcome significantly. In the few cases where soaking *is* beneficial, I've noted such in this book.

The third way to cook rice is to cook it like pasta (i.e., boiling it in lots of water). My parents tell me this is how they used to make it in India when they were growing up because the starchy cooking water could be used for other purposes (like ironing clothes or making ganji/kanji, a meager rice porridge). Interestingly, this traditional method may also be the simplest because it doesn't require any measuring and barely any monitoring. I don't know why this technique isn't more popular today. It just goes to show that despite our modern obsession with dissecting and perfecting cooking techniques, our grandmother's method is often the best.

To cook rice like pasta, simply bring a large pot of water to a boil, then pour in some rice that's been thoroughly washed. No need to measure the rice or water, just make sure you use lots of water in a large pot so the rice has plenty of space to move around (just like pasta). Cook the rice for 8 to 12 minutes (longer for brown rice), until the grains are fully tender when you bite into them—*not* al dente. Drain in a colander and let sit for a few minutes so the excess moisture can evaporate. That's it. Plain and simple.

Whatever your method for cooking, with regard to the *type* of rice to use, I always have three varieties in my kitchen: jasmine, basmati, and brown. I buy them in bulk and store them in airtight containers, which allows me to use them for months. Jasmine rice (sometimes called Thai jasmine) is what I use for everyday meals. It's fragrant, slightly sticky, and the perfect, simple palette for 90 percent of the dishes I cook. Basmati rice, although more traditionally Indian, is what I think of as "fancy rice." It's longer than jasmine, so it results in separated, fluffy grains that are ideal when you want drier rice in pulao (pilaf), biriyani, or other fried rice dishes. Basmati rice is what we've always served for dinner parties, while jasmine is what we eat as a family, day to day. Finally, there's brown rice, which I've been buying in recent years for its health benefits and robust, nutty flavor. I usually only make brown rice with vegetarian dishes like dal or chickpeas because I find this "sturdier" rice to be satisfying when there's no meat in the meal.

And one final note: Be sure to *mix the rice well* with your food. To get the full flavor of Indian food's distinctive gravies, you need to thoroughly combine them with rice on your plate, one small portion at a time. Just keep in mind, the rice you put in your mouth should never be white—it should be saturated with the luscious curries you've combined with it.

BREADS

It's always nice to have some Indian flatbread with your meal. Simply tear off a piece, fold it between your thumb and forefingers, and use it to pinch a bite of meat or veggies off your plate. There are many varieties of bread in India, but here in America, three are most common:

ROTI

This is the bread that we eat in my house every day. It's a plain, wheat flatbread, much like a tortilla. Although the recipe is incredibly simple (nothing more than flour and water, sometimes with a touch of oil and salt), it requires a great deal of practice to make good rotis. Rolling the dough to just the right thickness and getting it to puff up on a hot griddle may look easy when my aunties do it, but that's because they have a lifetime of experience.

So I buy my rotis at the Indian grocery store, and I suggest you do the same. Most stores carry both fresh rotis (often locally made), as well as factory-made packets, either on the shelf or in the freezer section. You can buy several dozen at a time and keep them in the freezer. Then, all you need to do is get a skillet or griddle screaming hot, take the roti directly from the freezer, and heat it for 30 to 45 seconds on each side, until it puffs up slightly.

Rotis are simple, everyday bread. I heat a stack nightly and dinner wouldn't be complete without it.

NAAN

Despite its popularity in Indian restaurants, naan is not made at home. That's because it requires a tandoor oven, which can only be found in restaurants. Luckily for us, though, these days you can purchase packaged naan in most American supermarkets (look for it in the bread, deli, or prepared food sections).

I'm thrilled that naan is one component of Indian cuisine that has crossed over into the mainstream. Aside from the fact that it's delicious, it has also made my life much more convenient. Now I'm confident that if I don't have rotis in my freezer, I can always pick up some naan at the grocery store for dinner. In the past, I would've had to settle for whole wheat tortillas (which, I admit, is not a bad option if you're in a pinch).

Much like "fancy" basmati rice vs. "everyday" jasmine rice, naan is what I reserve for dinner parties, while roti is what we eat on a daily basis. Naan is just a bit too heavy to eat every day, particularly if it's warmed with butter (and, really, is there any other way to enjoy it?). You can either heat each naan individually in a skillet with a pat of butter, or wrap a stack in aluminum foil and throw it in the oven for about 15 minutes at 350°F. And regardless of what the package may say, please don't microwave naan, unless you have a hankering for rubbery bread.

PARATHA

The final type of Indian bread to add to your arsenal is paratha, or stuffed bread. A paratha is made by rolling roti dough into a thick flatbread with pieces of vegetable or minced meat, along with herbs and spices. The bread is then cooked in a pan with some oil or butter (ghee). It's as delicious as it sounds. You can find packets of frozen parathas at the Indian grocery store (if you're lucky, you might stumble upon some locally made, fresh packets near the cash register).

The most common type of paratha is aloo (potato) paratha, which is basically bread that's been stuffed with mashed potatoes and spices. What could be better? Aloo paratha with a bowl of yogurt is a quintessential North Indian breakfast, made even better with a simple fried egg. It's enough to make my mouth water just writing about it.

DAL

Dal (commonly translated as "lentils," but technically, "legumes") is the treasure of an Indian diet. It would take a lifetime to learn and enjoy the countless varieties that are eaten in India. For a culture that was built on the principles of vegetarianism, dal was embraced brilliantly as a way to incorporate protein into the diet economically. In my opinion, Indians were way ahead of their time, as we in the West have only recently discovered the health and environmental benefits of steering away from animal-based proteins.

If you're familiar with dal from Indian restaurants, you're probably thinking of it as a thick lentil curry. But dal has so many more facets. It's used in both savory and sweet dishes, sometimes for subtle flavor in the background, and other times as the main star. Even the lentil curry common to Indian buffets can be made in countless ways, using a variety of different legumes.

When you go to the dal aisle(s) in an Indian grocery store, you'll be dazzled by the selection. But be sure to read the labels very closely. Not only are there many types of dal, but also each type comes in multiple varieties (e.g., whole, split, with

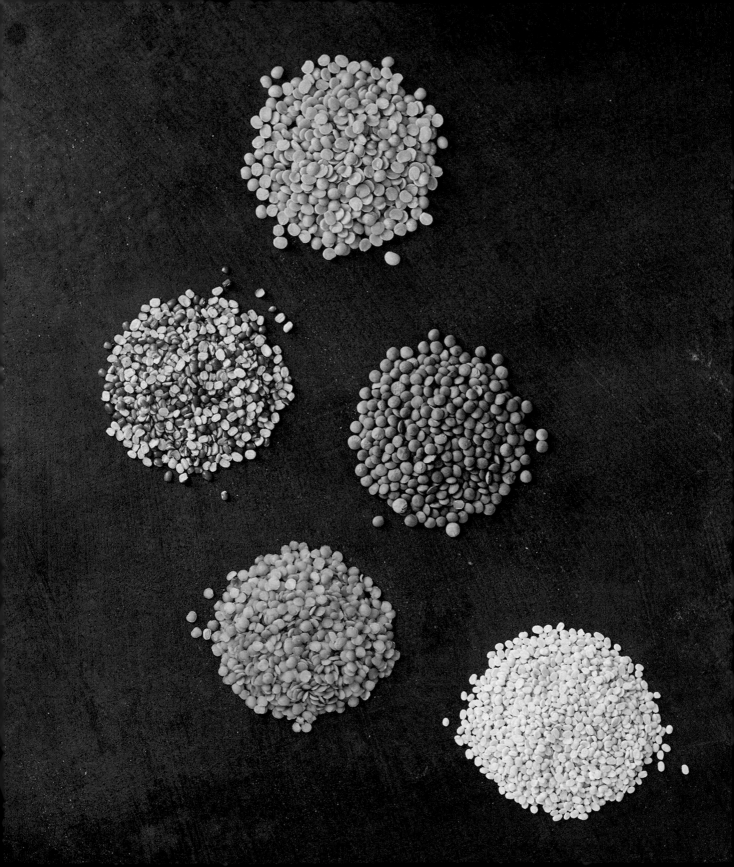

skin, without skin). And they're *not* interchangeable—if you buy the wrong kind, your recipe won't work.

In this book, we're only exploring the tip of the iceberg. I've chosen to use dal in the simplest, yet tastiest, preparations that don't require a pressure cooker (the standard way of cooking it in India). Here are the types of dal you'll encounter in this book and some of the recipes associated with them:

(Opposite, clockwise from top)
Toor Dal
Masoor Dal, whole
Urad Dal
Masoor Dal, split
Moong Dal

URAD DAL
SPLIT BLACK GRAM WITHOUT SKIN (WHITE)
USED IN: Chitrannam, Coconut Pachadi, Dondakaya, Dosas, Mallika Pinni's Beetroot, Upma

CHANA DAL
SPLIT INDIAN CHICKPEAS (YELLOW)
USED IN: Chitrannam, Coconut Pachadi, Dalcha, Tiffin Egg Curry

MASOOR DAL (WHOLE AND SPLIT)
WHOLE BROWN LENTILS; SPLIT RED/PINK LENTILS
USED IN: Himalayan Shepherd's Pie (whole), Masoor Dal (split)

MOONG DAL
SPLIT MUNG BEANS (YELLOW WITH GREEN HUSKS)
USED IN: Khichdi

TOOR DAL
SPLIT PIGEON PEAS (YELLOW/ORANGE)
USED IN: Hyderabadi Chaaru

HOMEMADE YOGURT

MAKES 4 CUPS

1 quart whole milk (you can also use 2%, but the yogurt will be thin)

⅓ cup plain yogurt, at room temperature (see Note)

Homemade yogurt is a comforting staple of Indian cuisine. Whether it's breakfast, lunch, or dinner, a lavish feast or simple family fare—a pot of yogurt can always be found at every meal. It's cooling, calming, and nutritious.

Preheat the oven to 200°F.

In a heavy saucepan or small Dutch oven, heat the milk over medium heat, stirring occasionally to make sure it doesn't scorch on the bottom of the pan. A skin of milk fat may form on top; that's okay—just stir it in. Once the milk comes to a gentle boil, remove the pan from the heat.

Wait for the milk to cool. Dip your little finger into it. It should feel warm to the touch, not hot.

Meanwhile, stir the yogurt in a small bowl until it's smooth and runny. Add the yogurt to the warm milk and stir gently. Cover the pan and place it in the oven. Turn the oven off. Leave the yogurt undisturbed overnight.

In the morning, place the pan in the fridge. If there's still some liquid (whey) in the yogurt, leave the lid off or ajar so the yogurt continues to set in the fridge as it cools. The yogurt will keep for up to two weeks. When serving, transfer a portion to a bowl and serve at room temperature. Avoid bringing the entire batch to room temperature or the yogurt will turn sour.

NOTES: For your starter, use any plain, unsweetened yogurt with active cultures. I recommend buying a side of yogurt (not raita) from an Indian restaurant. Once you start making your own, you can use leftovers to make your next batch.

If you find that the yogurt didn't set, try troubleshooting next time in one or more of the following ways: Make sure the milk is warm when you pour in the yogurt—not too hot and not cold (technically, 115°F); use a few more spoonfuls of starter yogurt; or place the yogurt in a warmer location to set (your oven may be drafty, especially in winter)—try wrapping the pot in a blanket and setting it near your heater. The longer the yogurt sits, the thicker and tarter it will become.

YOGURT

Indian yogurt is different in texture and taste from the kinds of yogurt we're used to encountering in America. In this book, I suggest using Greek yogurt as a close substitute because of its thick consistency and tangy flavor. You also can purchase containers of Indian yogurt in most Indian grocery stores.

But, honestly, it's so easy to make yogurt yourself that I suggest trying it at least once. I suspect you'll be making it regularly like I do when you discover how much more flavorful it is than any store-bought variety.

The "American" way to eat yogurt is to serve yourself a generous dollop on the side of your plate, as a way to cool the tongue while enjoying spicy Indian dishes. But you won't get the true satisfaction of homemade yogurt unless you end your meal with a generous serving of rice mixed with yogurt and lots of salt. I realize it may sound strange, and it's not for everyone—but for me, it's heaven. This was one of my very first meals (as you can see from the photo of me on page 3, sitting in a high chair with my face smeared in yogurt, the happiest I've ever been). To this day, there's nothing I find more comforting than a plate of salty yogurt-rice. It's how I finish dinner almost every day . . . which may explain why I can't seem to lose my pudgy belly.

CONDIMENTS

Here are two simple condiments to round out your meals:

"PICKLES" (CHUTNEYS)

"Pickles" are a ubiquitous condiment on every Indian dining table, akin to ketchup in America. Although they technically are pickled vegetables, they're probably better described as "chutneys" or "preserves" because of their consistency. They're tart and spicy—sometimes extremely—so just a scant teaspoon is plenty to add a nice kick to your meal.

Mango pickle is the most common variety, and the one I suggest you stock in your refrigerator. If you like it, there are many other flavors to try—garlic pickle, lemon and lime pickle, etc. Buy them at Indian grocery stores or online.

GHEE

A small pat of ghee, or clarified butter, on warm rice is the ultimate way to garnish your plate. It adds subtle richness to your meal while lowering the heat intensity of any dish. It's now available in many health food stores (look for it in glass jars in the baking section, or refrigerated with the butter). But it's relatively simple to make at home. Here's the way my mom has made ghee all my life:

GHEE

CLARIFIED BUTTER

**MAKES ABOUT
14 OUNCES**

1 pound butter, salted
or unsalted

Ghee dates back thousands of years; it was used in Hindu rituals for creating sacred fires. In Ayurvedic medicine, it's believed to have healing properties, and for this reason, it has recently become a trendy food product, purchased by yoga hipsters in places like Whole Foods and Trader Joe's.

Personally, I don't believe the hype. I grew up on ghee and I love it—not because it has mystical powers, but *because it's butter*, people. Rich, creamy, fatty butter. *That* is what's so sacred about it.

In a medium saucepan, melt the butter over medium heat. Bring the butter to a boil.

Decrease the heat and gently simmer, stirring occasionally, for 10 to 15 minutes. Keep a close eye on it, adjusting the heat as necessary, as the butter can burn if too hot. Milk solids will appear on top, then dissipate.

Foam will bubble to the surface. Allow the butter to continue simmering at this stage for an additional 5 to 7 minutes. The liquid underneath the foam will turn deeply golden (no longer yellow) and smell richly aromatic. This is when you know the ghee is done. Remove the pan from the heat immediately—leaving it any longer will overcook the ghee.

Carefully skim off the foam. Then spoon the clear, golden liquid into a jar, leaving any dark solids in the bottom of the pan. They say ghee can remain on your counter in an airtight container for up to a month, but I prefer to refrigerate mine, just to be safe.

INGREDIENTS

THE ESSENTIALS

Please don't be intimidated by the thought of cooking your own Indian food. Contrary to common perception, you only need a handful of spices to cook the most common, homestyle Indian dishes—and many of these ingredients are already familiar to you. Here's all you need to cook about 75 percent of the recipes in this book.

GARLIC PASTE AND GINGER PASTE

We use so much garlic and ginger in Indian food that most cooks these days rely on bottled pastes, which are nothing more than minced garlic or ginger. These two bottles are the most valuable items in my fridge because they save me from peeling (and smelling like) garlic all day. Honestly, this is just a shortcut ingredient, certainly not something you're obligated to use. The dishes will taste even better if you choose to use fresh garlic and ginger instead.
WHERE TO FIND IT: Indian grocery stores and Amazon (I recommend Laxmi and Swad brands); you can also find minced garlic and ginger in many supermarkets these days (in the produce section)
WHAT IT'S USED IN: Everything
SUBSTITUTE: Fresh minced garlic and peeled and grated fresh ginger, or garlic powder and ground ginger (approximately 1 teaspoon powder per 1 tablespoon paste)

INDIAN RED CHILLI POWDER

Not to be confused with chili powder used in Tex-Mex food (which is actually a blend of spices), Indian red chilli powder is ground red chillies. It is very similar in flavor and intensity to cayenne.
WHERE TO FIND IT: Indian grocery stores and Amazon
WHAT IT'S USED IN: Everything
SUBSTITUTE: Cayenne

TURMERIC

With its distinctive, beautiful yellow color (be careful because it can easily stain clothes and countertops), turmeric has been revered by Indians for centuries for its antiseptic attributes. Turmeric is bitter, so a little goes a long way.
WHERE TO FIND IT: Supermarkets
WHAT IT'S USED IN: Everything

GROUND CORIANDER

The seeds of the cilantro plant are known as coriander. When roasted and ground into a powder, coriander offers an earthy, lemony flavor that's imperative for Indian cooking. If you feel like the taste of your dish is "just missing something," the solution is often to add more ground coriander.
WHERE TO FIND IT: Supermarkets
WHAT IT'S USED IN: Everything

GROUND CUMIN AND CUMIN SEEDS

You're probably familiar with the smoky flavor of cumin from Mexican food, but it's equally prevalent in Indian cuisine. Ground cumin is the most commonly used form, while whole cumin seeds are sometimes preferable because they add a subtle crunch.

WHERE TO FIND IT: Supermarkets

WHAT IT'S USED IN: Almost everything

GROUND CINNAMON

Although we in the West are familiar with cinnamon in desserts, it offers warmth and spice to savory dishes as well.

WHERE TO FIND IT: Supermarkets

WHAT IT'S USED IN: Meat and poultry

GROUND CLOVES

Paired with cinnamon, cloves provide a sharp bite and intense flavor.

WHERE TO FIND IT: Supermarkets

WHAT IT'S USED IN: Meat and poultry

BLACK MUSTARD SEEDS

Many South Indian recipes begin by popping mustard seeds in hot oil, releasing their pungent flavor.

WHERE TO FIND IT: Many supermarkets, if not, Indian grocery stores and Amazon

WHAT IT'S USED IN: Vegetables and lentils

SUBSTITUTE: Yellow or brown mustard seeds

COCONUT POWDER

Unsweetened, desiccated coconut ground to a fine powder provides richness while mellowing the heat of curries. If you ever find that you overdid the spices in a dish, a quick fix is to add a spoonful or two of coconut powder. It can be purchased in shelf-stable packets or frozen.

WHERE TO FIND IT: Indian grocery stores and Amazon

WHAT IT'S USED IN: Most South Indian dishes

SUBSTITUTE: Many supermarkets carry unsweetened coconut flakes in the baking section, which you can pulse into a powder using a spice mill

DRIED BAY LEAVES

Bay leaves are used to infuse oil with their woodsy flavor. Just remember to remove them before serving.

WHERE TO FIND IT: I prefer the variety available in Indian grocery stores, but the kind sold in supermarkets works fine also

WHAT IT'S USED IN: Meat and poultry

CILANTRO

The universal herb of Indian cuisine, cilantro (called "coriander" in South Asia and Great Britain) is used not only as a garnish but also as an important cooking ingredient. I like to buy a large quantity of cilantro, wash, dry, and finely chop the leaves and stems, then freeze it flat in a plastic storage bag. Just break off a chunk whenever you need it.

WHERE TO FIND IT: I prefer the variety available in Indian grocery stores, but the kind sold in supermarkets works fine also

WHAT IT'S USED IN: Everything

VENTURING A LITTLE FURTHER . . .

Once you're ready to try your hand at a larger variety of Indian dishes, here are the additional ingredients you'll need, readily available at Indian grocery stores and online. The convenient thing is, you just need to go shopping once because all these items can be stored in your pantry, fridge, or freezer for months.

INDIAN GREEN CHILLIES

Indian green chillies are different from others you may have encountered (e.g., serrano, jalapeño, habanero). They are short (2 to 3 inches), thin, and dark green. They're also fiery hot. You can buy them by the pound and keep them in the freezer, as I do. If you want the flavor of the pepper but not the heat, use them whole. I usually break them in half to get some of the heat without going overboard. Always be sure to remove them before serving, or your guests will burn their tongue if they accidently bite down on one. Or—if you love it hot—mince the chillies and go to town.

SUBSTITUTE: Thai chilli (aka bird's-eye chilli) or cayenne

INDIAN DRIED RED CHILLIES

These gorgeous red pods are used to infuse oil and provide background heat to a dish.

SUBSTITUTE: Crushed red pepper flakes or cayenne

CURRY LEAVES

Unrelated to curry powder, curry leaves are herbs used primarily in South Indian vegetarian dishes; they are sautéed in oil prior to adding onions and spices. There really is no substitute for their unique flavor, so I always have several bunches in my freezer (they'll keep for months). Although curry leaves are technically edible, most people push them aside when eating.

TAMARIND PASTE

Tamarind is a sticky fruit that's intensely sour. My parents reminisce about sucking on pieces of tamarind like candy when they were kids. Traditionally, the fruit is soaked in water to extract its sour juice (you can purchase packets of tamarind fruit in ethnic grocery stores). It's easier, though, to buy a small jar or packet of tamarind paste. It's highly concentrated, so you'll typically use no more than ¼ teaspoon. Although you won't get quite the same taste as you do from soaking the fruit, the packaged paste is more convenient because it will keep in your refrigerator alongside your soy sauce and other condiments, and it doesn't require any prep.

SUBSTITUTE: Freshly squeezed lemon juice along with soy sauce

WHITE POPPY SEEDS AND WHITE SESAME SEEDS

Toasted and ground into a powder, these seeds are sometimes used to thicken and add flavor to seafood and vegetable preparations.

SUBSTITUTE: Black poppy seeds and black sesame seeds

ASAFOETIDA ("HING")

How to describe asafoetida? Well, its most distinguishing characteristic is its smell . . . and not in a good way. Although the yellow powder has a fetid aroma, when tempered in hot oil, it adds a wonderfully savory flavor to vegetarian dishes.

FENUGREEK SEEDS

These incredibly bitter seeds are used sparingly in some lentil and vegetable recipes.

CARDAMOM (GROUND OR WHOLE)

Cardamom is to Indian desserts what vanilla is to American desserts. When there is sweet, there is usually a pinch of cardamom. You're probably familiar with its strong flavor and aroma because it's commonly used in chai.

CHICKPEA FLOUR ("BESAN")

Indians have been using chickpea flour for ages, long before it became trendy among the gluten-free crowd. I always have a small bag in my pantry to use for breading fried or baked foods and for thickening curries. Although chickpea flour is commonly available in supermarkets these days, I prefer the variety in Indian grocery stores, which is made with chana dal.

Note that the two ingredients conspicuously absent from my list (and this entire book) are curry powder and garam masala.

Curry powder has no place in Indian cooking. It's a tepid blend of spices (mostly turmeric, hence its yellow color) developed by Western chefs as a way to poorly simulate Eastern flavors. If you have curry powder in your spice cabinet, I beg of you—please throw it away!

Garam masala is also a blend of spices, albeit a more authentic one. Garam masala is used by many Indian cooks because it's a "one-step solution" when you're looking for flavor. Each brand has a different mix of spices, but generally it includes cumin, coriander, cinnamon, cloves, cardamom, and pepper. Personally, I don't like using garam masala because it's much better to control how much and which of each spice you use for any particular recipe. Sure, garam masala is an easy shortcut, like sprinkling Lawry's seasoned salt on all your dishes, but everything will end up tasting generically the same. I realize many Indian cooks don't agree with my perspective, so you're welcome to buy a container of garam masala and experiment for yourself.

SHOPPING LISTS

YOUR LOCAL SUPERMARKET

- Turmeric
- Ground coriander
- Ground cumin
- Cumin seeds
- Ground cinnamon
- Ground cloves
- Paprika
- Cardamom
- Dried bay leaves
- White sesame seeds
- Cilantro
- Naan
- **Rice:**
  - Jasmine
  - Basmati
  - Brown

INDIAN GROCERY STORE (OR AMAZON)

All of the items on your supermarket grocery list, plus:

- Garlic paste*
- Ginger paste*
- Indian red chilli powder
- Black mustard seeds*
- Coconut powder*
- Indian green chillies
- Indian dried red chillies
- Curry leaves
- Tamarind paste
- White poppy seeds
- Fenugreek seeds
- Asafoetida (hing)
- Chickpea flour*
- Mango pickle
- Roti (fresh or frozen)
- Paratha (fresh or frozen)
- Snacks (e.g., frozen mini samosas, papad, mixture)
- **Dal:**
  - Masoor dal (whole and split)*
  - Moong dal (split with husks)
  - Chana dal (split)
  - Urad dal (split without skin)
  - Toor dal (split)

* Possibly available in your local supermarket

(Clockwise from top)
Black Mustard Seeds
Indian Dried Red Chillies
Turmeric
Indian Red Chilli Powder
Indian Green Chillies

(Center)
Curry Leaves

LIST OF RECIPES AND FILMS

(Films are in chronological order.)
v Vegetarian   **VG** Vegan   **GF** Gluten Free

INDEX